Geometry and Topology with Applications

Geometry and Topology with Applications

Guest Editor

Daniele Ettore Otera

MDPI

Basel • Beijing • Wuhan • Barcelona • Belgrade • Novi Sad • Cluj • Manchester

Guest Editor
Daniele Ettore Otera
Faculty of Mathematics
and Informatics
Vilnius University
Vilnius
Lithuania

Editorial Office
MDPI AG
Grosspeteranlage 5
4052 Basel, Switzerland

This is a reprint of the Special Issue, published open access by the journal *Mathematics* (ISSN 2227-7390), freely accessible at: https://www.mdpi.com/si/mathematics/5652O9S898.

For citation purposes, cite each article independently as indicated on the article page online and as indicated below:

Lastname, A.A.; Lastname, B.B. Article Title. *Journal Name* **Year**, *Volume Number*, Page Range.

ISBN 978-3-7258-3415-0 (Hbk)
ISBN 978-3-7258-3416-7 (PDF)
https://doi.org/10.3390/books978-3-7258-3416-7

Contents

About the Editor

Daniele Ettore Otera

Daniele Ettore Otera is Senior Researcher at the Institute of Data Science and Digital Technologies of Vilnius University. After his studies in Italy, he benefited from several post-doctoral fellowships, including the prestigious Marie Curie fellowship, in renowned research centers such as the University of Paris-Saclay and the Institut Fourier of Grenoble, in France, and the University of Neuchâtel, in Switzerland.

His research fields are geometric topology and geometric group theory, and he is an author of almost 40 scientific papers.

mathematics

MDPI

Editorial

Preface to "Geometry and Topology with Applications"

Daniele Ettore Otera

Institute of Data Science and Digital Technologies, Vilnius University, Akademijos St. 4, LT-08663 Vilnius, Lithuania; daniele.otera@mif.vu.lt

Citation: Otera, D.E. Preface to "Geometry and Topology with Applications". *Mathematics* **2024**, *12*, 3370. https://doi.org/10.3390/math12213370

Received: 30 September 2024
Accepted: 11 October 2024
Published: 28 October 2024

1. Motivation

Geometry is a very active research field in pure mathematics, with a history and tradition going back to the antiquity. One of its first goals was in connection with precise land measurements, and the work of Euclid has been fundamental for the systematic and abstract generalization of the concrete geometric concepts already known in that period. He created a model (nowadays called *Euclidean geometry*) that remained unsurpassed for hundreds of years.

More than a millennium later came Euler, Gauss, Lobachevsky, Riemann, Hilbert and Poincaré: their ideas led to the birth of works that brought together the various mathematical theories elaborated previously. New types of geometries were born (for instance, *non-Euclidean geometries*, *differential geometry*, *Riemannian geometry*, and *hyperbolic geometry*), and the interactions and applications with other branches of mathematics carried out to more profound, interesting and powerful developments.

These progresses have given rise to several new research fields in pure and applied mathematics (such as differential topology, complex analysis, algebraic geometry, the theory of general relativity, chaos theory, low-dimensional topology, geometric analysis, and algebraic topology) and deep problems and questions (such as the Riemann hypothesis, Hilbert's 23 problems, the n-body problem, or the notorious Poincaré conjecture).

In the second half of the recent century, geometry has experienced rapid growth thanks to its interactions with other areas of mathematics, such as analysis, algebra, and topology, as well as with applications, mostly in mathematical physics. However, recently it has also been used in statistics, graph theory, machine learning, information theory, and the study of complex networks.

Geometry is indeed a very broad subject. If we take in consideration all of its manifestations, then it can surely be regarded as one of the major areas of research in modern mathematics.

Geometry can be found almost everywhere, and geometric intuition can be used and exploited in many cases. With this approach, one can find a new perspective that introduces a geometric component, facilitating both pure research, visualization, and the proof writing.

This is just the leitmotif of the Special Issue "Geometry and Topology with Applications" in a broad sense.

Following this spirit, I will focus this brief exposition of geometry and topology on the two specific branches I prefer and know the most, and which seem to me to be very thorough: *geometric topology* and *geometric group theory*. Despite this, other research fields were also considered in this Special Issue.

2. The Development of Geometric Topology

The importance of research in geometry stems in part from its position at the crossroads of many active fields in mathematics, such as topology, analysis, partial differential equations, Lie groups and group theory, in part from its close connection to theoretical physics and mechanics.

On the other hand, the so-called (general) *topology* (literally the study of "places and forms") as an independent research branch of pure mathematics goes back to Hausdorff (even though it originates in the work of Euler and Riemann) and then to Poincaré himself, who can actually be considered the true founder and father of modern algebraic topology.

More recently, two of the greatest geometers of the recent century, namely William P. Thurston and Mikhail L. Gromov, have contributed in a revolutionary way to make an epochal turning point to the study of both geometry and topology by considering their interactions and ties.

Thurston gave an immense boost to the development of hyperbolic geometry, low-dimensional topology, and geometric topology, while Gromov's work ranged from Riemannian geometry to differential topology, from group theory to graph theory, and from analysis to probability.

2.1. *On Thurston's Work*

William Thurston has been the dominant figure in the study of geometry and topology in three dimensions. In 1982, he was awarded the Fields Medal for his contribution in these fields [1–3].Thurston's main contribution is the venerable *geometrization conjecture* (which includes that of Poincaré's) [4]. It is a three-dimensional version of the Riemann uniformization theorem proved at the end of the 19th century for surfaces. Thurston described eight basic types of geometric objects, and he hypothesized that any three-dimensional space could be obtained as a union of components of this type. Since then, the interactions between geometry, topology, and analysis have become more dense, and the branch called *geometric topology* has been subjected to immense development. The geometrization conjecture was finally proved by Grigori Perelman in 2003, with methods from geometric analysis and partial differential equations [4].

To be more precise, the Riemann uniformization theorem says that a simply connected Riemann surface supports one of the three classical geometries (Euclidean, spherical, or hyperbolic). On the other hand, not every 3-manifold can support a single geometry. Thurston's conjecture states instead that every 3-manifold can be canonically decomposed into pieces, each of which supports one and only one specific geometric structure among the eight possible geometries of the third dimension (called Thurston's geometries).

Thurston proved the geometrization conjecture for a large class of 3-manifolds, called Haken manifolds. Shortly after, Richard Hamilton proved it for closed 3-manifolds with a metric of a positive Ricci curvature. He also provided a detailed program aimed to prove the full geometrization conjecture by means of the so-called Ricci flow with surgery (a certain partial differential equation for a Riemannian metric with singularities), which was efficiently carried out by Perelman in 2003 and completed, in the following years, by several other mathematicians who filled in the complete details of their arguments.

So, thanks to the work of these mathematicians, we have now both a proof of the Poincaré conjecture and precise knowledge of the world of closed 3-manifolds.

2.2. *On Gromov's Work*

After leaving the USSR, working in the USA, and then as a permanent professor at the IHES near Paris, the Russian–French mathematician Mikhail Gromov was awarded the Oswald Veblen Prize in Geometry in 1981, the Wolf Prize in Mathematics in 1993, and finally, in 2009, won the prestigious Abel Prize "for his revolutionary contributions to geometry".

Besides his profound contributions to differential geometry [5], symplectic geometry, algebraic topology and analysis [6,7], Gromov also initiated and developed a new deep theory, which correlates geometric and topological invariants of spaces (manifolds, simplicial complexes, or graphs) to properties of algebraic objects (discrete groups or algebras) [8,9]. In his work on this subject, there were so much ideas, new techniques, and methods that a new branch of mathematics, called the *geometric group theory*, originated after it, (or, at least, its establishment as a distinct area of modern mathematics). Gromov's theorem on groups of polynomial growth [10] still remains the best and the main result in this field.

In his work, Gromov introduced, in addition to a variety of theories and countless profound results, the h-principle, the theory of convex integration, the notion of almost-flat manifolds, the Gromov–Hausdorff metric together with the Gromov–Hausdorff distance, the notion of hyperbolic group, the theory of random groups, and the theory of pseudo-holomorphic curves.

Asymptotic geometry, hyperbolic groups, expander graphs, and the study of random groups and graphs [11] are today among the branches of mathematics that experienced a big expansion in recent years, also thanks to his applications in contemporary sciences, informatics, and in applied mathematics too.

During the recent decades, various works, especially those of Cannon, Serre, Stallings, Sela, Rips, and Thurston himself, introduced new techniques of combinatorial and computational nature for the study of groups and graphs [12] with applications to computer science, complexity theory, and the theory of formal languages.

3. Some Details About This Special Issue

The aim of this Special Issue, titled "Geometry and Topology with Applications", was to attract and present new interesting papers concerning geometry and/or topology, in a broad sense, with applications. In total, 33 manuscripts were submitted to be considered for publication, and only 12 were accepted. These papers were written by scientists working in prestigious universities or known research centers in France, Italy, Lithuania, Croatia, Korea, South Africa, Serbia, Uzbekistan, Saudi Arabia, United Arab Emirates, China, and Jordan.

Let us mention that, among the published articles, there are two interesting survey papers: one dealing with the topology and geometry of discrete groups and the other one with the open problems of the topology in the fourth dimension. These two reviews perform an excellent job in providing a background, context, and a very readable discussion on these topics. They are certainly recommended for researchers interested in low-dimensional topology and related questions in the geometric group theory.

4. Conclusions

We hope that the published works will have a positive impact on the international scientific community working in geometry, topology, group theory, and their applications, inspiring other researchers to further develop the topics addressed in this Special Issue.

Funding: This research received no external funding.

Acknowledgments: As the Guest Editor, I am very grateful to all authors who have submitted their works to this Special Issue. In particular, I wish to thank V. Poenaru, R. Grimaldi, and L. Kocinac for their valuable contributions. Also, I would like to thank the MDPI publishing editorial team, who invited me to be the Guest Editor for this Special Issue, especially to Nemo Guan, who helped me all along the editorial process. Finally, I wish to thank all the referees who, with their less-than-visible work, helped keep the level of the publications within this Special Issue high: their interesting reviews and comments were greatly appreciated.

Conflicts of Interest: The author declares no conflicts of interest.

References

1. Thurston, W.P. Three-dimensional manifolds, Kleinian groups and hyperbolic geometry. *Bull. Amer. Math. Soc.* **1982**, *6*, 357–381. [CrossRef]
2. Thurston, W.P. On the geometry and dynamics of diffeomorphisms of surfaces. *Bull. Am. Math. Soc.* **1988**, *19*, 417–431. [CrossRef]
3. Thurston, W.P. *Three-Dimensional Geometry and Topology*; Princeton Mathematical Series, 35; Princeton University Press: Princeton, NJ, USA, 1997; Volume 1.
4. Morgan, J.; Tian, G. Clay Mathematics Monographs 5. In *The Geometrization Conjecture*; American Mathematical Society (AMS): Providence, RI, USA; Cambridge, MA, USA, 2014.
5. Gromov, M. *Metric Structures for Riemannian and Non-Riemannian Spaces*; Progress in Mathematics; Birkhäuser Boston, Inc.: Boston, MA, USA, 1999.
6. Gromov, M. Volume and bounded cohomology. *Publ. Math. Inst. Hautes Etud. Sci.* **1982**, *56*, 5–99.
7. Gromov, M. *Partial Differential Relations*; Springer: New York, NY, USA , 1986.
8. Gromov, M. Hyperbolic groups. In *Essays in Group Theory*; Mathematical Sciences Research Institute Publications; Springer: New York, NY, USA, 1987; Volume 8, pp. 75–263.

9. Gromov, M. Asymptotic invariants of infinite groups. In *Geometric Group Theory*; London Mathematical Society Lecture Note Series 182; Cambridge University Press: Cambridge, UK, 1993; Volume 2, pp. 1–295.
10. Gromov, M. Groups of polynomial growth and expanding maps. *Publ. Math. Inst. Hautes Etud. Sci.* **1981**, *53*, 53–73. [CrossRef]
11. Gromov, M. Random walk in random groups. *Geom. Funct. Anal.* **2003**, *13*, 73–146. [CrossRef]
12. Epstein, D.B.A.; Cannon, J.W.; Holt, D.F.; Levy, S.V.F.; Paterson, M.S.; Thurston, W.P. *Word Processing in Groups*; Jones and Bartlett Publishers: Boston, MA, USA, 1992.

mathematics

MDPI

Article

Curves Related to the Gergonne Point in an Isotropic Plane

Ema Jurkin [1,†] and Marija Šimić Horvath [2,*,†]

1 Faculty of Mining, Geology and Petroleum Engineering, University of Zagreb, Pierottijeva 6, HR-10000 Zagreb, Croatia; ema.jurkin@rgn.hr
2 Faculty of Architecture, University of Zagreb, Kačićeva 26, HR-10000 Zagreb, Croatia
* Correspondence: marija.simic@arhitekt.hr
† These authors contributed equally to this work.

Abstract: The notion of the Gergonne point of a triangle in the Euclidean plane is very well known, and the study of them in the isotropic setting has already appeared earlier. In this paper, we give two generalizations of the Gergonne point of a triangle in the isotropic plane, and we study several curves related to them. The first generalization is based on the fact that for the triangle ABC and its contact triangle $A_iB_iC_i$, there is a pencil of circles such that each circle k_m from the pencil the lines AA_m, BB_m, CC_m is concurrent at a point G_m, where A_m, B_m, C_m are points on k_m parallel to A_i, B_i, C_i, respectively. To introduce the second generalization of the Gergonne point, we prove that for the triangle ABC, point I and three lines q_1, q_2, q_3 through I there are two points $G_{1,2}$ such that for the points Q_1, Q_2, Q_3 on q_1, q_2, q_3 with $d(I, Q_1) = d(I, Q_2) = d(I, Q_3)$, the lines AQ_1, BQ_2 and CQ_3 are concurrent at $G_{1,2}$. We achieve these results by using the standardization of the triangle in the isotropic plane and simple analytical method.

Keywords: isotropic plane; Gergonne point; generalized Gergonne points

MSC: 51N25

1. Introduction

An isotropic plane is a projective plane with an absolute figure (f, F) consisting of a real line f and a real point $F \in f$. Isotropic lines are all lines incident with F, and isotropic points are all points incident with f. Two lines intersecting at an isotropic point are called parallel lines. Analogously, any pair of distinct points joined by an isotropic line is said to be parallel. The standard affine model of the isotropic plane is obtained by setting $x_0 = 0$ for the equation of f, and $(0, 0, 1)$ for the coordinates of F. In this model, the coordinates of points are defined by $x = \frac{x_1}{x_0}, y = \frac{x_2}{x_0}$. The isotropic lines are given by the equations $x = const$. The points $A = (x_A, y_A)$ and $B = (x_B, y_B)$ are parallel if $x_A = x_B$. The isotropic distance $d(A, B)$ of a pair of non-parallel points is defined by $d(A, B) = x_B - x_A$, as explained in [1].

We say that a triangle in the isotropic plane is allowable if all its sides are non-isotropic lines. It was shown in [2] that each allowable triangle can be set in the standard position by choosing an appropriate coordinate system. Such a triangle ABC is inscribed into the circle with the equation $y = x^2$ and has vertices of the form

$$A(a, a^2), \quad B(b, b^2), \quad C(c, c^2), \tag{1}$$

with $a + b + c = 0$.

The following abbreviations

$$p = abc, \quad q = ab + bc + ca, \tag{2}$$

Citation: Jurkin, E.; Šimić Horvath, M. Curves Related to the Gergonne Point in an Isotropic Plane. *Mathematics* **2023**, *11*, 1562. https://doi.org/10.3390/math11071562

Academic Editors: Daniele Ettore Otera and Gabriel Eduard Vilcu

Received: 14 February 2023
Revised: 19 March 2023
Accepted: 21 March 2023
Published: 23 March 2023

together with their repercussions

$$a^2 + b^2 + c^2 = -2q, \quad a^3 + b^3 + c^3 = 3p, \tag{3}$$

will be useful. In order to prove that some geometric fact is valid for each allowable triangle, it is sufficient to prove it for a standard triangle.

The Gergonne point of a triangle in the isotropic plane was studied in [3], where it was shown that the incircle (excircle) of the standard triangle ABC has the equation

$$k_i \quad \ldots \quad y = \frac{1}{4}x^2 - q, \tag{4}$$

and the contact points are given by

$$A_i(-2a, bc - 2q), \quad B_i(-2b, ca - 2q), \quad C_i(-2c, ab - 2q). \tag{5}$$

The common intersection point

$$\Gamma\left(-\frac{3p}{q}, -\frac{4q}{3}\right) \tag{6}$$

of the lines AA_i, BB_i, and CC_i is called the *Gergonne point* of the triangle ABC.

We study some curves related to the Gergonne point in the isotropic plane, and we present a sort of generalizations of the Gergonne point in the Euclidean case.

2. Materials and Methods

The Gergonne point of the triangle ABC in the Euclidean plane is the intersection point of three lines AA_i, BB_i, CC_i, where A_i, B_i, C_i are the contact points of the triangle and its incircle. In [4], the following generalization is given: let c be a circle concentric to the inscribed circle with the center I and let $\overline{A}_i, \overline{B}_i, \overline{C}_i$ be the intersections of c with IA_i, IB_i, IC_i, respectively. Then, the lines $A\overline{A}_i$, $B\overline{B}_i$, and $C\overline{C}_i$ are concurrent. The analogous situation in the isotropic plane is described in Theorem 1. In order to make the proofs simpler, we use the standardization of triangles. The calculation tool is purely analytical.

3. Results

Let $K(m)$ be the pencil of circles k_m with the equation of the form

$$k_m \quad \ldots \quad y = \frac{1}{4}x^2 + m, \tag{7}$$

where $m \in \mathbb{R}$. The inscribed circle k_i belongs to the pencil $K(m)$.

Theorem 1. *Let ABC be the standard triangle, $A_iB_iC_i$ its contact triangle, and k_m a circle of the pencil $K(m)$ given by the Equation (7). Let A_m, B_m, C_m be the points of k_m parallel to A_i, B_i, C_i, respectively. The lines AA_m, BB_m, CC_m are concurrent at a point G_m.*
When the circle k_m runs through the pencil $K(m)$, the points G_m form a special hyperbola.

Proof of Theorem 1. The points $A_m, B_m, C_m \in k_m$ parallel to A_i, B_i, C_i have the coordinates

$$A_m(-2a, a^2 + m), \quad B_m(-2b, b^2 + m), \quad C_m(-2c, c^2 + m).$$

Therefore, the lines AA_m, BB_m, CC_m have the equations

$$y = -\frac{m}{3a}x + a^2 + \frac{m}{3}, \quad y = -\frac{m}{3b}x + b^2 + \frac{m}{3}, \quad y = -\frac{m}{3c}x + c^2 + \frac{m}{3}.$$

They all pass through the point

$$G_m\left(\frac{3p}{m}, -q + \frac{m}{3}\right). \tag{8}$$

Indeed, the calculation $-\frac{m}{3a}\frac{3p}{m} + a^2 + \frac{m}{3} = -\frac{abc}{a} + a(-b-c) + \frac{m}{3} = -q + \frac{m}{3}$ gives a proof for the line AA_m.

All points G_m lie on the conic

$$xy + qx - p = 0,$$

which is according to [1], a special hyperbola, see Figure 1. □

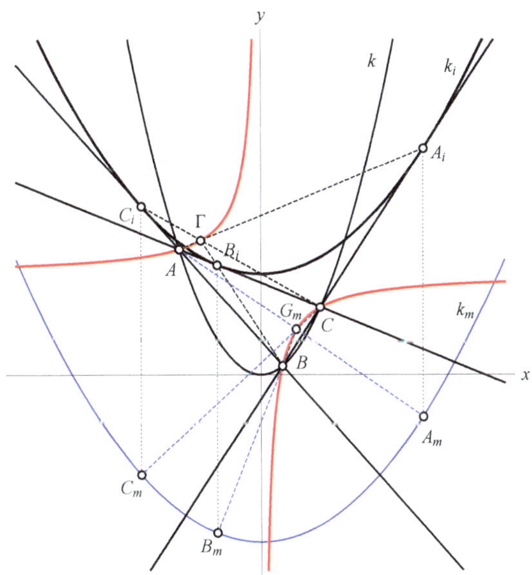

Figure 1. The locus of generalized Gergonne points of the triangle ABC.

The point G_m from Theorem 1 can be called the *generalized Gergonne point* for the triangle ABC and the circle k_m.

The Gergonne point Γ of the triangle ABC is identical to G_{-q}.

The locus of generalized Gergonne points also passes through the vertices of the triangle ABC since $G_{3bc} = A$, $G_{3ca} = B$, and $G_{3ab} = C$.

In [5,6], the authors gave some further generalizations of the concept of Gergonne point in the Euclidean case. Here, we study some analogues of these results in the isotropic case.

Theorem 2. *Let ABC be the standard triangle, I a point in the isotropic plane and q_1, q_2, q_3 three lines through I. There are at most two values $d \in \mathbb{R}\backslash\{0\}$ such that for points Q_1, Q_2, Q_3 on q_1, q_2, q_3 with $d(I, Q_1) = d(I, Q_2) = d(I, Q_3) = d$, the lines AQ_1, BQ_2 and CQ_3 are concurrent.*

Proof of Theorem 2. Let I be given by the coordinates $(\overline{x}, \overline{y})$, and let q_i have the equations $y = k_i(x - \overline{x}) + \overline{y}$, $i = 1,2,3$. All points T such that $d(I,T) = d$ lie on the isotropic line with the equation $x = \overline{x} + d$. Therefore, points Q_i have coordinates $(d + \overline{x}, k_i d + \overline{y})$, see Figure 2.

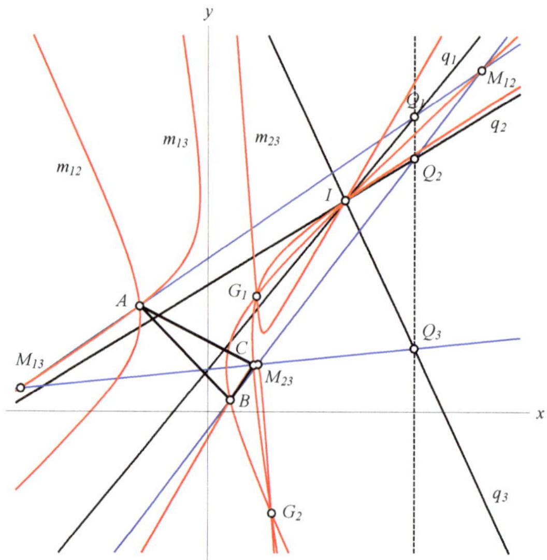

Figure 2. Generalized Gergonne points G_1, G_2 for the triangle ABC, point I and lines q_1, q_2, q_3 through I.

Thus,

$$
\begin{aligned}
AQ_1 \quad \ldots \quad y &= \frac{k_1 d + \overline{y} - a}{d + \overline{x} - a}(x - a) + a^2, \\
BQ_2 \quad \ldots \quad y &= \frac{k_2 d + \overline{y} - b}{d + \overline{x} - b}(x - b) + b^2, \\
CQ_3 \quad \ldots \quad y &= \frac{k_3 d + \overline{y} - c}{d + \overline{x} - c}(x - c) + c^2.
\end{aligned}
\tag{9}
$$

Let $M_{12} = AQ_1 \cap BQ_2$, $M_{23} = BQ_2 \cap CQ_3$, $M_{13} = AQ_1 \cap CQ_3$. Some trivial but long calculations deliver the following values of d for which these three points coincide

$$
d_{1,2} = \frac{-\mathcal{B} \pm \sqrt{\mathcal{B}^2 - 4\mathcal{A}\mathcal{C}}}{2\mathcal{A}},
\tag{10}
$$

where

$$
\begin{aligned}
\mathcal{A} &= k_1(c^2 - b^2) + k_2(a^2 - c^2) + k_3(b^2 - a^2) + k_1k_2(b - a) + k_2k_3(c - b) + k_1k_3(a - c), \\
\mathcal{B} &= k_1(c^3 - b^3) + k_2(a^3 - c^3) + k_3(b^3 - a^3) + (k_1k_2 + 2k_3\overline{x})(b^2 - a^2) \\
&\quad + (k_1k_3 + 2k_2\overline{x})(a^2 - c^2) + (k_2k_3 + 2k_1\overline{x})(c^2 - b^2) + (k_1k_2\overline{x} - k_3\overline{y})(b - a) \\
&\quad + (k_2k_3\overline{x} - k_1\overline{y})(c - b) + (k_1k_3\overline{x} - k_2\overline{y})(a - c), \\
\mathcal{C} &= (p - \overline{xy})[k_1(c - b) + k_2(a - c) + k_3(b - a)] + \overline{x}\left[k_1(c^3 - b^3) + k_2(a^3 - c^3) + k_3(b^3 - a^3)\right] \\
&\quad + (\overline{x}^2 - \overline{y})\left[k_1(c^2 - b^2) + k_2(a^2 - c^2) + k_3(b^2 - a^2)\right].
\end{aligned}
$$

The numbers $d_{1,2}$ are real and different, real and identical, or a pair of complex conjugate numbers depending on the value of $\mathcal{B}^2 - 4\mathcal{AC}$. □

The values $d_{1,2}$ determine the points $G_{1,2}$, the common points of the lines AQ_1, BQ_2, and CQ_3. The points G_1 and G_2 can be real and different, complex conjugate, or coinciding depending on the value of $\mathcal{B}^2 - 4\mathcal{AC}$. They are called generalized Gergonne points for the triangle ABC and point I and lines q_1, q_2, q_3, through it.

Remark: By eliminating the parameter d from the first two equations of (9), we obtain the equation

$$\frac{(\overline{y}-a)(x-a)-(\overline{x}-a)(y-a^2)}{y-a^2-k_1(x-a)} = \frac{(\overline{y}-b)(x-b)-(\overline{x}-b)(y-b^2)}{y-b^2-k_2(x-b)}. \quad (11)$$

It represents the locus m_{12} of points M_{12} when d runs through $\mathbb{R}$. The curve m_{12} is obviously a conic. In the same manner, we conclude that the loci of M_{13} and M_{23} are conics as well. According to Theorem 2, three loci m_{12}, m_{13} and m_{23} share two further common points $G_{1,2}$ except the fixed point I, see Figure 2.

Note that, if directions k_1, k_2, k_3 are given, $\mathcal{B}^2 - 4\mathcal{AC}$ from (10) is a quadratic function of $I(\overline{x}, \overline{y})$. This means that there will be two, one, or none real points $G_{1,2}$ depending on whether the point I is located outside, on or inside the conic i with the equation $\mathcal{B}^2 - 4\mathcal{AC} = 0$, see Figure 3.

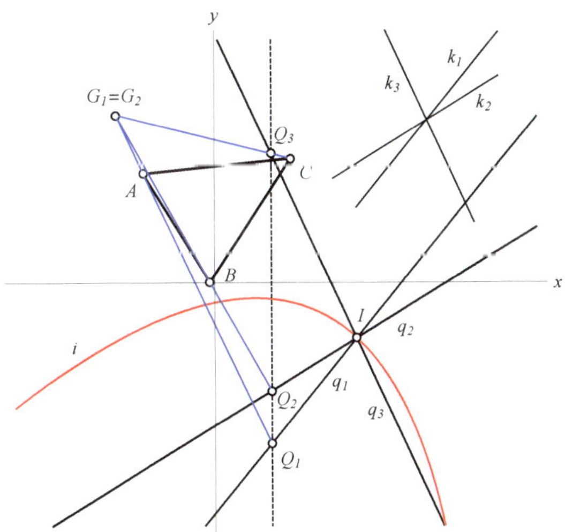

Figure 3. The locus i of all points I for which two generalized Gergonne points G_1, G_2 of the triangle ABC in directions k_1, k_2, k_3 coincide.

Now, we can also state:

Theorem 3. *Let ABC be the standard triangle and k_1, k_2, k_3 three directions. All points I for which there is a unique value $d \in \mathbb{R}\backslash\{0\}$ such that for points Q_1, Q_2, Q_3 on lines q_1, q_2, q_3 in directions k_1, k_2, k_3 with $d(I,Q_1) = d(I,Q_2) = d(I,Q_3) = d$ the lines AQ_1, BQ_2, and CQ_3 are concurrent lie on a parabola.*

Proof of Theorem 3. It is left to prove that the conic i with the equation $\mathcal{B}^2 - 4\mathcal{A}\mathcal{C} = 0$ is a parabola. After replacing $\overline{x}, \overline{y}$ with x, y and introducing notations

$$\begin{aligned}\mathcal{D} &= k_1(c^2 - b^2) + k_2(a^2 - c^2) + k_3(b^2 - a^2),\\ \mathcal{F} &= k_1(c - b) + k_2(a - c) + k_3(b - a),\end{aligned}$$

the terms of the highest degree in the equation of i are

$$[(\mathcal{A} - \mathcal{D})x - \mathcal{F}y]^2.$$

Thus, the conic i touches the absolute line in one point, the isotropic point of the line $y = \dfrac{\mathcal{A} - \mathcal{D}}{\mathcal{F}}x$. □

4. Discussion and Conclusions

This study gives a contribution to the very rich base of triangle properties in the isotropic plane. We have proved that for a triangle ABC and its contact triangle $A_iB_iC_i$, there is a pencil of circles K_m such that for each circle k_m from the pencil the lines AA_m, BB_m, CC_m are concurrent at a point G_m, where A_m, B_m, C_m are points on k_m parallel to A_i, B_i, C_i, respectively. When k_m runs through $K(m)$, the generalized Gergonne points G_m form a special hyperbola.

Further on, to each triangle ABC, a point I and three lines q_1, q_2, q_3 through I we have associated three conics intersecting at I and two generalized Gergonne points G_1 and G_2. The existence of G_1 and G_2 follows from the existence of two values d such that for points Q_1, Q_2, Q_3 on q_1, q_2, q_3 with $d(I, Q_1) = d(I, Q_2) = d(I, Q_3) = d$ the lines AQ_1, BQ_2 and CQ_3 are concurrent. For arbitrary directions, the points I, such that G_1, G_2 coincide, lie on a parabola.

In the papers [7,8], the authors studied some further curves related to Gergonne points; they studied the loci of Gergonne points in different pencils of triangles in the isotropic plane. Hence, this paper completes the investigations given there.

Author Contributions: Conceptualization, E.J. and M.Š.H.; investigation, E.J.; methodology, E.J. and M.Š.H.; writing—original draft preparation, E.J. and M.Š.H.; and writing—review and editing, E.J. and M.Š.H. All authors have read and agreed to the published version of the manuscript.

Funding: This research received no external funding.

Institutional Review Board Statement: Not applicable.

Data Availability Statement: No new data were created or analyzed in this study. Data sharing is not applicable to this article.

Conflicts of Interest: The authors declare no conflict of interest.

Abbreviations

The following abbreviations are used in this manuscript:

MDPI	Multidisciplinary Digital Publishing Institute
DOAJ	Directory of Open-Access Journals

References

1. Sachs, H. *Ebene Isotrope Geometrie*; Wieweg: Braunschweig/Wiesbaden, Austria, 1987.
2. Kolar-Šuper, R.; Kolar-Begović, Z.; Volenec, V.; Beban-Brkić, J. Metrical relationships in a standard triangle in an isotropic plane. *Math. Commun.* **2005**, *10*, 149–157.
3. Beban-Brkić, J.; Volenec, V.; Kolar-Begović, Z.; Kolar-Šuper, R. On Gergonne point of the triangle in isotropic plane. *Rad HAZU. Matematičke Znanosti* **2013**, *17*, 95–106.
4. Konečný, V.; Heuver, J.; Pfiefer, R.A. Problem 132 and solutions. *Math. Mag.* **1990**, *63*, 130–131.
5. Gorjanc, S.; Hoffmann, M. The Gergonne Conic. *J. Geom. Graph.* **2011**, *15*, 19–28.

6. Hoffmann, M.; Gorjanc, S. On the Generalized Gergonne Point and Beyond. *Forum Geom.* **2008**, *8*, 151–155.
7. Jurkin, E. Loci of centers in pencils of triangles in the isotropic plane. *Rad HAZU. Matematičke Znanosti* **2022**, *26*, 155–169. [CrossRef]
8. Katić Žlepalo, M.; Jurkin, E. Curves of centroids, Gergonne points and symmedian centers in triangle pencils in isotropic plane. *Rad HAZU. Matematičke Znanosti* **2018**, *22*, 119–127. [CrossRef]

mathematics

MDPI

Article

A Differential Relation of Metric Properties for Orientable Smooth Surfaces in $\mathbb{R}^3$

Sungmin Ryu

Department of Mechanical Engineering, Incheon National University, Academy-ro 119, Incheon 22012, Republic of Korea; sungminryu@inu.ac.kr

Abstract: The Gauss–Bonnet formula finds applications in various fundamental fields. Global or local analysis on the basis of this formula is possible only in integral form since the Gauss–Bonnet formula depends on the choice of a simple region of an orientable smooth surface S. The objective of the present paper is to construct a differential relation of the metric properties concerned at a point on S. Pointwise analysis on S is possible through the differential relation, which is expected to provide new geometrical insights into existing studies where the Gauss–Bonnet formula is applied in integral form.

Keywords: orientable smooth surfaces; Gaussian curvature; angles of intersection

MSC: 53A05; 53A25; 26E05

1. Introduction

Let S be an orientable smooth surface in $\mathbb{R}^3$ and R a region of S with boundary. Then the Gauss–Bonnet formula, which can be found in textbooks of classical differential geometry (e.g., [1,2]), states that:

$$\iint_R K + \int_{\partial R} \kappa_g = 2\pi\chi(R), \tag{1}$$

where K is the Gaussian curvature over S, κ_g is the geodesic curvature over the boundary ∂R of R in S, and $\chi(R)$ is the Euler–Poincaré characteristic of R. Common to various applications of the Gauss–Bonnet formula so far, any local or global analysis is viable only in integral form, since the relation between geometry and topology depends on the choice of R. For instance, the deflection angle of light by gravitational lensing has been calculated on the basis of the Gauss–Bonnet formula, and the setup for integral regions is indispensable for this calculation [3–17]. As a pioneering example of such an application, Gibbons and Werner considered two regions of a static, spherically symmetric spacetime [5]: one is bounded by two geodesics connecting the source and observer, and the other is a simply connected, asymptotically flat region. The integral of Gaussian curvature over the former is the key term for the calculation of the deflection angle. More precisely, the deflection angle of light can be calculated for asymptotically flat spacetimes, as follows:

$$\alpha = -\iint_{S_o} \mathcal{K} d\sigma, \tag{2}$$

where $\mathcal{K}$ is the Gaussian curvature over an optical surface and $d\sigma$ is its element. This formula can have different forms depending on physical situations (see, e.g., [4,9,12,13]), but the integral of $\mathcal{K}$ is essential in common.

Turning the point of view from a simple region of S to its single point p, five metric properties are concerned at p: the Gaussian curvature, the normal to S, the geodesic curvatures of intersecting curves at p, their speeds, and the angles of intersection between

Citation: Ryu, S. A Differential Relation of Metric Properties for Orientable Smooth Surfaces in $\mathbb{R}^3$. *Mathematics* **2023**, *11*, 2337. https://doi.org/10.3390/math11102337

Academic Editor: Daniele Ettore Otera

Received: 16 April 2023
Revised: 14 May 2023
Accepted: 15 May 2023
Published: 17 May 2023

those curves. To the best of our knowledge, the differential relation between these five geometric objects has not been uncovered so far. If this differential relation is constructed, it will be employable for pointwise analysis on S. Further, as those five properties are associated in the Gauss–Bonnet formula, it could provide new geometrical insights into existing applications of the formula that inevitably relied on integral analysis. The objective of the present paper is thus to construct a differential relation between the above-described five geometric objects for a general extension of application of the Gauss–Bonnet formula to differential analysis.

2. Preliminaries and the Main Results

Let $\mathbf{r}: U \to S$ be a parametrization of S in an open set $U \subseteq \mathbb{R}^2$. We consider a rectangular domain $D \subset U$: $[u_c - \Delta u/2, u_c + \Delta u/2] \times [v_c - \Delta v/2, v_c + \Delta v/2]$, where (u_c, v_c) is the coordinate of the center σ_c of D. In addition, we use P to denote the image under $\mathbf{r}(u,v)$ of D. This image has four external angles and these are denoted by θ_i, $i = 1,2,3,4$, which are ordered in the positive orientation from the angle formed at the lower right vertex of P. In addition, the positively oriented boundary of P consists of four curves and these are denoted by c_i, $i = 1,2,3,4$, which are ordered in the same orientation from the upper one. Apart from these curves, we use γ_i, $i = 1,2,3,4$, to denote the subsets of $\mathbf{r}(u,v)$ corresponding to the sides of D. These are represented as follows:

$$\gamma_1(u) := \mathbf{r}(u, v_c + \Delta v/2), u \in [u_c - \Delta u/2, u_c + \Delta u/2]; \tag{3}$$

$$\gamma_2(v) := \mathbf{r}(u_c - \Delta u/2, v), v \in [v_c - \Delta v/2, v_c + \Delta v/2]; \tag{4}$$

$$\gamma_3(u) := \mathbf{r}(u, v_c - \Delta v/2), u \in [u_c - \Delta u/2, u_c + \Delta u/2]; \tag{5}$$

$$\gamma_4(v) := \mathbf{r}(u_c + \Delta u/2, v), v \in [v_c - \Delta v/2, v_c + \Delta v/2]. \tag{6}$$

The trajectories of the boundary paths c_1 and c_2 are overlapped with those of $\gamma_1(u)$ and $\gamma_2(v)$, respectively, but with opposite orientation. On the other hand, c_3 and c_4 are compatible with $\gamma_3(u)$ and $\gamma_4(v)$, respectively. Figure 1 illustrates the introduced notations on D and P.

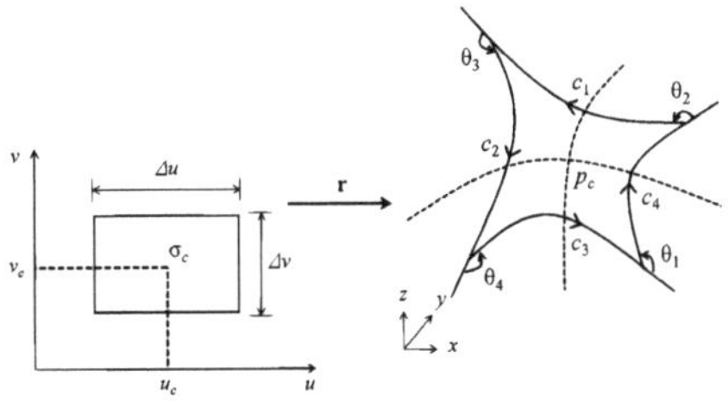

Figure 1. A rectangular region in the uv-plane and the image under $\mathbf{r}$ of the rectangle.

Remark 1. *It can be easily seen that P is a simple region of S and $\chi(P) = 1$.*

We present two definitions for the surface S and the parametrization $\mathbf{r}(u,v)$.

Definition 1. *We define two real-valued functions $F_a, F_b : \mathbf{r}^{-1}(S) \to \mathbb{R}$, as follows:*

$$F_a(u,v) := \kappa_g\big(\mathbf{r}(u, v = const)\big)\big|\mathbf{r}'(u, v = const)\big|, (u,v) \in U; \tag{7}$$

$$F_b(u,v) := \kappa_g\big(\mathbf{r}(u = const, v)\big)\big|\mathbf{r}'(u = const, v)\big|, (u,v) \in U, \tag{8}$$

where κ_g is the geodesic curvature of a coordinate curve on the map of $\mathbf{r}(u,v)$ and $|\mathbf{r}'(u, v = const)|$ and $|\mathbf{r}'(u = const, v)|$ are the speeds of the coordinate curves $v = const.$ and $u = const.$, respectively.

Remark 2. *Given that S is orientable and smooth, it can be easily seen that $F_a(u,v)$ and $F_b(u,v)$ are at least of class $C^1(U)$. First, these two functions are explicitly written as follows:*

$$F_a(u,v) = \frac{\langle \mathbf{r}_{uu}, \mathbf{n} \wedge \mathbf{r}_u \rangle}{|\mathbf{r}_u|^2}, \tag{9}$$

$$F_b(u,v) = \frac{\langle \mathbf{r}_{vv}, \mathbf{n} \wedge \mathbf{r}_v \rangle}{|\mathbf{r}_v|^2}, \tag{10}$$

where the subscripts u, v, uu, and vv denote the first- and second-order derivatives of $\mathbf{r}(u,v)$ with respect to u and v and $\mathbf{n}$ is the unit normal to S. The coordinates of $\mathbf{r}(u,v)$ are of class $C^\omega(U)$ since S is smooth. In addition, every 2-form on S is positive by the definition of an orientable surface in [2], so that $|\mathbf{r}_u|, |\mathbf{r}_v| \neq 0$ in U. These two facts yield that the first-order derivatives of $F_a(u,v)$ and $F_b(u,v)$ with respect to u and v are continuous in U.

Definition 2. *Two intersecting coordinate lines at some point $(u,v) \in U$ quadrisect a region centered at the point, and the images under $\mathbf{r}(u,v)$ of the coordinate lines form an oriented angle of intersection on each quadrant. These are measured by the positively turning displacements from $\mathbf{r}_u$ to $\mathbf{r}_v$, from $\mathbf{r}_v$ to $-\mathbf{r}_u$, from $-\mathbf{r}_u$ to $-\mathbf{r}_v$, and from $-\mathbf{r}_v$ to $\mathbf{r}_u$, where $\mathbf{r}_u$ and $\mathbf{r}_v$ are the tangent vectors to the coordinate curves $v = const.$ and $u = const.$, respectively. For such angles on each point of S, we define four intersection angle functions such that $\phi_i : \mathbf{r}^{-1}(S) \to \mathbb{R}$, $i = 1,2,3,4$, which are ordered in the positive orientation from the angle formed on the first quadrant. Figure 2 illustrates ϕ_i at $p_c = \mathbf{r}(\sigma_c)$.*

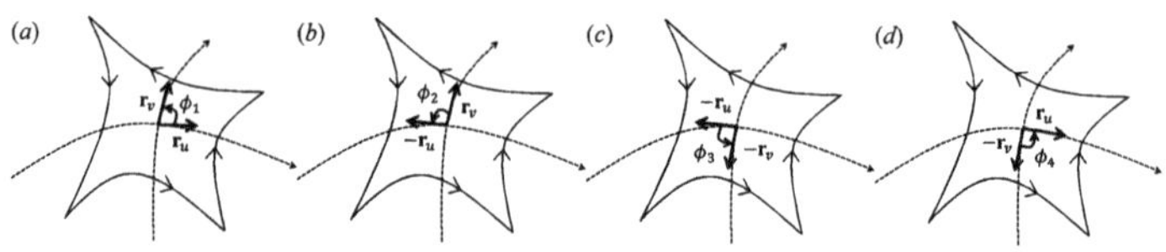

Figure 2. The intersection angle formed by two intersecting coordinate curves on (**a**–**d**) each of the four quadrants.

Remark 3. *The four intersection angle functions are related to each other; ϕ_1 and ϕ_2 are vertically opposite to ϕ_3 and ϕ_4, respectively, and ϕ_1 and ϕ_3 are adjacent to ϕ_2 and ϕ_4, respectively. Therefore, three relations between ϕ_i are established: $\phi_1 = \phi_3$, $\phi_2 = \phi_4$, and $\phi_2 = \pi - \phi_1$. In order to reduce the notations ϕ_i, we substitute ϕ_1 with ϕ and then, the others are naturally expressed in terms of ϕ by those three relations: $\phi_1 = \phi_3 = \phi$ and $\phi_2 = \phi_4 = \pi - \phi$.*

The definition of ϕ_i seems redundant, but it helps the reader to systematically understand the process of expressing the sum of θ_i in differential form in the proof of Theorem 1. The following states our main results.

Theorem 1. *Let S be an orientable smooth surface in $\mathbb{R}^3$, and let $\mathbf{r} : U \to S$ be a parametrization of S in an open set $U \subseteq \mathbb{R}^2$. Then for each $(u,v) \in U$*

$$K|\mathbf{N}| + \left(\frac{\partial F_b}{\partial u} - \frac{\partial F_a}{\partial v}\right) - \frac{\partial^2 \phi}{\partial u \partial v} = 0, \tag{11}$$

where K is the Gaussian curvature over S, $\mathbf{N}$ is the normal to S, F_a and F_b are the products of the geodesic curvatures of the coordinate curves $v = const.$ and $u = const.$ and the speeds of those curves, respectively, and ϕ is the positively oriented angle of intersection from the coordinate curve $v = const.$ to $u = const.$ on S.

Corollary 1. *The Gaussian curvature, which is explicitly expressed from the differential relation of Theorem (1), is intrinsic for orientable smooth surfaces in $\mathbb{R}^3$.*

3. Real Analyticity of ϕ

We present a lemma that states the real analyticity of ϕ. For the proof of this lemma, we recall three propositions proven in [18].

Proposition 1 ([18], Proposition 2.2.3). *Let f be a real analytic function defined on an open set $U \subseteq \mathbb{R}^m$. Then f is continuous and has continuous, real analytic partial derivatives of all orders. Further, the indefinite integral of f with respect to any variable is real analytic.*

Proposition 2 ([18], Proposition 2.2.2). *Let $U, V \subseteq \mathbb{R}^m$ be open. If $f : U \to \mathbb{R}$ and $g : V \to \mathbb{R}$ are real analytic, then $f + g$, $f \cdot g$ are real analytic on $U \cap V$, and f/g is real analytic on $U \cap V \cap \{x : g(x) \neq 0\}$.*

Proposition 3 ([18], Proposition 2.2.8). *If $f_1, f_2, \ldots, f_m$ are real analytic in some neighborhood of the point $\alpha \in \mathbb{R}^k$ and g is real analytic in some neighborhood of the point $(f_1(\alpha), f_2(\alpha), \ldots, f_m(\alpha)) \in \mathbb{R}^m$, then $g[f_1(x), f_2(x), \ldots, f_m(x)]$ is real analytic in a neighborhood of α.*

Lemma 1. *The intersection angle function $\phi(u,v)$ is real analytic in U.*

Proof. As mentioned in Remark 2, $|\mathbf{r}_u|, |\mathbf{r}_v| \neq 0$ in U. Accordingly, when $\mathbf{r}(u,v)$ is given as $(f(u,v), g(u,v), h(u,v))$, $\phi(u,v)$ can be explicitly written by the formula of the angle between two nonzero vectors, as follows:

$$\phi(u,v) = \arccos\left(\frac{\langle \mathbf{r}_u, \mathbf{r}_v \rangle}{|\mathbf{r}_u||\mathbf{r}_v|}\right) = \arccos\left(\frac{f_u f_v + g_u g_v + h_u h_v}{\sqrt{f_u^2 + g_u^2 + h_u^2}\sqrt{f_v^2 + g_v^2 + h_v^2}}\right), \tag{12}$$

where the subscripts u and v denote the first-order derivatives of $f(u,v)$, $g(u,v)$, and $h(u,v)$ with respect to u and v. We shall prove this lemma by showing that the composite arc cosine function in Equation (12) is real analytic in U, and this will proceed in a bottom-up way.

Since S is smooth, $f(u,v)$, $g(u,v)$, and $h(u,v)$ are real analytic in U. By Proposition 1, any derivatives of these functions with respect to u and v are thus real analytic, and further, by Proposition 2, any products of these derivatives and any sums of these products are also real analytic. The numerator of the input for $\arccos(x)$ is thus real analytic in U. For the denominator, $\sqrt{f_u^2 + g_u^2 + h_u^2}$ and $\sqrt{f_v^2 + g_v^2 + h_v^2}$ are the compositions of $\sqrt{x}$ and $f_u^2 + g_u^2 + h_u^2$ and $\sqrt{x}$ and $f_v^2 + g_v^2 + h_v^2$, respectively. The inputs for $\sqrt{x}$ are real analytic in U for the same reason above. Further, these inputs cannot be equal to zero in U (as mentioned at the beginning of this proof). Taking into account that the elementary function $\sqrt{x}$, $x \in \mathbb{R}^+$, is real analytic in $\mathbb{R}^+_*$, by Proposition 3, $\sqrt{f_u^2 + g_u^2 + h_u^2}$ and $\sqrt{f_v^2 + g_v^2 + h_v^2}$ are real analytic in U. Further, by Proposition 2, so is the product of these two composite square root functions. When put together, the numerator and denominator, again by Proposition 2, the resultant rational function is real analytic in U. According to the Cauchy–Schwarz inequality, the rational function, which is the input for $\arccos(x)$, can have an absolute value less than or equal to 1 in U. However, $\mathbf{r}_u$ and $\mathbf{r}_v$ are linearly independent by the definition of an orientable surface, so that the absolute value is always less than 1 in U. Taking into consideration that $\arccos(x)$, $|x| \leq 1$, is real analytic in $|x| < 1$, by Proposition 3 this fact yields that the composite arc cosine function is real analytic in U. □

4. Proofs

The outline for the proof of Theorem 1 is as follows. At a build-up stage, the Gauss–Bonnet formula is applied to P to obtain a base equation. At the latter part, the base equation is discretized and then the differential relation is derived by taking the limit of the discretized equation as $(\Delta u, \Delta v) \to (0,0)$.

Proof of Theorem 1. The Gauss–Bonnet formula is rewritten for P:

$$\iint_P K dA + \int_{\partial P} \kappa_g(s) ds + \sum_{i=1}^{4} \theta_i = 2\pi. \tag{13}$$

First, the integral of Gaussian curvature over P is given by the integral over D, as follows:

$$\iint_P K dA = \iint_D K|\mathbf{N}| du dv. \tag{14}$$

Second, the integrals of geodesic curvature along the positively oriented boundary paths of P are written. The geodesic curvature of an oriented regular curve contained in an oriented surface changes sign when the orientation of the curve is reversed [1]. Accordingly, the geodesic curvatures of c_1 and c_2 can be represented by those of $\gamma_1(u)$ and $\gamma_2(v)$ with opposite signs, respectively:

$$\kappa_g(c_1) = -\kappa_g(\gamma_1(u)), \tag{15}$$

$$\kappa_g(c_2) = -\kappa_g(\gamma_2(v)). \tag{16}$$

On the other hand, the geodesic curvatures of c_3 and c_4 are compatible with those of $\gamma_3(u)$ and $\gamma_4(v)$:

$$\kappa_g(c_3) = \kappa_g(\gamma_3(u)), \tag{17}$$

$$\kappa_g(c_4) = \kappa_g(\gamma_4(v)). \tag{18}$$

The integral of geodesic curvature along c_i may be represented by that over γ_i, as follows:

$$\int_{c_1} \kappa_g(s) ds = -\int_{u_c+\frac{\Delta u}{2}}^{u_c-\frac{\Delta u}{2}} -\kappa_g(\gamma_1(u))|\gamma_1'(u)| du, \tag{19}$$

$$\int_{c_2} \kappa_g(s) ds = -\int_{v_c+\frac{\Delta v}{2}}^{v_c-\frac{\Delta v}{2}} -\kappa_g(\gamma_2(v))|\gamma_2'(v)| dv, \tag{20}$$

$$\int_{c_3} \kappa_g(s) ds = \int_{u_c-\frac{\Delta u}{2}}^{u_c+\frac{\Delta u}{2}} \kappa_g(\gamma_3(u))|\gamma_3'(u)| du, \tag{21}$$

$$\int_{c_4} \kappa_g(s) ds = \int_{v_c-\frac{\Delta v}{2}}^{v_c+\frac{\Delta v}{2}} \kappa_g(\gamma_4(v))|\gamma_4'(v)| dv. \tag{22}$$

By means of Definition 1, the integrands in the right sides of Equations (19)–(22) are substitutable with $F_a(u, v_c + \Delta v/2)$, $F_b(u_c - \Delta u/2, v)$, $F_a(u, v_c - \Delta v/2)$, and $F_b(u_c + \Delta u/2, v)$, respectively. Accordingly, the above four integrals are rewritten in terms of $F_a(u,v)$ and $F_b(u,v)$:

$$\int_{c_1} \kappa_g(s) ds = \int_{u_c+\frac{\Delta u}{2}}^{u_c-\frac{\Delta u}{2}} F_a\left(u, v_c + \frac{\Delta v}{2}\right) du, \tag{23}$$

$$\int_{C_2} \kappa_g(s)ds = \int_{v_c+\frac{\Delta v}{2}}^{v_c-\frac{\Delta v}{2}} F_b\left(u_c - \frac{\Delta u}{2}, v\right)dv, \tag{24}$$

$$\int_{C_3} \kappa_g(s)ds = \int_{u_c-\frac{\Delta u}{2}}^{u_c+\frac{\Delta u}{2}} F_a\left(u, v_c - \frac{\Delta v}{2}\right)du, \tag{25}$$

$$\int_{C_4} \kappa_g(s)ds = \int_{v_c-\frac{\Delta v}{2}}^{v_c+\frac{\Delta v}{2}} F_b\left(u_c + \frac{\Delta u}{2}, v\right)dv. \tag{26}$$

By adding up these integrals,

$$\sum_{i=1}^{4} \int_{C_i} \kappa_g(s)ds = \oint_{\partial D} (F_a du + F_b dv). \tag{27}$$

Since the positively oriented boundary ∂D of D is a simple closed, piecewise smooth curve, and as stated in Remark 2, $\partial F_b/\partial u$ and $\partial F_a/\partial v$ are continuous in U, Green's theorem holds for the above integral. Accordingly, the integral along ∂D may be transformed into that over D, as follows:

$$\oint_{\partial D} (F_a du + F_b dv) = \iint_D \left(\frac{\partial F_b}{\partial u} - \frac{\partial F_a}{\partial v}\right) du dv. \tag{28}$$

Third, the sum of the external angles of P is expressed in differential form. Since the domain for P is a rectangle, those external angles are measured by the positively turning displacements from $\mathbf{r}_u$ to $\mathbf{r}_v$, from $\mathbf{r}_v$ to $-\mathbf{r}_u$, from $-\mathbf{r}_u$ to $-\mathbf{r}_v$, and from $-\mathbf{r}_v$ to $\mathbf{r}_u$ at the vertices of P, respectively. This implies that the external angles θ_i can be represented in terms of $\phi_i(u, v)$. Further, by the two relations established in Remark 3, θ_i is consequently expressed in terms of ϕ:

$$\theta_1 = \phi_1\left(u_c + \frac{\Delta u}{2}, v_c - \frac{\Delta v}{2}\right) = \phi\left(u_c + \frac{\Delta u}{2}, v_c - \frac{\Delta v}{2}\right), \tag{29}$$

$$\theta_2 = \phi_2\left(u_c + \frac{\Delta u}{2}, v_c + \frac{\Delta v}{2}\right) = \pi - \phi\left(u_c + \frac{\Delta u}{2}, v_c + \frac{\Delta v}{2}\right), \tag{30}$$

$$\theta_3 = \phi_3\left(u_c - \frac{\Delta u}{2}, v_c + \frac{\Delta v}{2}\right) = \phi\left(u_c - \frac{\Delta u}{2}, v_c + \frac{\Delta v}{2}\right), \tag{31}$$

$$\theta_4 = \phi_4\left(u_c - \frac{\Delta u}{2}, v_c - \frac{\Delta v}{2}\right) = \pi - \phi\left(u_c - \frac{\Delta u}{2}, v_c - \frac{\Delta v}{2}\right). \tag{32}$$

Since $\phi(u, v)$ is real analytic in U (as stated in Lemma 1), $\phi(\sigma)$, where $\sigma \in D$ is some point in the neighborhood of σ_c, may be expanded at σ_c as a convergent Taylor-series if σ lies within the region of convergence centered at σ_c. At this stage, it may be assumed that D is small enough to satisfy that its vertices lie within the region of convergence. When the values of $\phi(u, v)$ corresponding to the vertices of D are expanded as Taylor-series at σ_c, this assumption ensures their convergence. The four Taylor-series expansions are written as follows:

$$\begin{aligned}\phi\left(u_c+\tfrac{\Delta u}{2},v_c-\tfrac{\Delta v}{2}\right)&=\phi(\sigma_c)+\left.\tfrac{\partial\phi}{\partial u}\right|_{\sigma_c}\left(\tfrac{\Delta u}{2}\right)-\left.\tfrac{\partial\phi}{\partial v}\right|_{\sigma_c}\left(\tfrac{\Delta v}{2}\right)\\&+\tfrac{1}{2}\left\{\left.\tfrac{\partial^2\phi}{\partial u^2}\right|_{\sigma_c}\left(\tfrac{\Delta u}{2}\right)^2-2\left.\tfrac{\partial^2\phi}{\partial u\partial v}\right|_{\sigma_c}\left(\tfrac{\Delta u}{2}\right)\left(\tfrac{\Delta v}{2}\right)+\left.\tfrac{\partial^2\phi}{\partial v^2}\right|_{\sigma_c}\left(\tfrac{\Delta v}{2}\right)^2\right\}\\&+\textstyle\sum_{n=3}^{\infty}\left\{\tfrac{1}{n!}\sum_{k=0}^{n}\left(\tfrac{n!}{(n-k)!k!}\right)\left.\tfrac{\partial^{(n)}\phi}{\partial u^{(n-k)}\partial v^{(k)}}\right|_{\sigma_c}(-1)^k\left(\tfrac{\Delta u}{2}\right)^{n-k}\left(\tfrac{\Delta v}{2}\right)^k\right\},\end{aligned} \tag{33}$$

$$\begin{aligned}\phi\left(u_c+\tfrac{\Delta u}{2},v_c+\tfrac{\Delta v}{2}\right)&=\phi(\sigma_c)+\left.\tfrac{\partial\phi}{\partial u}\right|_{\sigma_c}\left(\tfrac{\Delta u}{2}\right)+\left.\tfrac{\partial\phi}{\partial v}\right|_{\sigma_c}\left(\tfrac{\Delta v}{2}\right)\\&+\tfrac{1}{2}\left\{\left.\tfrac{\partial^2\phi}{\partial u^2}\right|_{\sigma_c}\left(\tfrac{\Delta u}{2}\right)^2+2\left.\tfrac{\partial^2\phi}{\partial u\partial v}\right|_{\sigma_c}\left(\tfrac{\Delta u}{2}\right)\left(\tfrac{\Delta v}{2}\right)+\left.\tfrac{\partial^2\phi}{\partial v^2}\right|_{\sigma_c}\left(\tfrac{\Delta v}{2}\right)^2\right\}\\&+\textstyle\sum_{n=3}^{\infty}\left\{\tfrac{1}{n!}\sum_{k=0}^{n}\left(\tfrac{n!}{(n-k)!k!}\right)\left.\tfrac{\partial^{(n)}\phi}{\partial u^{(n-k)}\partial v^{(k)}}\right|_{\sigma_c}\left(\tfrac{\Delta u}{2}\right)^{n-k}\left(\tfrac{\Delta v}{2}\right)^k\right\},\end{aligned} \tag{34}$$

$$\begin{aligned}\phi\left(u_c-\tfrac{\Delta u}{2},v_c+\tfrac{\Delta v}{2}\right)&=\phi(\sigma_c)-\left.\tfrac{\partial\phi}{\partial u}\right|_{\sigma_c}\left(\tfrac{\Delta u}{2}\right)+\left.\tfrac{\partial\phi}{\partial v}\right|_{\sigma_c}\left(\tfrac{\Delta v}{2}\right)\\&+\tfrac{1}{2}\left\{\left.\tfrac{\partial^2\phi}{\partial u^2}\right|_{\sigma_c}\left(\tfrac{\Delta u}{2}\right)^2-2\left.\tfrac{\partial^2\phi}{\partial u\partial v}\right|_{\sigma_c}\left(\tfrac{\Delta u}{2}\right)\left(\tfrac{\Delta v}{2}\right)+\left.\tfrac{\partial^2\phi}{\partial v^2}\right|_{\sigma_c}\left(\tfrac{\Delta v}{2}\right)^2\right\}\\&+\textstyle\sum_{n=3}^{\infty}\left\{\tfrac{1}{n!}\sum_{k=0}^{n}\left(\tfrac{n!}{(n-k)!k!}\right)\left.\tfrac{\partial^{(n)}\phi}{\partial u^{(n-k)}\partial v^{(k)}}\right|_{\sigma_c}(-1)^{n-k}\left(\tfrac{\Delta u}{2}\right)^{n-k}\left(\tfrac{\Delta v}{2}\right)^k\right\},\end{aligned} \tag{35}$$

$$\begin{aligned}\phi\left(u_c-\tfrac{\Delta u}{2},v_c-\tfrac{\Delta v}{2}\right)&=\phi(\sigma_c)-\left.\tfrac{\partial\phi}{\partial u}\right|_{\sigma_c}\left(\tfrac{\Delta u}{2}\right)-\left.\tfrac{\partial\phi}{\partial v}\right|_{\sigma_c}\left(\tfrac{\Delta v}{2}\right)\\&+\tfrac{1}{2}\left\{\left.\tfrac{\partial^2\phi}{\partial u^2}\right|_{\sigma_c}\left(\tfrac{\Delta u}{2}\right)^2+2\left.\tfrac{\partial^2\phi}{\partial u\partial v}\right|_{\sigma_c}\left(\tfrac{\Delta u}{2}\right)\left(\tfrac{\Delta v}{2}\right)+\left.\tfrac{\partial^2\phi}{\partial v^2}\right|_{\sigma_c}\left(\tfrac{\Delta v}{2}\right)^2\right\}\\&+\textstyle\sum_{n=3}^{\infty}\left\{\tfrac{1}{n!}\sum_{k=0}^{n}\left(\tfrac{n!}{(n-k)!k!}\right)\left.\tfrac{\partial^{(n)}\phi}{\partial u^{(n-k)}\partial v^{(k)}}\right|_{\sigma_c}(-1)^{n}\left(\tfrac{\Delta u}{2}\right)^{n-k}\left(\tfrac{\Delta v}{2}\right)^k\right\}.\end{aligned} \tag{36}$$

By introducing these expanded series into Equations (29)–(32) and then adding up the resultant equations,

$$\sum_{i=1}^{4}\theta_i=2\pi-\left.\frac{\partial^2\phi}{\partial u\partial v}\right|_{\sigma_c}\Delta u\Delta v+\tilde{R}, \tag{37}$$

where $\tilde{R}$ is the sum of the remainders:

$$\begin{aligned}\tilde{R}=\textstyle\sum_{n=3}^{\infty}&\left[\tfrac{1}{n!}\sum_{k=0}^{n}\left(\tfrac{n!}{(n-k)!k!}\right)\left.\tfrac{\partial^{(n)}\phi}{\partial u^{(n-k)}\partial v^{(k)}}\right|_{\sigma_c}\left\{(-1)^k+(-1)\right.\right.\\&\left.\left.+(-1)^{n-k}+(-1)^{n+1}\right\}\left(\tfrac{\Delta u}{2}\right)^{n-k}\left(\tfrac{\Delta v}{2}\right)^k\right].\end{aligned} \tag{38}$$

The sum of Equations (14), (28) and (37) follows from the Gauss–Bonnet formula:

$$\iint_D\left\{K|\mathbf{N}|+\left(\frac{\partial F_b}{\partial u}-\frac{\partial F_a}{\partial v}\right)\right\}dudv-\left.\frac{\partial^2\phi}{\partial u\partial v}\right|_{\sigma_c}\Delta u\Delta v+\tilde{R}=0, \tag{39}$$

where 2π has been canceled out. Since S is orientable and smooth, the integrand of the double integral in Equation (39) is continuous in D. The mean value theorem for definite integrals thus holds for the integral term in Equation (39). Accordingly, there exists some point σ^* in the open region of D, such that

$$\iint_D \left\{K|\mathbf{N}| + \left(\frac{\partial F_b}{\partial u} - \frac{\partial F_a}{\partial v}\right)\right\}dudv = \left\{K(\sigma^*)|\mathbf{N}(\sigma^*)| + \left(\left.\frac{\partial F_b}{\partial u}\right|_{\sigma^*} - \left.\frac{\partial F_a}{\partial v}\right|_{\sigma^*}\right)\right\}\Delta u\Delta v. \quad (40)$$

By introducing the right side of Equation (40) into Equation (39),

$$\left\{K(\sigma^*)|\mathbf{N}(\sigma^*)| + \left(\left.\frac{\partial F_b}{\partial u}\right|_{\sigma^*} - \left.\frac{\partial F_a}{\partial v}\right|_{\sigma^*}\right)\right\}\Delta u\Delta v - \left.\frac{\partial^2 \phi}{\partial u \partial v}\right|_{\sigma_c}\Delta u\Delta v + \tilde{R} = 0. \quad (41)$$

The above equation is then divided by $\Delta u\Delta v$:

$$\left\{K(\sigma^*)|\mathbf{N}(\sigma^*)| + \left(\left.\frac{\partial F_b}{\partial u}\right|_{\sigma^*} - \left.\frac{\partial F_a}{\partial v}\right|_{\sigma^*}\right)\right\} - \left.\frac{\partial^2 \phi}{\partial u \partial v}\right|_{\sigma_c} + \frac{\tilde{R}}{\Delta u\Delta v} = 0. \quad (42)$$

By taking the limit of this equation as $(\Delta u, \Delta v) \to (0,0)$,

$$\begin{aligned}\lim_{(\Delta u,\Delta v)\to(0,0)} \left\{K(\sigma^*)|\mathbf{N}(\sigma^*)| + \left(\left.\tfrac{\partial F_b}{\partial u}\right|_{\sigma^*} - \left.\tfrac{\partial F_a}{\partial v}\right|_{\sigma^*}\right)\right\} - \left.\tfrac{\partial^2 \phi}{\partial u \partial v}\right|_{\sigma_c} \\ + \lim_{(\Delta u,\Delta v)\to(0,0)}\left(\tfrac{\tilde{R}}{\Delta u\Delta v}\right) = 0.\end{aligned} \quad (43)$$

Let $I(u,v)$ be the integrand of the double integral in Equation (39). Since $I(u,v)$ is continuous in D (as mentioned above), the extreme value theorem holds for $I(u,v)$. Accordingly, there exist σ_m and σ_M in D, such that

$$I(\sigma_m) \le I(\sigma) \le I(\sigma_M), \ \forall \sigma \in D. \quad (44)$$

By the way,

$$\lim_{(\Delta u,\Delta v)\to(0,0)} I(\sigma_m) = \lim_{(\Delta u,\Delta v)\to(0,0)} I(\sigma_M) = I(\sigma_c). \quad (45)$$

Since $I(\sigma_m) \le I(\sigma^*) \le I(\sigma_M)$, by the squeeze theorem

$$\lim_{(\Delta u,\Delta v)\to(0,0)} I(\sigma^*) = I(\sigma_c). \quad (46)$$

Therefore, σ^* tends to σ_c as $(\Delta u, \Delta v) \to (0,0)$. On the other hand, the remainder term in Equation (42) is written as follows:

$$\begin{aligned}\tfrac{\tilde{R}}{\Delta u\Delta v} = \textstyle\sum_{n=3}^{\infty}\Bigg[\tfrac{1}{n!}\textstyle\sum_{k=0}^{n}\left(\tfrac{n!}{(n-k)!k!}\right)\left.\tfrac{\partial^{(n)}\phi}{\partial u^{(n-k)}\partial v^{(k)}}\right|_{\sigma_c}\Big\{(-1)^k + (-1) \\ +(-1)^{n-k} + (-1)^{n+1}\Big\}\left(\tfrac{1}{4}\right)\left(\tfrac{\Delta u}{2}\right)^{n-k-1}\left(\tfrac{\Delta v}{2}\right)^{k-1}\Bigg].\end{aligned} \quad (47)$$

In the above equation, the sum of the power terms of (-1) in the braces vanishes for all k for odd n and for even k for even n. All terms multiplied by this sum thus vanish irrespective of Δu and Δv. On the other hand, all terms for odd k for even n tend to zero as $(\Delta u, \Delta v) \to (0,0)$. Together, $\tilde{R}/(\Delta u\Delta v)$ vanishes as $(\Delta u, \Delta v) \to (0,0)$. Finally, the differential relation at σ_c is obtained as follows:

$$K(\sigma_c)|\mathbf{N}(\sigma_c)| + \left(\left.\frac{\partial F_b}{\partial u}\right|_{\sigma_c} - \left.\frac{\partial F_a}{\partial v}\right|_{\sigma_c}\right) - \left.\frac{\partial^2 \phi}{\partial u \partial v}\right|_{\sigma_c} = 0. \quad (48)$$

Since the point σ_c is arbitrary, the above relation holds for each $\sigma \in U$. This completes the proof. □

As a preliminary setup for the proof of Corollary 1, the coefficients of the first and second fundamental forms of $\mathbf{r}(u,v)$ are denoted as follows:

$$E = \langle \mathbf{r}_u, \mathbf{r}_u \rangle, \quad F = \langle \mathbf{r}_u, \mathbf{r}_v \rangle, \quad G = \langle \mathbf{r}_v, \mathbf{r}_v \rangle, \tag{49}$$

$$L = \langle \mathbf{r}_{uu}, \mathbf{n} \rangle, \quad M = \langle \mathbf{r}_{uv}, \mathbf{n} \rangle, \quad N = \langle \mathbf{r}_{vv}, \mathbf{n} \rangle. \tag{50}$$

According to Gauss' Theorema Egregium, the Gaussian curvature of an orientable smooth surface embedded in $\mathbb{R}^3$ is intrinsic. As is well known, this is proved by showing that the Gaussian curvature is represented in terms only of E,F,G, and their derivatives. The proof of Corollary 1 will proceed in a similar fashion.

Proof of Corollary 1. First, the Gaussian curvature K is expressed as a functional from Equation (11),

$$K = \frac{\left(\frac{\partial F_a}{\partial v} - \frac{\partial F_b}{\partial u}\right) + \frac{\partial^2 \phi}{\partial u \partial v}}{|\mathbf{N}|}. \tag{51}$$

The two entities ϕ and $|\mathbf{N}|$ in this equation are straightforwardly written in terms of E, F, and G:

$$\phi = \arccos\left(\frac{F}{\sqrt{EG}}\right), \tag{52}$$

$$|\mathbf{N}| = \sqrt{EG - F^2}. \tag{53}$$

To express F_a as a whole in the desired form, each of the terms consisting of F_a in Equation (9) is first rewritten:

$$\begin{aligned} \mathbf{n} \wedge \mathbf{r}_u &= \frac{\mathbf{r}_u \wedge \mathbf{r}_v}{|\mathbf{r}_u \wedge \mathbf{r}_v|} \wedge \mathbf{r}_u \\ &= \frac{1}{\sqrt{EG - F^2}} (\langle \mathbf{r}_u, \mathbf{r}_u \rangle \mathbf{r}_v - \langle \mathbf{r}_v, \mathbf{r}_u \rangle \mathbf{r}_u) \\ &= \frac{E\mathbf{r}_v - F\mathbf{r}_u}{\sqrt{EG - F^2}} \end{aligned} \tag{54}$$

and

$$\mathbf{r}_{uu} = \Gamma^u_{uu} \mathbf{r}_u + \Gamma^v_{uu} \mathbf{r}_v + L\mathbf{n}, \tag{55}$$

where Γ^k_{ij} are the Christoffel symbols of S. Then

$$\begin{aligned} F_a &= \frac{\langle \mathbf{r}_{uu}, \mathbf{n} \wedge \mathbf{r}_u \rangle}{|\mathbf{r}_u|^2} \\ &= \frac{\langle \Gamma^u_{uu} \mathbf{r}_u + \Gamma^v_{uu} \mathbf{r}_v + L\mathbf{n}, \frac{E\mathbf{r}_v - F\mathbf{r}_u}{\sqrt{EG-F^2}} \rangle}{E} \\ &= \frac{1}{E\sqrt{EG - F^2}} (\Gamma^u_{uu} \langle \mathbf{r}_u, E\mathbf{r}_v - F\mathbf{r}_u \rangle + \Gamma^v_{uu} \langle \mathbf{r}_v, E\mathbf{r}_v - F\mathbf{r}_u \rangle) \\ &= \frac{1}{E\sqrt{EG - F^2}} \left(\Gamma^u_{uu}(EF - FE) + \Gamma^v_{uu}(EG - F^2)\right) \\ &= \frac{\sqrt{EG - F^2}}{E} \Gamma^v_{uu}. \end{aligned} \tag{56}$$

We recall the expression of the Christoffel symbol Γ^{v}_{uu}, as follows:

$$\Gamma^{v}_{uu} = -\frac{E(E_v - 2F_u) + E_u F}{2(EG - F^2)}. \tag{57}$$

By introducing this expression into the above equation,

$$F_a = -\frac{E(E_v - 2F_u) + E_u F}{2E\sqrt{EG - F^2}}. \tag{58}$$

Similarly,

$$F_b = \frac{G(G_u - 2F_v) + G_v F}{2G\sqrt{EG - F^2}}. \tag{59}$$

In substituting the rewritten expressions of ϕ, $|\mathbf{N}|$, F_a, and F_b into the explicit expression of K and then manipulating the derivatives contained therein, it involves only E, F, G, and their derivatives. This completes the proof. □

5. Concluding Remarks and Examples

In summary, for orientable smooth surfaces in $\mathbb{R}^3$ we constructed a differential relation between five metric properties: K, $|\mathbf{N}|$, F_a, F_b, and ϕ. The differential relation can be applied to those surfaces given by either orthogonal or non-orthogonal parameterizations since Theorem 1 has no loss of generality for parametrization. In representing the Gaussian curvature explicitly from the differential relation of Theorem 1, the resultant equation may be regarded as a specific form of the Brioschi formula. However, it is emphasized that the objective of this study is not to establish a new expression for the Gaussian curvature, but to facilitate a general extension of the application of the Gauss–Bonnet formula via a differential relation of the metric properties of S.

We present examples of the differential relation of Theorem 1 by means of two surfaces given by orthogonal and non-orthogonal parameterizations, respectively. For a systematic investigation, we hereafter denote the three budgets of Equation (11) by I_K, I_{κ_g}, and I_ϕ in order, respectively.

Example 1. *Let S_1 be a unit sphere, and let $\mathbf{r}_1$ be a parametrization of S_1 such that $\mathbf{r}_1(u,v) = (\sin u \cos v, \sin u \sin v, \cos u)$, $(u,v) \in (0,\pi) \times (0,2\pi)$. Taking into account that $\mathbf{r}_1(u,v)$ is orthogonal and the geodesic curvature of the great circle $v = const.$ over S_1 is equal to zero, the differential relation of Equation* (11) *is reduced to a particularly elementary form, as follows:*

$$K|\mathbf{N}| + \frac{\partial F_b}{\partial u} = 0. \tag{60}$$

For a computer-aided investigation, we consider a subset of U as a test interval: $0 < u < \pi$ at $v = \pi/6$. We computed I_K, I_{κ_g}, I_ϕ, and their sum for the considered interval. First, we confirmed that the root-mean-square (r.m.s.) value of the sum is zero. Figure 3a shows the variations of the three budgets as a function of u. The values of I_ϕ are trivially zero since $\mathbf{r}_1$ is orthogonal. On the other hand, the values of I_K counteract exactly those of I_{κ_g}.

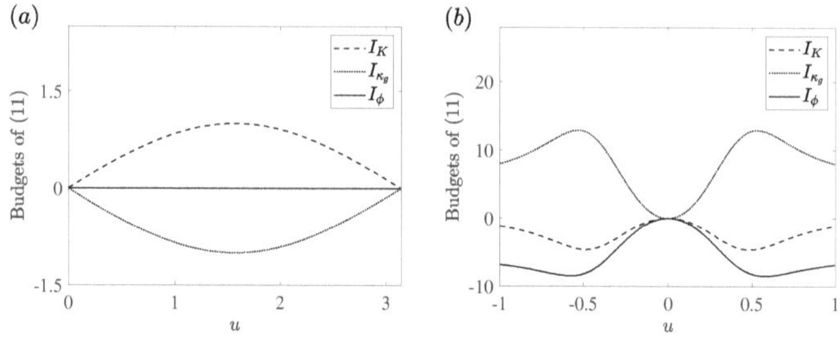

Figure 3. Budgets of the differential Equation (11) as a function of u for two surfaces: (**a**) at $v = \pi/6$ for a unit sphere and (**b**) at $v = 0$ for the monkey saddle.

Example 2. *Let S_2 be the "monkey saddle" given by $\mathbf{r}_2(u,v) = (u, v, u^3 - 3v^2u)$, $(u,v) \in (-\infty,\infty) \times (-\infty,\infty)$. It is well known that S_2 is an orientable smooth surface. We computed I_K, I_{K_g}, and I_ϕ for a test interval: $-1 \leq u \leq 1$ at $v = 0$. For this case, the order of the r.m.s. value of the sum is identified as 10^{-14}, and we attribute this error to the floating-point precision in our computation. As observed in Figure 3b, the sum of the three budgets agrees with the differential relation of Equation* (11)*, but now with the non-trivial values of I_ϕ.*

Funding: This research received no external funding.

Data Availability Statement: Not applicable.

Conflicts of Interest: The author declares no conflicts of interest.

References

1. Do Carmo, M.P. *Differential Geometry of Curves and Surfaces*, 2nd ed.; Dover Publications: New York, NY, USA, 2016.
2. O'Neill, B. *Elementary Differential Geometry*, 2nd ed.; Academic Press: New York, NY, USA, 2006.
3. Arakida, H. Light deflection and Gauss-Bonnet theorem: Defintion of total deflection angle and its applications. *Gen. Relativ. Gravit.* **2018**, *50*, 48. [CrossRef]
4. Crisnejo, G.; Gallo, E. Weak lensing in a plasma medium and gravitational deflection of massive particles using the Gauss-Bonnet theorem. A unified treatment. *Phys. Rev. D* **2018**, *97*, 124016. [CrossRef]
5. Gibbons, G.W.; Werner, M.C. Applications of the Gauss–Bonnet theorem to gravitational lensing. *Class. Quantum Grav.* **2008**, *25*, 235009. [CrossRef]
6. Ishihara, A.; Suzuki, Y.; Ono, T.; Asada, H. Finite-distance corrections to the gravitational bending angle of light in the strong deflection limit. *Phys. Rev. D* **2017**, *95*, 044017. [CrossRef]
7. Ishihara, A.; Suzuki, Y.; Ono, T.; Kitamura, T.; Asada, H. Gravitational bending angle of light for finite distance and the Gauss-Bonnet theorem. *Phys. Rev. D* **2016**, *94*, 084015. [CrossRef]
8. Jusufi, K.; Övgün, A. Gravitational lensing by rotating wormholes. *Phys. Rev. D* **2018**, *97*, 024042. [CrossRef]
9. Jusufi, K.; Övgün, A.; Saavedra, J.; Vásquez, Y.; González, P.A. Deflection of light by rotating black holes using the Gauss-Bonnet theorem. *Phys. Rev. D* **2018**, *97*, 124024. [CrossRef]
10. Jusufi, K.; Werner, M.C.; Banerjee, A.; Övgün, A. Light deflection by a rotating global monopole spacetime. *Phys. Rev. D* **2017**, *95*, 104012. [CrossRef]
11. Ono, T.; Ishihara, A.; Asada, H. Deflection angle of light for an observer and source at finite distance from a rotating wormhole. *Phys. Rev. D* **2018**, *98*, 044047. [CrossRef]
12. Övgün, A. Light deflection by Damour-Solodukhin wormholes and Gauss-Bonnet theorem. *Phys. Rev. D* **2018**, *98*, 044033. [CrossRef]
13. Övgün, A. Weak field deflection angle by regular black holes with cosmic strings using the Gauss-Bonnet theorem. *Phys. Rev. D* **2019**, *99*, 104075. [CrossRef]
14. Övgün, A. Deflection angle of photons through dark matter by black holes and wormholes using Gauss–Bonnet theorem. *Universe* **2019**, *5*, 115. [CrossRef]
15. Övgün, A.; Gyulchev, G.; Jusufi, K. Weak gravitational lensing by phantom black holes and phantom wormholes using the Gauss–Bonnet theorem. *Ann. Phys.* **2019**, *406*, 152–172. [CrossRef]

16. Övgün, A.; Sakalli, I.; Saavedra, J. Shadow cast and deflection angle of Kerr-Newman-Kasuya spacetime. *J. Cosmol. Astropart. Phys.* **2018**, *10*, 041. [CrossRef]
17. Övgün, A.; Sakalli, I.; Saavedra, J. Weak gravitational lensing by Kerr-MOG black hole and Gauss–Bonnet theorem. *Ann. Phys.* **2019**, *411*, 167978. [CrossRef]
18. Krantz, S.G.; Parks, H.R. *A Primer of Real Analytic Functions*, 2nd ed.; Birkhäuser Advanced Texts: Boston, MA, USA, 2002.

mathematics

MDPI

Article

The Problems of Dimension Four, and Some Ramifications

Valentin Poénaru

Laboratoire de mathematiques, Université Paris-Sud XI, CEDEX, 91405 Orsay, France;
valpoe@yahoo.com or valpoe@hotmail.com

Abstract: In this short note, I present a very quick review of the peculiarities of dimension four in geometric topology. I consider, in particular, the role of geometric simple connectivity (which means handle decomposition without handles of index one) for both closed manifolds and open manifolds and for finitely presented groups, together with some of recent developments in geometric group theory.

Keywords: DIFF category; geometric simple connectivity; 4-dimensional topology; finitely presented groups; QSF property

MSC: 20F65; 20F55; 05C40

Citation: Poénaru V. The Problems of Dimension Four, and Some Ramifications. *Mathematics* **2023**, *11*, 3826. https://doi.org/10.3390/math11183826

Academic Editor: Jay Jahangiri

Received: 16 August 2023
Revised: 30 August 2023
Accepted: 5 September 2023
Published: 6 September 2023

1. Introduction

Since about 1950, geometric topology has seen spectacular advances. However, deep mysteries still remain, exactly in dimension four—the present main topic in this short paper. In addition, since geometric topology is very closely related to group theory, I discuss that as well here.

As soon as we are in dimensions strictly larger than three, there are three related contexts in which manifolds can be studied: differentiable (DIFF), piecewise linear (PL) and topological (TOP). We cannot go here into the deep interconnections between these three distinct categories, and to a large extent, I restrict the discussion here to the DIFF case; whenever not, this is explicitly stated. Of course, DIFF means C^∞.

I think that at the origin of this topic is the famous Poincaré Conjecture [1] from 1904, stating that each closed simply connected 3-manifold is homeomorphic to the 3-sphere $\mathbb{S}^3$. In the 1930s, this was extended to the generalized Poincaré Conjecture: each closed n-manifold homotopically equivalent to $\mathbb{S}^n$ is actually homeomorphic to $\mathbb{S}^n$.

Very soon, mathematicians found out that as soon as one gets to n equals 3, things get very hard, and it was believed that difficulties only increased with dimensions. However, in about 1957, there was a big breakthrough that totally changed the perspective. Steve Smale discovered that in dimensions 5 and more, things become even easier, and so he proved the generalized Poincaré Conjecture in dimensions $n \geq 5$ [2,3].

Soon, John Stallings found a different approach for the same problem [4]; many big breakthroughs followed (see for instance [5,6]), and high-dimensional topology became a rather well understood topic.

For further purposes, I only mention here another related important theorem of Stallings [7]: there is a unique DIFF structure on the Euclidean space $\mathbb{R}^n$, for any $n \geq 5$. More generally, John Milnor and Michel Kervaire [8,9] showed that, in those dimensions, the possible DIFF structures are actually controlled by algebraic topology.

Then, around 1983, Mike Freedman proved the 4-dimensional TOP Poincaré Conjecture, and then he also essentially cleaned up the structure of compact, simply connected 4-manifolds in the TOP case [10,11].

Next, using Freedman's work and also the equations of Yang-Mills from quantum field theory, Simon Donaldson showed, among many other things, that there are even uncountably many DIFF structures on the 4-dimensional Euclidean space $\mathbb{R}^4$ [12,13].

Finally, in 2002–2003, Grisha Perelman, using the Ricci flow, a nonlinear partial differential equation in infinite dimensions stemming from differential geometry, proved the 3-dimensional Poincaré Conjecture and, at the same time, Thurston's Conjecture on the geometrization of all closed 3-manifolds [14–16].

This is a very brief account of the glamorous successes of geometric topology, too brief indeed and incomplete, but sufficient to understand how things have been in recent decades. Now, we can move to the open problems.

2. Open Problems and Dimension Four

The first problem (the very obvious one) is the DIFF 4-dimensional Poincaré Conjecture. This is still a deep mystery, and the fact is that dimension four is really very special.

Here below, I present a list of items that make dimension four really very different from all the others.

(A) Already in Smale's work cited above, the notion of *geometric simple connectivity* (GSC) arose, which I very briefly explain now (more about it is written in the Appendix at the end of the paper).

The notion of handle-body decomposition is equivalent to a Morse function where higher index singularities occur only for higher values of the function. A handle of index λ (a λ-handle), is a copy of

$$B^{\lambda} \times B^{n-\lambda}$$

that is attached to some union of lower index handles, along $\partial B^{\lambda} \times B^{n-\lambda}$, and a manifold is *geometrically simply connected* if it admits a handle-body decomposition where all the 1-handles are cancellable by appropriate 2-handles; in the Appendix to the paper, I offer a more precise definition.

In any case, we have an obvious implication

$$GSC \implies \pi_1 = 0,$$

but what about the converse implication?

Here is the complete answer for compact n-manifolds:

(A1) For $n \geq 5$, the answer is yes, $\pi_1 = 0$ implies GSC. This was actually one of the main steps in Smale's proof of the high-dimensional Poincaré Conjecture.

(A2) For $n = 4$, the answer is no. Very explicitly, the Po-Mazur manifolds, which are non-trivial factors of the 5-ball discovered long ago by the present author and by Barry Mazur [17,18] and which clearly are simply-connected, were shown many years later not to be GSC by Andrew Casson. He never published his argument, but many people knew about it, and personally, I learned it from Mike Freedman.

(A3) Finally, for n equal 3, the answer is again yes. Very explicitly, the corresponding implication is equivalent to the original Poincaré Conjecture, proved by Perelman [14–16].

Similar results to (A1) and (A3) are true for open manifolds, provided one adds the condition of simple connectivity at infinity (a space is said to be simply connected at infinity if loops close to infinity can be collapsed to a point still staying close to infinity); see here, for instance, the paper by Po-Tanasi [19].

When one moves then to the non-compact manifolds with a non-empty boundary, then we enter largely uncharted territory, except for the very special spaces endowed with high symmetry coming from geometric group theory. This is a territory which, together with others, I have explored a great deal, and we return to it later.

(B) When we go to the issue of DIFF structures versus TOP structures on a given n-manifold, then dimension four is again very special.

For the dimensions $n = 1, 2$ or 3, on a given manifold, one can largely ignore the distinction between the two, while for $n \geq 5$, the difference between DIFF and TOP is controlled by algebraic topology.

On the other hand, when we move to dimension four, the situation is completely different. The uncountable infinity of different DIFF structures on $\mathbb{R}^4$, already mentioned earlier, lays this in front of us. Clearly, algebraic topology is powerless here; is there maybe some still-to-be-discovered quantum topology that could help us here? I certainly do not know, and I do not know either whether there is some earthly connection between the present item (B) and the previous one (A). However, there is a connection between our (B) and the next item (C).

(C) It is only in dimension four that the Yang-Mills equations (and hence the Maxwell equations) make sense. This is so because only in dimension four is the Hodge dual of a 2-form again a 2-form. Of course, some people might add that four is the dimension of our space-time, but that argument does not very much appeal to me.

(D) Largely connected with the Poincaré Conjecture is the classical Schoenflies problem, of about the same vintage. The issue here is whether an $\mathbb{S}^{n-1}$ embedded in $\mathbb{S}^n$ divides it into two copies of $\mathbb{B}^n$.

Again, of course, there are the contexts DIFF, PL and TOP. In any case, since the 1920s, things were clear for n equal to three or less, and complete mystery lay beyond that. Then, in the late 1950s, a few years before Smale, came the big breakthrough of Barry Mazur [20,21], who was barely 18 at that time. Below is what Barry proved.

If X^n is any of the two manifolds into which $\mathbb{S}^{n-1}$ divides $\mathbb{S}^n$, then we have a homeomorphism f from $X^n - \{\text{a boundary point}\}$ to $\mathbb{B}^n - \{\text{a boundary point}\}$, extending of course to the boundary point as well, and this f is infinitely differentiable, except maybe at that boundary point.

A few years later, using the heaviest artillery of high-dimensional topology, Smale and Milnor-Kervaire proved that for dimensions n equal to 5 or more, the map f is C^∞ even at that boundary point.

Hence, if $n \geq 5$, via Mazur, Smale and Milnor-Kervaire, we have that

$$X^n \underset{DIFF}{=} \mathbb{B}^n,$$

holding actually for all dimensions, EXCEPT for $n = 4$, where it is still a big open mystery!

I have managed to prove that in the 4-dimensional Schoenflies context, the Schoenflies ball X^4 is GSC [22]. Now, if we would manage to show that any DIFF compact 4-manifold homotopically equivalent to the 4-ball is GSC, this would be a big step towards the DIFF 4-dimensional Poincaré Conjecture; see [23]. Personally, I have some doubts concerning the truth of the conjecture in question.

For more details on the topology of dimension 4 and its particularities, we refer to the classic books by Akbulut [24], Freedman-Quinn [11], Gompf-Stipsicz [25] and Scorpan [26].

3. Discrete Groups

We end this short review paper with some words concerning geometric group theory—a topic that is very closely connected with the things we have just discussed.

It concerns finitely presented groups (no other ones will be considered here) and the geometric and topological properties of the universal covering spaces of the compact spaces having as fundamental group, the group in question. According to the viewpoint of the quasi-isometries of Misha Gromov [27], the groups and those universal covering spaces are in fact equivalent objects, and so many topological properties make sense for groups as well (see e.g., [28,29]).

Now, when Grisha Perelman proved the Poincaré Conjecture and Thurston's geometrization, this had very important consequences for group theory as well. For instance, it actually implied that any fundamental group of a compact 3-manifold is simply connected at infinity, whereas, on the other hand, this turns out to be a very rare property among discrete groups [30].

However, in the realm of group theory, descending from the old classical work of Max Dehn, there is the notion of quasi-simple filtration (QSF), which for fundamental groups of 3-manifolds is equivalent to simple connectivity at infinity; in the appendix here below, I define QSF rigorously.

A few years ago, I managed to prove that all groups are QSF; see here the trilogy [31–33] and also the review papers by Daniele Otera and myself [34,35]. Now, GSC also makes sense for groups, and it is a stronger property than QSF.

Louis Funar, Daniele Otera and myself are currently working on a project to show that all groups are actually GSC, continuing our previous research in this direction [36,37]. On this topic, see also my forthcoming paper "On the Whitehead nightmare and related topics" which will appear in an issue of the European Mathematical Journal dedicated to the 80th birthday of the recent Abel prize winner Dennis Sullivan.

4. Appendix (Explaining Some Technical Terms)

4.1. On GSC

For a manifold M^n of dimension n, we consider a decomposition starting with an n-ball if M^n is compact, or with a regular neighborhood of an infinite tree if M^n is not; then, in increasing order of indices λ come handles

$$H^\lambda = B^\lambda \times B^{n-\lambda}, \quad (\partial H^\lambda = \partial B^\lambda \times B^{n-\lambda} \cup B^\lambda \times \partial B^{n-\lambda}),$$

with $\partial B^\lambda \times B^{n-\lambda}$ being the attaching zone to lower index handles and $B^\lambda \times \partial B^{n-\lambda}$ being the "lateral surface". For two handles H^2_α, H^1_β, we consider the incidence number $a_{\alpha,\beta}$, which counts how many times the attaching zone of the 2-handle goes through the lateral surface of the 1-handle; no signs are involved here.

We say that the manifold M^n is GSC if for the family of 1-handles

$$\sum_{i \in I} H^1_i$$

we can find a family of 2-handles $\sum_{j \in J} H^2_j$ with $I \approx J$, such that the corresponding geometric incidence matrix a_{ji} has the property "easy id + nilpotent" (equivalent to id + nilpotent in the finite case), namely

$$a_{ji} = \delta_{ji} + b_{ji}, \quad b_{ji} \in \mathbb{Z}_+, \quad \text{with } b_{ji} > 0 \implies j > i.$$

For more detailed information about this fundamental notion in geometric topology, low-dimensional topology and geometric group theory, see [19,28,38,39].

4.2. On Yang-Mills Equations

We consider a closed oriented 4-manifold M^4 endowed with a complex bundle of structure group G, having a connection A. This comes with a curvature form F_A with values in the 2-forms

$$\Omega(M^4, \mathcal{L}G).$$

With this, we have Bianchi's theorem

$$d_A F_A = 0.$$

If $\star$ is the Hodge operator between 2-forms, we also have the Yang-Mills equations (written here without the source term), namely

$$d_A \star F_A = 0.$$

In a more basic form, this means (with $\epsilon =$ charge, $\mathcal{I} =$ current (or source)) that

$$\partial F_{\mu\nu} / \partial x_\nu + 2\epsilon [A_\nu \times F_{\mu\nu}] + \mathcal{I}_\mu = 0.$$

The unknown here is the connection A, and as soon as G involves two dimensions or more, the equations are non-linear. For $G = U(1)$, we find Maxwell.

Note also that the Yang-Mills equations are at the core of the Standard Model of elementary particles, but that is another story. For all the details of this interesting field, we refer the reader to and recommend Donaldson's wonderful book [13].

4.3. On QSF

A locally compact complex X is QSF (*quasi-simply filtrated*) if for every compact subset k of X there is some abstract simply connected finite complex K coming with a commutative diagram

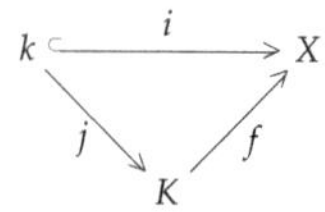

where j is an inclusion map, and f is some simplicial map satisfying the Dehn-type property $j(k) \cap M_2(f) = \emptyset$ (where $M_2(f) \subset K$ denotes the set of double points of f).

This notion was introduced by Stephen Brick and Mike Mihalik in [40] (but see also [28,29,41]), and they also proved the following useful concepts:

- If K_1 and K_2 are two finite complexes with the same fundamental group G, then $\tilde{K}_1$ if QSF if and only if $\tilde{K}_2$ is QSF. In this case we say that the group G is QSF.
- For fundamental groups of finite 3-complexes, QSF is equivalent to simple connectivity at infinity.

5. Conclusions

In this short survey paper, we have stressed once again that four-dimensional topology is very special indeed and deserves to be further studied in depth. In addition, in dimension 4, as far as geometric topology is concerned, there are still big questions waiting to be explored and solved. Furthermore, all these questions concern several distinct branches of mathematics: we have differential geometry and topology, calculus, Riemannian geometry, geometric topology, global analysis, combinatorial topology, algebraic topology, wild topology, group theory, geometric group theory, mathematical physics, theoretical physics and partial differential equations. It is a rich and vast research area, with connections to the real world and applications in physics.

Funding: This research received no external funding.

Data Availability Statement: Not applicable.

Conflicts of Interest: The author declares no conflict of interest.

References

1. Poincaré, H. Cinquième complément à l'analysis situs. *Rend. Circ. Mat. Palermo* **1904**, *18*, 45–110. [CrossRef]
2. Smale, S. On the Struture of Manifolds. *Am. J. Math.* **1962**, *84*, 387–399. [CrossRef]
3. Smale, S. The Story of the Higher Dimensional Poincaré Conjecture (What actually happened on the beaches of Rio). *Math. Intell.* **1990**, *12*, 44–51. [CrossRef]
4. Stallings, J.R. Polyhedral homotopy-spheres. *Bull. Am. Math. Soc.* **1960**, *66*, 485–488. [CrossRef]
5. Zeeman, E.C. The generalised Poincaré conjecture. *Bull. Am. Math. Soc.* **1961**, *67*, 270. [CrossRef]
6. Zeeman, E.C. The Poincaré Conjecture for n greater than or equal to 5. In *Topology of 3-Manifolds and Related Topics*; (Proc. The Univ. of Georgia Institute, 1961); Prentice-Hall: Upper Saddle River, NJ, USA, 1962; pp. 198–204.
7. Stallings, J.R. The piecewise linear structure of Euclidean spaces. *Proc. Cambr. Math. Soc.* **1962**, *58*, 481–488. [CrossRef]
8. Kervaire, M.; Milnor, J.W. Groups of homotopy spheres I. *Ann. Math.* **1963**, *77*, 504–537. [CrossRef]
9. Milnor, J.W. On manifolds homeomorphic to the 7-sphere. *Ann. Math.* **1956**, *64*, 399–405. [CrossRef]
10. Freedman, M. The Topology of four-dimensional manifolds. *J. Diff. Geom.* **1983**, *17*, 279–315. [CrossRef]
11. Freedman, M.H.; Quinn, F. *Topology of 4-Manifolds*; Princeton mathematical Series 39; Princeton University Press: Princeton, NJ, USA, 1990.
12. Donaldson, S.K. An application of gauge theory to four-dimensional topology. *J. DIff. Geom.* **1983**, *18*, 278–315. [CrossRef]
13. Donaldson, S.K.; Kronheimer, P.B. *The Geometry of Four-Manifolds*; Oxford Mathematical Monographs; Oxford University Press: New York, NY, USA, 1990.

14. Perelman, G. The entropy formula for the Ricci flow and its geometric applications. *arXiv* **2002**, arXiv:math/0211159.
15. Perelman, G. Ricci flow with surgery on three-manifolds. *arXiv* **2003**, arXiv:math/0303109.
16. Perelman, G. Finite extinction time for the solutions of the Ricci flow on certain three-manifolds. *arXiv* **2003**, arXiv:math/0307245.
17. Mazur, B. A note on some contractible 4-manifolds. *Ann. Math.* **1961**, *73*, 221–228. [CrossRef]
18. Poénaru, V. Les décompositions de l'hypercube en produit topologique. *Bull. Soc. Math. France* **1960**, *88*, 113–129. [CrossRef]
19. Poénaru, V.; Tanasi, C. Some remarks on geometric simple connectivity. *Acta Math. Hung.* **1998**, *81*, 1–12. [CrossRef]
20. Poénaru, V. What is ... an infinite swindle. *Notices AMS* **2007**, *54*, 619–622.
21. Mazur, B. On embeddings of spheres. *Bull. AMS* **1959**, *65*, 59–65. [CrossRef]
22. Poénaru, V. All smooth four-dimensional Schoenflies balls are geometrically simply connected. *arXiv* **2016**, arXiv:1609.05094.
23. Poénaru, V. *All Smooth Four-Dimensional Schoenflies Balls Are Geometrically Simply Connected*; Surveys in geometry I; Springer: Cham, Switzerland, 2022; pp. 269–307.
24. Akbulut, S. *4-Manifolds*; Oxford University Press: Oxford, UK, 2016.
25. Gompf, R.E.; Stipsicz, A. *4-Manifolds and Kirby Calculus*; Issue 20 of the book Graduate studies in mathematics; American Mathematical Society: Providence, RI, USA, 1999.
26. Scorpan, A. *The Wild World of 4-Manifolds*; American Mathematical Society: Providence, RI, USA, 2005.
27. Gromov, M. Asymptotic invariants of infinite groups. In *Geometric Group Theory, Volume 2*; London Math. Society Lecture Note Series 182; Cambridge University Press: Cambridge, UK, 1993; pp. 1–295.
28. Otera, D.E. Topological tameness conditions of groups. Results and developments. *Lith. Math. J.* **2016**, *3*, 357–376. [CrossRef]
29. Otera, D.E. On simplicial resolutions of groups. *Rev. Real Acad. Cienc. Exactas Fis. Nat. Ser. Mat.* **2022**, *116*, 138. [CrossRef]
30. Davis, M.W. Groups generated by reflections and aspherical manifolds not covered by Euclidean spaces. *Ann. Math.* **1983**, *117*, 293–324. [CrossRef]
31. Poénaru, V. Equivariant, locally finite inverse representations with uniformly bounded zipping length, for arbitrary finitely presented groups. *Geom. Dedicata* **2013**, *167*, 91–121. [CrossRef]
32. Poénaru, V. Geometric simple connectivity and finitely presented groups. *arXiv* **2014**, arXiv:1404.4283.
33. Poénaru, V. All finitely presented groups are QSF. *arXiv* **2014**, arXiv:1409.7325.
34. Otera, D.E.; Poénaru, V. *Topics in Geometric Group Theory, Part I*; Handbook of Group Actions, Volume V, Advanced Lectures in Mathematics; University of Chicago Press: Chicago, IL, USA, 2020; Volume 48, pp. 307–353.
35. Poénaru, V. *Topics in Geometric Group Theory, Part II*; Handbook of Group Actions, Volume V, Advanced Lectures in Mathematics; University of Chicago Press: Chicago, IL, USA, 2020; Volume 48, pp. 347–398.
36. Otera, D.E.; Poénaru, V. "Easy" Representations and the QSF property for groups. *Bull. Belgian Math. Soc. Simon Stevin* **2012**, *19*, 385–398. [CrossRef]
37. Otera, D.E.; Poénaru, V. Finitely presented groups and the Whitehead nightmare. *Groups Geom. Dyn.* **2017**, *11*, 291–310. [CrossRef]
38. Otera, D.E.; Poénaru, V.; Tanasi, C. On Geometric Simple Connectivity. *Bull. Mathématique Société Des Sci. Mathématiques Roum. Nouv. Série* **2010**, *101*, 157–176.
39. Otera, D.E.; Russo, F.G.; Tanasi, C. On 3-dimensional WGSC inverse-representations of groups. *Acta Math. Hung.* **2017**, *151*, 379–390. [CrossRef]
40. Brick, S.G.; Mihalik, M.L. The QSF property for groups and spaces. *Math. Z.* **1995**, *220*, 207–217. [CrossRef]
41. Stallings, J.R. Brick's quasi-simple filtrations for groups and 3-manifolds. In *Geometric Group Theory, Volume 1*; Volume 181 of London Mathematical Society Lecture Note Series; Cambridge University Press: Cambridge, UK, 1993; pp. 188–203.

mathematics

MDPI

Article

On *c*-Compactness in Topological and Bitopological Spaces

Rehab Alharbi [1], Jamal Oudetallah [2], Mutaz Shatnawi [2] and Iqbal M. Batiha [3,4,*]

[1] Department of Mathematics, Jazan University, Jazan 2097, Saudi Arabia; ralharbi@jazanu.edu.sa
[2] Department of Mathematics, Irbid National University, Irbid 21110, Jordan; dr_jamal@inu.edu.jo (J.O.); m.shatnawi@inu.edu.jo (M.S.)
[3] Department of Mathematics, Al Zaytoonah University of Jordan, Amman 11733, Jordan
[4] Nonlinear Dynamics Research Center (NDRC), Ajman University, Ajman 346, United Arab Emirates
* Correspondence: i.batiha@zuj.edu.jo

Abstract: The primary goal of this research is to initiate the pairwise *c*-compact concept in topological and bitopological spaces. This would make us to define the concept of *c*-compact space with some of its generalization, and present some necessary notions such as the *H*-closed, the quasi compact and extremely disconnected compact spaces in topological and bitopological spaces. As a consequence, we derive numerous theoretical results that demonstrate the relations between *c*-separation axioms and the *c*-compact spaces.

Keywords: pairwise compact; pairwise *c*-compact; pairwise *H*-closed; pairwise quasi compact space

MSC: 54D35

Citation: Alharbi, R.; Oudetallah, J.; Shatnawi, M.; Batiha, I.M. On *c*-Compactness in Topological and Bitopological Spaces. *Mathematics* **2023**, *11*, 4251. https://doi.org/10.3390/math11204251

Academic Editor: Daniele Ettore Otera

Received: 6 September 2023
Revised: 6 October 2023
Accepted: 9 October 2023
Published: 11 October 2023

1. Introduction

Compactness owns a significant role in topology and also so for a certain of its more grounded and weaker kinds. Among those kinds is *H*-closedness, whereby the theory of such kinds was studied by Alexandroff et al. in 1929 [1]. Thirty years after that date, Singal et al. discussed the spaces of nearly-compact type. In 1976, the *S*-compact space was established as another type of compact spaces [2]. Many other researchers have explored a few other types of compactness from time to time [3]. In this work, we intend to introduce many new theoretical results of the weaker type of compact spaces for the purpose of defining the *c*-compact space, and then generalizing such space to pairwise *c*-compact space.

The notion of bitopological spaces is a set endowed with two topologies, and it might be written as $\chi = (\chi, \beta_1, \beta_2)$, where β_1, β_2 are topologies on χ. Typically, if the set is χ and the topologies are β_1 and β_2, then the bitopological space is referred to as (χ, β_1, β_2). Corresponding to well-known properties of topological spaces, there are versions for bitopological spaces. We state some of them below for completeness:

- A bitopological space (χ, β_1, β_2) is pairwise compact if each cover $\{U_i \mid i \in I\}$ of χ with $U_i \in \beta_1 \cup \beta_2$ contains a finite subcover. In this case, $\{U_i \mid i \in I\}$ must contain at least one member from β_1 and at least one member from β_2.
- A bitopological space (χ, β_1, β_2) is pairwise Hausdorff if for any two distinct points $x, y \in \chi$ there exist disjoint $U_1 \in \beta_1$ and $U_2 \in \beta_2$ with $x \in U_1$ and $y \in U_2$.
- A bitopological space (χ, β_1, β_2) is pairwise zero-dimensional if opens in (χ, β_1) which are closed in (χ, β_2) form a basis for (χ, β_1), and opens in (χ, β_2) which are closed in (χ, β_1) form a basis for (χ, β_2).

The notion of bitopological space is associated with several previous studies that have been performed on bitopological spaces through which every single one of topologies is just a set of points that satisfies a set of axioms. With some common standard theoretical findings characterized by Tietze extension, the so-called pairwise normal spaces, pairwise regular and pairwise Hausdorff were studied well in 1963 by Kelly [4]. Afterward, Kim (1968) and Patty (1967) carried some further works out in the field of bitopological spaces [5,6]. Expand ability, nearly expand ability and feebly expand ability of bitoplogical spaces were explained by Oudetallah in [7,8]. In addition, the space of pairwise r-compact was defined well in bitopological spaces in [9].

For the reason of that the subject of c-compactness is one of the topological spaces' subjects, we intend to deeply explore this subject in the bitopological spaces. Accordingly, there will be a lot of theoretical results and findings that can be satisfied in these bitopological spaces. We think that the results derived in this paper can find their applications in some applications in the field of real analysis due to it is known, e.g., that $(\mathbb{R}, \tau_u)$ doesn't represent a compact space, but $(\mathbb{R}, \tau_u, \tau_u)$ is a c-bitopological compact space. For instance, this assertion ultimately allows one to apply the Heine-Borel Theorem, which is regarded very important in the field of real analysis. In this article, we intend to propose a new class of compact spaces, named the pairwise c-compact space (or simply p-c-compact) in topological spaces and bitopological spaces. Accordingly, numerous results are generated from this concept related to the H-closed, the quasi compact and extremely disconnected compact spaces in the considered spaces. In addition, numerous other results associated with relations between c-separation axioms and the c-compact spaces are derived as well. However, the rest of this article is organized in the subsequent order: In the next part, we define the p-c-compact space, and then we establish numerous results on the basis of this space. In Section 3, we derive other several theorems associated with the connection of the c-separation axioms with the c-compact spaces. Finally, the last section summarizes the main points of this work.

2. On p-c-Compact Spaces

In this part, we aim to set a definition for the p-c-compact concept in topological spaces and bitopological spaces. As a consequence, numerous other definitions related to this concept are defined well. Those definitions are then used to derive numerous generalizations and novel results associated with the H closed, the quasi compact and extremely disconnected compact spaces in topological spaces and bitopological spaces. Herein, it is noteworthy to highlight that all preliminaries stated below, are considered an important part of the contribution of this work. In particular, such preliminaries would help us in establishing Theorems 2 and 3 stated at the end of this section in which the first theorem determines a strong condition that makes the topological space χ is c-compact, while the second theorem outlines another strong condition that can make the bitopological space χ is p-compact.

Definition 1 ([10]). *If $B \subseteq \chi$ and (χ, β) is a topological space. Then*

(i) *If $B = \overset{o}{\overline{B}}$, then B is regular open set of χ.*
(ii) *$B = \overline{B^o}$ if and only if B is regular closed set of χ.*
(iii) *There exists an open set F in which $F \subseteq B \subseteq \overline{F}$ if and only if B is a semi-open set in χ.*

Definition 2. *Consider (χ, β_1, β_2) is a bitopological space and $B \subseteq \chi$. We say that*

(i) *B is a p-regular open set if $B = Int_{\beta_1}(CL_{\beta_1}(B))$ and $B = Int_{\beta_2}(CL_{\beta_2}(B))$.*
(ii) *B is a p-regular closed set if $B = CL_{\beta_1}(Int_{\beta_1}(B))$ and $B = CL_{\beta_2}(Int_{\beta_2}(B))$.*
(ii) *B is a p-semi-open set if there exists an open set ω in which $\omega_{\beta_1} \subseteq B \subseteq CL_{\beta_1}(\omega)$ and $\omega_{\beta_2} \subseteq B \subseteq CL_{\beta_2}(\omega)$.*

Remark 1. *If (χ, β_1, β_2) is a bitopological space and $B \subseteq \chi$, we have*

- *If $\chi - B$ is a p-regular open set, then B is called a p-regular closed set.*
- *If $\chi - B$ is a p-regular closed set, then B is called a p-regular open set.*

Theorem 1. *Consider (χ, β_1, β_2) is a bitopological space. Each p-open set is a p-semi-open set.*

Proof. Consider B is a p-regular open set. Then, we have $Int_{\beta_i}(B) \subseteq B \subseteq CL_{\beta_i}(B)$, for all $i = 1,2$. So, we obtain $\omega \subseteq B \subseteq CL_{\beta_i}(\omega)$, for all $i = 1,2$. Therefore, B is a p-semi-open set. □

Definition 3 ([2]). *If every open cover of χ has a finite subfamily whose closures cover χ, then the topological space (χ, β) is called quasi H-closed space.*

Definition 4 ([2]). *If every β_i-open cover of χ has a finite subfamily whose closures cover χ, the bitopological space $\chi = (\chi, \beta_1, \beta_2)$ is called p-quasi H-closed space, for all $i = 1,2$.*

Definition 5 ([11]). *If every open cover has a finite subfamily such that the interior of the closures of which covers χ, then the space (χ, β) is called nearly compact space.*

Definition 6. *If every β_i-open cover of χ has a finite subfamily so that the interior of closures of which covers χ, then the bitopological space $\chi = (\chi, \beta_1, \beta_2)$ is called a p-nearly compact space, for all $i = 1,2$.*

Definition 7 ([2,12]). *If every semi-open cover of χ has a finite subfamily whose closure covers χ, then the space (χ, β) is called S-closed space.*

Definition 8. *If every β_i-semi open cover of χ has a finite subfamily whose closure covers χ, then the bitopological space $\chi = (\chi, \beta_1, \beta_2)$ is called a p-S-closed space, for all $i = 1,2$.*

Definition 9. *Consider $\chi = (\chi, \beta_1, \beta_2)$ is a bitopological space. It is said that χ is a p-c-compact space if for all $i, j = 1,2$ and $\underset{\sim}{F} = \{\omega_\alpha : \alpha \in \wedge\}$ is a β_i-open cover of A, there exists a finite collection of β_i-open sets $\omega_{\alpha_1}, \omega_{\alpha_2}, \ldots, \omega_{\alpha_n}$ such that $A \subset \bigcup_{k=1}^{n} \overline{\omega_{\alpha_k}}$, for all $i = 1,2$.*

Definition 10 ([2,4]). *A Housderff space $\chi = (\chi, \beta)$ is defined as a p-H-closed space if for all open cover $\underset{\sim}{F} = \{\omega_\alpha : \alpha \in \wedge\}$ of χ, there exists a finite collection $\{\omega_{\alpha_k}\}_{k=1}^{n}$ in which $A \subset \bigcup_{k=1}^{n} \overline{\omega_{\alpha_k}}$.*

Definition 11. *A p-Housderff space $\chi = (\chi, \beta_1, \beta_2)$ is defined as a p-H-closed space if β_i-open cover $\underset{\sim}{F} = \{\omega_\alpha : \alpha \in \wedge\}$ has a finite β_i-collection $\{\omega_{\alpha_k}\}_{k=1}^{n}$ such that $A \subset \bigcup_{k=1}^{n} \overline{\omega_{\alpha_k}}$, for all $i, j = 1,2$.*

Definition 12 ([2]). *A set A of a bitopological space is defined as regular open set if $Int(\overline{A}) = A$.*

Definition 13. *If $Int(\overline{A}) = A$ in β_1 and $Int(\overline{A}) = A$ in β_2, then the subset A of bitopological space (χ, β_1, β_2) is called a p-regular open set.*

Theorem 2. *Consider $\chi = (\chi, \beta)$ is a topological space. Then, the space χ is c-compact if and only if for all A subset of χ and for every $\underset{\sim}{F} = \{\omega_\alpha : \alpha \in \wedge\}$ in which ω_α is a regular open set and covers A, there exists a finite collection $\{\omega_{\alpha_k}\}_{k=1}^{n}$ of $\underset{\sim}{F}$ in which $A \subset \bigcup_{k=1}^{n} \overline{\omega_{\alpha_k}}$.*

Proof. $\Rightarrow$ Consider χ is a c-compact space. Consider $A \subset \chi$ and $\underset{\sim}{F} = \{\omega_\alpha : \alpha \in \wedge\}$ such that F_α is a regular open set and covers A. Then, we have $Int(\overline{\omega_\alpha}) = \omega_\alpha$, for all $\alpha \in A$. Since $Int(\overline{\omega_\alpha})$ is open set for all $\alpha \in \wedge$, then by the c-compactness of χ the result is hold.

$\Leftarrow$ Consider the condition here is to prove that χ is a c-compact space. For this purpose, we consider that $\underset{\sim}{F} = \{\omega_\alpha : \alpha \in \wedge\}$ is an open cover of A, $\forall A \subset \chi$. So, we have

$$A \subset \bigcup_{\alpha \in \wedge} \omega_\alpha \subset \bigcup_{\alpha \in \wedge} \overline{\omega_\alpha} \subset \bigcup_{\alpha \in \wedge} Int(\overline{\omega_\alpha}).$$

Thus, $\{Int(\overline{\omega_\alpha}), \alpha \in \wedge\}$ forms an open cover of A called $Int(\overline{\omega_\alpha}) = v_\alpha$, for all $\alpha \in \wedge$. Therefore, $A \subset \bigcup_{\alpha \in \wedge} v_\alpha$. Consequently, by the conditions of this theorem, we can have $A \subset \bigcup_{\alpha \in \wedge} v_{\alpha_k}$, and hence χ is a c-compact space. □

Theorem 3. *Consider $\chi = (\chi, \beta_1, \beta_2)$ is a bitopological space. The space χ is p-space if and only if $\forall A$ subset of χ and for every β_i, $\underset{\sim}{F} = \{\omega_\alpha : \alpha \in \wedge\}$ such that ω_α is regular open set and covers A, there exists a β_i-finite collection $\{\omega_{\alpha_k}\}_{k=1}^n$ of $\underset{\sim}{F}$ such that $A \subset \bigcup_{k=1}^{n} \overline{\omega_{\alpha_k}}$, for all $i = 1, 2$.*

Proof. $\Rightarrow$ Consider χ is a p-c-compact space. Consider $A \subset \chi$ and $\underset{\sim}{F} = \{\omega_\alpha : \alpha \in \wedge\}$ such that ω_α is regular open set and β_i covers A, for all $i = 1, 2$. So, we have $Int(\overline{\omega_\alpha}) = \omega_\alpha$, for all $\alpha \in \wedge$ in β_i, for all $i = 1, 2$. Now, since $Int(\overline{\omega_\alpha})$ is β_i-open set for all $\alpha \in \wedge$ and for all $i = 1, 2$, then by the p-c-compactness of χ, the result is hold.
$\Leftarrow$ Consider the state here is to show that χ is a p-c-compact space. To this end, we consider $\underset{\sim}{F} = \{\omega_\alpha : \alpha \in \wedge\}$ is a β_i-open cover of A, for all $A \subset \chi$ and for all $i = 1, 2$. So, we have

$$A \subset \bigcup_{\alpha \in \wedge} \omega_\alpha \subset \bigcup_{\alpha \in \wedge} \overline{\omega_\alpha} \subset \bigcup_{\alpha \in \wedge} Int(\overline{\omega_\alpha}).$$

Consequently, $\{Int(\overline{\omega_\alpha}), \alpha \in \wedge\}$ forms an open cover of A called $Int(\overline{\omega_\alpha}) = v_\alpha$, $\forall \alpha \in \wedge$. Therefore, we obtain $A \subset \bigcup_{\alpha \in \wedge} v_\alpha$. Thus, by the conditions of this theorem, we can have $A \subset \bigcup_{\alpha \in \wedge} v_{\alpha_k}$, and therefore χ is a p-c-compact space. □

3. Relations between c-Separation Axioms and c-Compact Spaces

In the following content, we continue deriving numerous results theoretically, but this time to demonstrate the relations between c-separation axioms and the c-compact spaces. In what follows, we state two important definitions in relation to the topological and bitopological spaces in which they would be very useful to establish the next theorems.

Definition 14. *Consider $\chi = (\chi, \beta)$ is a topological space. The space χ is said to be*

(i) *$c - T_0$-space if for all $\theta \neq \vartheta \in \chi$, there exists an open set ω_θ in χ in which $\theta \in \overline{\omega_\theta}$ and $\vartheta \notin \overline{\omega_\theta}$, and there exists an open set v_θ in which $\vartheta \in \overline{v_\theta}$ and $\theta \notin \overline{v_\theta}$.*
(ii) *c-compact T_1-space if for all $\theta \neq \vartheta$ in χ, there exists an open set ω_θ in χ in which $\theta \in \overline{\omega_\theta}$ and $\vartheta \notin \overline{\omega_\theta}$, and there exists an open set v_θ in χ in which $\vartheta \notin \overline{v_\theta}$ and $\theta \notin \overline{v_\theta}$.*
(iii) *c-compact T_2-space if for all $\theta \neq \vartheta$ in χ, there exist two open sets ω_θ and v_θ in χ in which $\theta \in \overline{\omega_\theta}$, $\vartheta \in \overline{v_\theta}$ and $\overline{\omega_\theta} \cap \overline{v_\theta} = \phi$.*
(iv) *c-regular space if for all $\theta \notin A$ such that A is a closed subset in χ, there exist two open sets ω_θ and v_θ in which $\theta \in \omega_\theta$, $A \subset \overline{v_A}$ and $\overline{\omega_\theta} \cap \overline{v_\theta} = \phi$.*
(v) *$c - T_3$-space if χ is a $c - T_1$-space and c-regular space.*
(vi) *$c - T_4$-space if χ is c-normal space and c-T_1-space.*
(vii) *c-normal space if $\forall$ closed sets A and B in which $A \cap B = \phi$, there exist two open sets ω_θ and v_θ in which $A \subset \overline{\omega_\theta}$, $B \subset \overline{v_\theta}$ and $\overline{\omega_\theta} \cap \overline{v_\theta} = \phi$.*

Definition 15. *Consider $\chi = (\chi, \beta_1, \beta_2)$ is a bitopological space. The space χ is said to be*

(i) *a p-c-T_0-space if for all $\theta \neq \vartheta \in \chi$, $\exists\omega_\theta$ of a β_i-open set in χ in which $\theta \in \overline{\omega_\theta}$ and $\vartheta \notin \overline{\omega_\theta}$, and $\exists v_\vartheta$ of a β_j-open set in which $\vartheta \in \overline{v_\vartheta}$ and $\theta \notin \overline{v_\vartheta}$ for all $i, j = 1$.*

(ii) *a p-c-compact T_1-space if $\forall\theta \neq \vartheta$ in χ, $\exists\omega_\theta$ of a β_i-open set in χ in which $\theta \in \overline{\omega_\theta}$ and $\vartheta \notin \overline{\omega_\theta}$, and $\exists v_\theta$ of a β_j-open set in χ in which $\vartheta \notin \overline{v_\vartheta}$ and $\theta \notin \overline{v_\vartheta}$, for all $i, j = 1, 2$.*

(iii) *a p-c-compact T_2-space, if for all $\theta \neq \vartheta$ in χ, $\exists\omega_\theta$ of a β_i-open set and v_ϑ of a β_j-open set in χ in which $\theta \in \overline{\omega_\theta}$, $\vartheta \in \overline{v_\vartheta}$ and $\overline{\omega_\theta} \cap \overline{v_\vartheta} = \phi$, $\forall i, j = 1, 2$.*

(iv) *a p-c-regular space if for all $\theta \notin A$ and a βi-closed subset of χ, $\exists\omega_\theta$ of a β_i-open set and v_θ of a β_j-open set in which $\theta \in \omega_\theta$, $A \subset \overline{v_A}$ and $\overline{\omega_\theta} \cap \overline{v_\vartheta} = \phi$, for all $i, j = 1, 2$.*

(v) *a p-c-T_3-space if χ is a p-c-T_1-space and a p-c-regular space.*

(vi) *a p-c-normal space if for all A of a β_i-closed set and for all B of a β_j-closed set in which $A \cap B = \phi$, $\exists\beta_i$-open set and β_j-open set in which $A \subset \overline{\omega_\theta}$, $B \subset \overline{v_\vartheta}$ and $\overline{\omega_\theta} \cap \overline{v_\vartheta} = \phi$, for all $i, j = 1, 2$.*

(vii) *a p-c-T_4-space if χ is a p-c-normal space and a p-c-T_1-space.*

Theorem 4. *Consider B is a c-compact subset in c-T_2-space. For all $\theta \neq \vartheta$, there exist two open sets ω_θ and v_B in which $\theta \in \overline{\omega_\theta}$, $B \subset \overline{v_B}$ and $\overline{\omega_\theta} \cap \overline{v_A} \doteq \phi$.*

Proof. Consider $b \in B$ and $\theta \neq a$. Since $\underline{\theta \notin B}$ and χ is $\underline{c\text{-}T_2\text{-space}}$. So, there exist two open sets $\omega_\theta(b)$ and $v(b)$ in which $\overline{\omega_\theta(b)}$ and $b \in \overline{v(b)}$ with $\overline{\omega_\theta(b)} \cap \overline{v_{\alpha_k}(b)} = \phi$. So, $\underset{\sim}{v} = \{v(b) : a \in B\}$ is an open cover of B. Due to $\overline{A} \subset \chi$, then there exists a collection $\{v_{\alpha_\theta}\}_{k=1}^n$ in which $\overline{B} \subset \bigcup_{k=1}^n \overline{v_{\alpha_k}(b)}$. Thus, we have $\theta \in \overline{v_{\alpha_k}(b)}$ and $B \subset \overline{v}$, where $\overline{v} = \bigcup_{k=1}^n \overline{v_{\alpha_k}(b)}$. As a result, we can obtain

$$\overline{\omega(b)} \cap \overline{v} = \overline{\omega(b)} \cap \bigcup_{k=1}^n \overline{v_{\alpha_k}(b)} = \bigcup_{k=1}^n \overline{\omega(b)} \cap \overline{v_{\alpha_k}(b)} = \bigcup_{k=1}^n \phi = \phi,$$

and hence the result is hold. □

Theorem 5. *Consider B is a p-c-compact subset of a p-c-T_2-space. For all $\theta \neq \vartheta$, $\exists\beta_i$-open set ω_θ and β_j-open set v_B in which $\theta \in \overline{\omega_\theta}$ and $B \subset \overline{v_B}$ with $\overline{\omega_\theta} \cap \overline{v_B} \doteq \phi$, for all $i = 1, 2$.*

Proof. Consider $b \in B$ and $\theta \neq a$. Since $\theta \notin B$ and χ is a p-c-T_2-space, then $\exists\beta_i$-open set $\omega_\theta(b)$ and β_j-open set $v(b)$ in which $\overline{\omega_\theta(b)}$ and $b \in \overline{v(b)}$ with $\overline{\omega_\theta(b) \cap v(b)} = \phi$, for $i \neq j$, $i, j = 1, 2$. Therefore, $\underset{\sim}{v} = \{v(b) : a \in B\}$ is an open cover of B, and due to $\overline{B} \subset \chi$, so there exists a collection $\{v_{\alpha_\theta}\}_{k=1}^n$ in which $\overline{B} \subset \bigcup_{k=1}^n \overline{v_{\alpha_k}(b)}$. Thus, we obtain $\theta \in \overline{v_{\alpha(b)}}$ and $B \subset \overline{v}$, where $\overline{v} = \bigcup_{k=1}^n \overline{v_{\alpha k}(b)}$. This implies

$$\overline{\omega(b)} \cap \overline{v} = \overline{\omega(b)} \cap \bigcup_{k=1}^n \overline{v_{\alpha(b)}} = \bigcup_{k=1}^n \overline{\omega(b)} \cap \overline{v_{\alpha(b)}} = \bigcup_{k=1}^n \phi = \phi.$$

□

Theorem 6. *Consider A and B are two disjoint c-compact subsets of a p-T_2-space $\chi = (\chi, \beta)$. We can sperate A and B by two disjoint open sets ω_A and v_B in which $A \subset \omega_A$ and $B \subset v_B$.*

Proof. Consider we have two disjoint c-compact subsets A and B. Consider $\chi = (\chi, \beta)$ is a T_2-space. Now, for all $a \in A$, we can obtain $a \notin B$ as $A \cap B = \phi$. Since B is a c-compact subset of χ, so by Theorem 5, there exist two B_j-open sets $\omega(a)$ and $v(B)$ in which $a \in \omega(a)$ and $B \subset v(B)$ with $\omega(a) \cap v(B) = \phi$. Therefore, $\underset{\sim}{F} = \{\omega(a) : a \in A\}$

represents an open cover of A, and hence $A = \bigcup_{a\in A}(\omega(a))$. Due to A is c-compact subset, there exists a regular open set $\{\omega_k(a) : k = 1,2,\ldots,n, \omega_k(a)\}$ in which $A \subset \bigcup_{k=1}^{n} Int(\overline{\omega_k(a)})$, (say $\bigcup_{k=1}^{n} Int(\overline{\omega_k(a)}) = \omega_A$). So, we have $A \subset \omega_A$ and $B \subset v_B$ in which ω_A, v_B are two open sets. Thus, it is enough to show $\omega_A \cap v_B = \phi$. To do so, one might have

$$\omega_A \cap v_B = (\bigcup_{k=1}^{n} Int(\omega_k(a)) \cap V_B = \bigcup_{k=1}^{n} Int(\overline{\omega_k(a)}) \cap V_B.$$

But we have $\omega_k(a)) \cap v_B = \phi$ and $Int(\overline{\omega_k(a)}) \subset \omega_k(a)$. Therefore, we get

$$Int(\overline{\omega_k(a)}) \cap V_B = \phi,$$

and hence $\omega_A \cap v_B = \bigcup_{k=1}^{n} \phi = \phi$. □

Theorem 7. *Consider we have two disjoint B_i-c-compact subsets A and B of a p-T_2-space $\chi = (\chi, \beta_1, \beta_2)$. We can sperate A and B by two disjoint B_j-open sets ω_A and v_B in which $A \subset \omega_A$ and $B \subset v_B$, for all $i \neq j$, $i, j = 1,2$.*

Proof. Consider we have two disjoint $B_i-c-compact$ subsets A and B, for all $i = 1,2$. Consider $\chi = (\chi, \beta_1, \beta_2)$ is a p-T_2-space. For all $a \in A$, we have $a \notin B$as $A \cap B = \phi$. Since B is B_i-c-compact subset of χ, so by Theorem 6, $\exists B_j$-open sets $\omega(a)$ and $v(B)$ in which $a \in \omega(a)$ and $B \subset v(B)$ with $\omega(a) \cap v(B) = \phi$, for all $i, j = 1,2$. Thus, $\underset{\sim}{F} = \{\omega(a) : a \in A\}$ represents an B_j-open cover of A, and so $A = \bigcup_{a\in A}(\omega(a))$. Due to A is a B_i-c-compact subset, so there exists a regular open set $\{\omega_k(a) : k = 1,2,\ldots,n, \omega_k(a)\}$ in which $A \subset \bigcup_{k=1}^{n} Int(\overline{\omega_k(a)})$, (say $\bigcup_{k=1}^{n} Int(\omega_k(a)) = \omega_A$), for all $i = 1,2$. Accordingly, $A \subset \omega_A$ and $B \subset v_B$ such that ω_A and v_B are two B_i-open sets, for all $i = 1,2$. From this point, it is enough to show $\omega_A \cap v_B = \phi$. To do so, we have

$$\omega_A \cap v_B = (\bigcup_{k=1}^{n} Int(\overline{\omega_k(a)}) \cap V_B = \bigcup_{k=1}^{n} Int(\overline{\omega_k(a)}) \cap v_B.$$

But $\omega_k(a)) \cap v_B = \phi$ and $Int(\overline{\omega_k(a)}) \subset \omega_k(a)$. Consequently, we have $Int(\overline{\omega_k(a)}) \cap v_B = \phi$, and hence

$$\omega_A \cap v_B = \bigcup_{k=1}^{n} \phi = \phi.$$

□

In subsequent paragraphs, we first introduce a specific definition that illustrates the concept of p-extremely disconnected bitopological space, followed by a certain theoretical result associated with such a definition. Afterward, we continue exploring further results in connection with the relationships between the c-separation axioms and the c-compact spaces.

Definition 16. *If every β_i-open set is a β_i-clopen set, then the bitopological space $\chi = (\chi, \beta_1, \beta_2)$ is called p-extremely disconnected, for all $i = 1,2$.*

Theorem 8. *The space $\chi = (\chi, \beta_1, \beta_2)$ is a p-extremely disconnected compact space if and only if it is a p-c-compact space.*

Proof. Consider $\underset{\sim}{F} = \{\omega_\alpha : \alpha \in \wedge\}$ is a β_i-open cover of A, for all $i = 1,2$. Consider $\chi = (\chi, \beta_1, \beta_2)$ is a p-extremely disconnected compact space and A be a subset of χ. Then, $A = \bigcup\limits_{\alpha \in \wedge} \omega_\alpha$ and $\chi = (\chi - A) \cup A$ implies

$$\chi = (\chi - A) \cup (\bigcup_{\alpha \in \wedge} \omega_\alpha).$$

As a result, $U\underset{\sim}{F}^* = \{\chi - A, \omega_\alpha : \alpha \in \wedge\}$ represents an open cover of χ. Due to χ is a p-compact space, then χ has a β_i-finite subcover, say

$$\chi = (\chi - A) \cup (\bigcup_{\alpha \in \wedge} \omega_{\alpha_k}) : k = 1, 2, \ldots, n,$$

for all $i = 1,2$. Consequently, we get $\chi = (\chi - A) \cup \bigcup\limits_{k=1}^{n} \omega_{\alpha_k}$. Thus, we attain $A = \bigcup\limits_{k=1}^{n} \omega_{\alpha_k}$. Due to χ is a p-disconnected space, then $\overline{\omega_{\alpha_k}} = \omega_{\alpha_k}$, for all $k = 1, 2, \ldots, n$. Thus, $A = \bigcup\limits_{k=1}^{n} \overline{\omega_{\alpha_k}}$ for χ is a p-c-compact space. Now, consider $\chi = (\chi, \beta_1, \beta_2)$ is a p-extremely disconnected c-compact space. Consider $\underset{\sim}{F} = \{\omega_\alpha : \alpha \in \wedge\}$ is a β_i-open cover of χ, for $i = 1,2$ and $A \subset \chi$. So, $\underset{\sim}{F}$ is a β_i-open cover of A, for all $i = 1,2$. It means that $A = \bigcup\limits_{k=1}^{n} \omega_{\alpha_k}$. But, we have

$$\chi = A \cup (\chi - A) = (\bigcup_{k=1}^{n} \omega_{\alpha_k}) \cup (\chi - A).$$

So $\{\chi - A, \omega_{\alpha_k} : k = 1, 2, \ldots, n\}$ is a finite subcover of χ, and therefore χ is a p-compact space. □

Theorem 9. *Every compact space $\chi = (\chi, \beta)$ is a c-compact space.*

Proof. Consider $\underset{\sim}{F} = \{\omega_\alpha : \alpha \in \wedge\}$ is an open cover of A, where A is a subset of χ. So, $\{\omega_\alpha : \chi - A : \alpha \in \wedge\}$ forms an open cover of χ. Due to χ is a compact space, we have $\chi \subset (\bigcup\limits_{k=1}^{n} \omega_{\alpha_k}) \cup (\chi - A)$, and so $A \subset \bigcup\limits_{k=1}^{n} \omega_{\alpha_k} \subset \bigcup\limits_{k=1}^{n} \overline{\omega_{\alpha_k}}$. Therefore, $\{\omega_{\alpha_1}, \omega_{\alpha_2}, \ldots, \omega_{\alpha_n}\}$ is a collection of $\underset{\sim}{F}$ and $A \subset \bigcup\limits_{k=1}^{n} \overline{\omega_{\alpha_k}}$. Therefore, χ is a c-compact space. □

Theorem 10. *Every p-compact space $\chi = (\chi, \beta_1, \beta_2)$ is a p-c-compact space.*

Proof. Consider $i = 1,2$, and $\underset{\sim}{F} = \{\omega_\alpha : \alpha \in \wedge\}$ is a βi-open cover of A, where A is a subset of χ. So, $\{\omega_\alpha : \chi - A : \alpha \in \wedge\}$ forms a βi-open cover of χ, for all $i = 1,2$. Due to χ is a p-compact space, then $\chi \subset (\bigcup\limits_{k=1}^{n} \omega_{\alpha_k}) \cup (\chi - A)$, and so $A \subset \bigcup\limits_{k=1}^{n} \omega_{\alpha_k} \subset \bigcup\limits_{k=1}^{n} \overline{\omega_{\alpha_k}}$. Therefore, $\{\omega_{\alpha_1}, \omega_{\alpha_2}, \ldots, \omega_{\alpha_n}\}$ is a βi-collection of $\underset{\sim}{F}$ and $A \subset \bigcup\limits_{k=1}^{n} \overline{\omega_{\alpha_k}}$, for all $i = 1,2$. Hence, χ is a p-c-compact space. □

Theorem 11. *Every extremely disconnected nearly compact space $\chi = (\chi, \beta)$ is a c-compact space.*

Proof. Consider (χ, β) is an extremely disconnected nearly compact space. Consider $A \subset \chi$ and $\underset{\sim}{F} = \{\omega_\alpha : \alpha \in \wedge\}$ is an open cover of A, so $A \subset \bigcup_{\alpha\in\wedge} \omega_\alpha$ and $\chi - A$ covers it set. Thus, $\{\omega_\alpha, \chi - A : \alpha \in \wedge\}$ forms an open cover of χ. But χ is extremely disconnected, then ω_α is a clopen set $\forall\alpha \in \wedge$. Thus, we have $\omega_\alpha = \overline{\omega_\alpha}$, and so $\omega_\alpha^\circ = \overline{\omega_\alpha}$. Hence, we get $\omega_\alpha = \overline{\omega_\alpha^\circ}$, which gives $\chi \subset (\bigcup_{\alpha\in\wedge} \overline{\omega_\alpha^\circ}) \cup (\chi - A)$. Now, since χ is a nearly compact space, we have $\chi \subset (\bigcup_{\alpha\in\wedge} \overline{\omega_\alpha^\circ}) \cup (\chi - A)$, and so we have

$$A \subset (\bigcup_{k=1}^{n} \overline{\omega_\alpha^\circ}) =\subset (\bigcup_{k=1}^{n} \overline{\omega_\alpha^\circ}).$$

Hence, χ is a c-compact space. □

Theorem 12. *Every p-extremely disconnected nearly compact space* $\chi = (\chi, \beta_1, \beta_2)$ *is a p-c-compact space.*

Proof. Consider (χ, β_1, β_2) is a p-extremely disconnected nearly compact space. Consider that $A \subset \chi$ and $\underset{\sim}{F} = \{\omega_\alpha : \alpha \in \wedge\}$ is a βi-open cover of A, for all $i = 1,2$. So, $A \subset \bigcup_{\alpha\in\wedge} \omega_\alpha$ and $\chi - A$ covers it set. So, we have $\{\omega_\alpha, \chi - A : \alpha \in \wedge\}$ forms a βi-open cover of χ, for all $i = 1,2$. But, χ is p-extremely disconnected, which implies that ω_α is a βi-clopen set for all $\alpha \in \wedge$ and for all $i = 1,2$. Therefore, $\omega_\alpha = \overline{\omega_\alpha}$, and so $\omega_\alpha^\circ = \overline{\omega_\alpha}$. Thus, we get $\omega_\alpha = \overline{\omega_\alpha^\circ}$, and consequently we obtain $\chi \subset (\bigcup_{\alpha\in\wedge} \overline{\omega_\alpha^\circ}) \cup (\chi - A)$. Now, since χ is a p-nearly compact space, then $\chi \subset (\bigcup_{\alpha\in\wedge} \overline{\omega_\alpha^\circ}) \cup (\chi - A)$. This immediately gives

$$A \subset \bigcup_{k=1}^{n} \overline{\omega_\alpha^\circ}.$$

Hence, χ is a p-c-compact space. □

Theorem 13. *Every quasi H-closed space* $\chi = (\chi, \beta)$ *is a c-compact space.*

Proof. Consider (χ, β) is a quasi H-closed space. Consider $A \subset \chi$ and $\underset{\sim}{F} = \{\omega_\alpha : \alpha \in \wedge\}$ is an open cover of A. As a consequence, $\{\omega_\alpha, \chi - A\} : \alpha \in \wedge\}$ forms an open cover of χ, which is a quasi H-closed. Consequently, we have $\chi \subset (\bigcup_{k=1}^{n} \overline{\omega_{\alpha_k}}) \cup (\overline{\chi - A})$. Now, due to $(\overline{\chi - A})$ covers $\chi - A$, then $A \subset (\bigcup_{k=1}^{n} \overline{\omega_{\alpha_k}})$, and hence χ is a c-compact space. □

Theorem 14. *Every quasi p-H-closed space* $\chi = (\chi, \beta_1, \beta_2)$ *is a p-c-compact space.*

Proof. Consider (χ, β_1, β_2) is a p-quasi H-closed space. Consider $A \subset \chi$ and $\underset{\sim}{F} = \{\omega_\alpha : \alpha \in \wedge\}$ is a βi-open cover of A, for all $i = 1,2$. Then, $\{\omega_\alpha, \chi - A : \alpha \in \wedge\}$ forms a p-open cover of χ. Due to χ is quasi H-closed, we have $\chi \subset (\bigcup_{k=1}^{n} \overline{\omega_{\alpha_k}}) \cup (\overline{\chi - A})$. Also, due to $(\overline{\chi - A})$ covers $\chi - A$, then $A \subset (\bigcup_{k=1}^{n} \overline{\omega_{\alpha_k}})$, and hence χ is a p-c-compact space. □

Theorem 15. *If* $\chi = (\chi, \beta)$ *is an H-closed and S-closed space, then it is a c-compact space.*

Proof. Consider $\chi = (\chi, \beta)$ is an H-closed and S-closed space. Consider A is a subset of χ and $\underset{\sim}{F} = \{\omega_\alpha : \alpha \in \wedge\}$ is an open cover of A. Then, there exists $\alpha \in \wedge$ in which $\omega_\alpha \subset A \subset \overline{\omega_\alpha}$ as χ is an S-closed space. Thus, we have

$$\bigcup_{\alpha\in\wedge} \omega_\alpha \subset A \subset \bigcup_{\alpha\in\wedge} \overline{\omega_\alpha}.$$

This implies that $\{\overline{\omega_\alpha} : \alpha \in \wedge\}$ forms a cover of χ, which is also a closure of χ. In the same regard, since χ is an H-closed space, we get $A \subset \bigcup_{k=1}^{n} \overline{\omega_{\alpha_k}}$, and hence χ is a c-compact space. □

Theorem 16. *Consider $\chi = (\chi, \beta_1, \beta_2)$ is a p-H-closed and a p-S-closed space, then it is a c-compact space.*

Proof. Consider $\chi = (\chi, \beta_1, \beta_2)$ is a p-H-closed and a p-S-closed space. Consider A is a subset of χ and $\underset{\sim}{F} = \{\omega_\alpha : \alpha \in \wedge\}$ is a βi-open cover of A, for all $i = 1, 2$. So, $\exists \alpha \in \wedge$ in which $\omega_\alpha \subset A$ as χ is a p-S-closed space. As a consequence $\bigcup_{\alpha\in\wedge} \omega_\alpha \subset A \subset \bigcup_{\alpha\in\wedge} \overline{\omega_\alpha}$. Therefore, $\{\overline{\omega_\alpha} : \alpha \in \wedge\}$ forms a βi-H-closed cover of χ, for all $i = 1, 2$. Thus, because of χ is p-H-closed space, then $A \subset \bigcup_{k=1}^{n} \overline{\omega_{\alpha_k}}$. Hence, χ is a p-c-compact. □

Theorem 17. *If $\chi = (\chi, \beta)$ is an extremely disconnected space, then the statements below are equivalent:*

(i) *χ is c-compact with respect to the closed subspace.*
(ii) *χ is nearly compact.*
(iii) *χ is a quasi H-closed space.*

Proof. (i→ii) Consider χ is c-compact and $\underset{\sim}{F} = \{\omega_\alpha : \alpha \in \wedge\}$ is an open cover of χ. Now, $\forall B \subset \chi$, we have $\underset{\sim}{F}$ is a cover of B. This means $B \subset \bigcup_{\alpha\in\wedge} \omega_\alpha$. But χ is a c-compact space, so $B \subset \bigcup_{k=1}^{n} \omega_\alpha$. Due to χ is an extremely disconnected space, so $\chi - B$ and ω_{α_k} are clopen sets, for all $k = 1, 2, \ldots, n$. Thus, $\overline{\omega^\circ_{\alpha_k}} = \omega_{\alpha_k}$, for all $k = 1, 2, \ldots, n$. This implies $B \subset \overline{\omega^\circ_{\alpha_k}}$, which means $\chi \subset (\bigcup_{k=1}^{n} \overline{\omega^\circ_{\alpha_k}}) \cup (\overline{\chi - B})$. Consequently, $\{\overline{\omega^\circ_{\alpha_k}}\, \overline{\chi - B}, k = 1, 2, \ldots, n\}$ is a subcover of $\underset{\sim}{F}$ that covers χ. Thus, χ is nearly compact space.

(ii→iii) Consider χ is a nearly compact space and $\underset{\sim}{F} = \{\omega_\alpha : \alpha \in \wedge\}$ is an open cover of χ, so it has a finite subcover of interior of closure set, say $\{\overline{\omega^\circ_{\alpha_k}}\, \overline{\chi - B}, k = 1, 2, \ldots, n\}$. With the use of nearly compactness of χ, we attain $\chi \subset (\bigcup_{k=1}^{n} \overline{\omega^\circ_{\alpha_k}})$. Since χ is an extremely disconnected space, then ω_{α_k} is a clopen set, for all $k = 1, 2, \ldots, n$. Hence, $\overline{\omega^\circ_{\alpha_k}} = \overline{\omega_{\alpha_k}}$, and so $\chi \subset \bigcup_{k=1}^{n} \overline{\omega_\alpha}$. This means that χ is an H-closed space.

(iii→i) Consider χ is an H-closed space and $\underset{\sim}{F} = \{\omega_\alpha : \alpha \in \wedge\}$ is an open cover of B, where B is a closed subspace of χ. Thus, $\underset{\sim}{F}$ is an open cover of B. Since χ is an H-closed space, so $B \subset \chi \subset \bigcup_{k=1}^{n} \overline{\omega_{\alpha}}$. Also, due to χ is an extremely disconnected space, we obtain $B \subset \bigcup_{k=1}^{n} \overline{\omega_{\alpha}}$. Hence, χ is a c-compact space.

□

Theorem 18. *Consider $\chi = (\chi, \beta_1, \beta_2)$ is a p-extremely disconnected space, then the following are equivalent:*

(i) *χ is p-c-compact with respect to βi-closed subspace, for all $i = 1, 2$.*
(ii) *χ is p-nearly compact.*
(iii) *χ is a p-quasi H-closed space.*

Proof. (i→ii) Consider χ is p-c-compact and $\underset{\sim}{F} = \{\omega_\alpha : \alpha \in \wedge\}$ is a βi-open cover of χ, for all $i = 1, 2$. Now, for all βi-closed set $B \subset \chi$, we have $\underset{\sim}{F}$ is a βi-cover of B, for all $i = 1, 2$. This means $B \subset \bigcup_{\alpha \in \wedge} \omega_\alpha$. But χ is a p-c-compact, which implies $B \subset \bigcup_{k=1}^{n} \omega_\alpha$. In this regard, since χ is a p-extremely disconnected space, so $\chi - B$ and ω_{α_k} are βi-clopen sets, for all $k = 1, 2, \ldots, n$ and for all $i = 1, 2$. Thus, one might get $\overline{\omega^{\circ}_{\alpha_k}} = \omega_{\alpha_k}$, for all $k = 1, 2, \ldots, n$. As a result, $B \subset \overline{\omega^{\circ}_{\alpha_k}}$, which immediately yields $\chi \subset (\bigcup_{k=1}^{n} \overline{\omega^{\circ}_{\alpha_k}}) \cup (\overline{\chi - B})$. As a result, we have $\{\overline{\omega^{\circ}_{\alpha_k}}, \overline{\chi - B}, k = 1, 2, \ldots, n\}$ is a βi-subcover of $\underset{\sim}{F}$ of interior of closure of βi-open set that covers χ, for all $i = 1, 2$. Hence, χ is a p-nearly compact space.

(ii→iii) Consider χ is a p-nearly compact space and $\underset{\sim}{F} = \{\omega_\alpha : \alpha \in \wedge\}$ is a βi-open cover of χ, for all $i = 1, 2$. Then, it possesses a finite βi-subcover of interior of closure set, say $\{\overline{\omega^{\circ}_{\alpha_k}}, \overline{\chi - B}, k = 1, 2, \ldots, n\}$, for all $i = 1, 2$. By p-nearly compactness of χ, we have $\chi \subset (\bigcup_{k=1}^{n} \overline{\omega^{\circ}_{\alpha_k}})$. Since χ is a p-extremely disconnected space, then ω_{α_k} is a βi-clopen set, for all $k = 1, 2, \ldots, n$ and for all $i = 1, 2$. Hence, we have $\overline{\omega^{\circ}_{\alpha_k}} = \overline{\omega_{\alpha_k}}$, which consequently leads to $\chi \subset \bigcup_{k=1}^{n} \overline{\omega_{\alpha}}$. Therefore, χ is a p-H-closed space.

(iii→i) Consider χ is a p-H-closed space and $\underset{\sim}{F} = \{\omega_\alpha : \alpha \in \wedge\}$ is an βi-open cover of B in which B is a βi-closed subspace of χ, for all $i = 1, 2$. Therefore, $\underset{\sim}{F}$ is a βi-open cover of B, for all $i = 1, 2$. Due to χ is a p-H-closed space, then $B \subset \chi \subset \bigcup_{k=1}^{n} \overline{\omega_{\alpha}}$. Also, due to χ is a p-extremely disconnected space, then $B \subset \bigcup_{k=1}^{n} \overline{\omega_{\alpha}}$, and hence χ is a p-c-compact space.

□

Theorem 19. *The c-compactness possesses a hereditary property with respect to the closed subspace.*

Proof. Consider χ is a c-compact space. Consider B is a closed subspace of χ and C is a subset of B. Consider $\underset{\sim}{F} = \{\omega_\alpha : \alpha \in \wedge\}$ is an open cover of β. Thus, we have $\chi = C \cup (\chi - C)$. Because of $C \subset B$, then $\chi = C \cup (\chi - B)$. Therefore, we obtain $\chi = (\bigcup_{\alpha \in \wedge} \omega_\alpha) \cup (\chi - B)$. This means that $\{\omega_\alpha, \chi - B : \alpha \in \wedge\}$ forms an open cover. Since χ is

c-compact, then every subset of χ might be covered by a finite subcover of closure of subset of $\underset{\sim}{F}$. So, we have $\beta \subset \bigcup_{k=1}^{n} \overline{\omega_{\alpha_k}}$, and hence B is a c-compact space. □

Theorem 20. *The p-c-compactness possesses a hereditary property with respect to βi-closed subspace, for all $i = 1, 2$.*

Proof. Consider χ is a p-c-compact space. Consider B is a βi-closed subspace of χ and C is a βi-subset of B, for all $i = 1, 2$. Consider $\underset{\sim}{F} = \{\omega_\alpha : \alpha \in \wedge\}$ is an βi-open cover of β, for all $i = 1, 2$. Then, $\chi = C \cup (\chi - C)$. Since $C \subset B$, then $\chi = C \cup (\chi - B)$. This consequently yields that $\chi = (\bigcup_{\alpha \in \wedge} \omega_\alpha) \cup (\chi - B)$, which gives $\{\omega_\alpha, \chi - B : \alpha \in \wedge\}$ forms a βi-open cover, for all $i = 1, 2$. Now, since χ is a p-c-compact space, then every subset of χ might be covered by a finite βi-subcover of closure of subset of $\underset{\sim}{F}$, for all $i = 1, 2$. So, we have $\beta \subset \bigcup_{k=1}^{n} \overline{\omega_{\alpha_k}}$, which means that B is a p-c-compact space. □

Theorem 21. *If $\chi = (\chi, \beta)$ is a c-compact, $c - T_2$- and c-extremely disconnected space, then χ is $c - T_4$-space.*

Proof. Consider $\chi = (\chi, \beta)$ is a c-compact and c-T_2-space. It is clearly that $\chi = (\chi, \beta)$ is a c-T_1-space. Now, consider A and B be c-closed subsets of χ in which $A \cap B = \phi$. Due to χ is a c-compact space, so by Theorem 20, A and B are two c-compact subsets of c-T_2-space χ. Also, by Theorem 20, there exist two c-open sets ω_A and υ_B in which $A \subseteq \overline{\omega_A}$ and $B \subseteq \overline{\upsilon_B}$ with $\overline{\omega_A} \cap \overline{\upsilon_B} = \phi$. Thus, χ is a c-T_4-space. □

Theorem 22. *If $\chi = (\chi, \beta_1, \beta_2)$ is a p-c-compact, p-c-T_2- and p-c-extremely disconnected space, then χ is a p-c-T_4-space.*

Proof. Consider $\chi = (\chi, \beta_1, \beta_2)$ is a p-c-compact and p-c-T_2-space. It is quite clear that $\chi = (\chi, \beta_1, \beta_2)$ is a p-c-T_1-space. Now, consider A and B are two β_i-c-closed subsets of χ in which $A \cap B = \phi$, for all $i = 1, 2$. As a consequence, due to χ is a p-c-compact space, then with the use of Theorem 21, A and B are β_i-c-compact subsets of p-c-T_2-space, for all $i = 1, 2$. So, with the use of Theorem 21, there exist two β_i-c-open sets ω_A and υ_B in which $A \subseteq \overline{\omega_A}$ and $B \subseteq \overline{\upsilon_B}$ with $\overline{\omega_A} \cap \overline{\upsilon_B} = \phi$, for all $i = 1, 2$. Thus, χ is a p-c-T_4-space. □

Theorem 23. *Consider $\chi = (\chi, \beta)$ is a c-T_2- and c-extremely disconnected space. Every subset of χ is closed set.*

Proof. Consider A is a c-compact subset of χ and $\theta \notin A$. So, with the use of Theorem 22, there exist two c-open sets ω_θ and υ_A in which $\theta \in \omega_\theta$ and $A \subseteq \upsilon_A$ with $\omega_\theta \cap \upsilon_A = \phi$. Consequently, we have $\omega \subseteq (\upsilon_A)^c$, and because of $A \subseteq \upsilon$ yields $\upsilon^c \subseteq A^c$, then we have $\theta \in \omega_\theta \subseteq \upsilon^c \subset A^c$. As a result, due to ω is a c-open set, then A^c is r-open set, which means that A is c-closed set. □

Theorem 24. *Consider $\chi = (\chi, \beta_1, \beta_2)$ is a p-c-T_2- and p-c-extremely disconnected space. Every subset of χ is a β_i-closed set, for all $i = 1, 2$.*

Proof. Consider A is a β_i-c-compact subset of χ and $\theta \notin A$, for all $i = 1, 2$. So, with the help of Theorem 23, there exist two β_i-c-open sets ω_θ and υ_A in which $\theta \in \omega_\theta$ and $A \subseteq \upsilon_A$ with $\omega_\theta \cap \upsilon_A = \phi$, for all $i = 1, 2$. Therefore, we have $\omega \subseteq (\upsilon_A)^c$. Because of $A \subseteq \upsilon$ leads to $\upsilon^c \subseteq A^c$, then we have $\theta \in \omega_\theta \subseteq \upsilon^c \subset A^c$. Also, due to ω is a β_i-c-open set, then A^c is a β_i-c-open set, for all $i = 1, 2$. Thus, A is β_i-r-closed set, for all $i = 1, 2$. □

Theorem 25. *If $\chi = (\chi, \beta)$ is a c-compact, c-T_2- and c-extremely disconnected space, then every subset of χ is c-compact if and only if it is c-closed set.*

Proof. $\Rightarrow$ Consider A is a c-compact subset of χ, so with the help of Theorem 24, A is c-closed set.
$\Leftarrow$ Consider A is a c-closed of a c-T_2-extremely disconnected space, then by Theorem 24, A is c-compact. □

Theorem 26. *If $\chi = (\chi, \beta_1, \beta_2)$ is a p-c-compact, p-c-T_2- and p-c-extremely disconnected space, then every β_i-subset of χ is a p-c-compact if and only if it is a β_i-c-closed set, for all $i = 1, 2$.*

Proof. $\Rightarrow$ Consider A is a p-c-compact subset of χ, so with the help of Theorem 25, A is a β_i-c-closed set, for all $i = 1, 2$.
$\Leftarrow$ Consider A is a β_i-c-closed of a p-c-compact, p-c-T_2-extremely disconnected space, so with the help of Theorem 25, A is a β_i-c-compact, for all $i = 1, 2$. □

4. Conclusions

In this work, we have initiated a novel concept, named the p-c-compact in topological and bitopological spaces. Accordingly, we have defined the concept of c-compact space and inferred some novel generalizations and results related to the H-closed, the quasi compact and extremely disconnected compact spaces in topological and bitopological spaces. In addition, we have derived several theoretical results that demonstrate the relations between c-separation axioms and the c-compact spaces. However, this study can be extended to the c-compactness in tritopological space $(\chi, \beta_1, \beta_2, \beta_3)$, where β_1, β_2 and β_3 are topologies on χ. Based on this conception, many properties and results can be then inferred and derived from such a study, which would be left to the future for further considerations.

Author Contributions: Conceptualization, R.A.; Methodology, J.O. and I.M.B.; Validation, M.S.; Formal analysis, R.A.; Investigation, J.O. and I.M.B.; Resources, R.A.; Data curation, J.O.; Writing – original draft, M.S.; Visualization, M.S.; Supervision, I.M.B. All authors have read and agreed to the published version of the manuscript.

Funding: This research received no external funding.

Data Availability Statement: Not applicable.

Conflicts of Interest: The authors declare no conflict of interest.

References

1. Nagata, J.-I. *Modern General Topology*; Elsevier Science: Amsterdam, The Netherlands, 1985.
2. Willard, S. *General Topology*; Addison-Wesley Publishing Company, Inc.: London, UK, 1970.
3. Levine, N. Semi-Open Sets and Semi-Continuity in Topological Spaces. *Am. Math. Mon.* **1963**, *70*, 36–41. [CrossRef]
4. Kelly, J. General topology, Van Nostrand Company. *Kyungpook Math. J.* **1955**, *32*, 273–284.
5. Kim, Y.W. Pairwise Compactness. *Publ. Math. Debrecen* **1968**, *15*, 87–90. [CrossRef]
6. Shehadeh, H.A.; Jebril, I.H.; Wang, X.; Chu, S.-C.; Idris, M.Y.I. Optimal topology planning of electromagnetic waves communication network for underwater sensors using multi-objective optimization algorithms (MOOAs). *Automatika* **2023**, *64*, 315–326. [CrossRef]
7. Oudetallah, J. On Feebly Pairwise Expandable Space. *J. Math. Comput. Sci.* **2021**, *11*, 6216–6225.
8. Oudetallah, J. Nearly Expandability in bitopological spaces. *Adv. Math. Sci. J.* **2021**, *10*, 705–712. [CrossRef]
9. Oudetallah, J.; Alharbi, R.; Batiha, I.M. On r-Compactness in Topological and Bitopological Spaces. *Axioms* **2023**, *12*, 210. [CrossRef]
10. Dugundji, J. *Topology*; Allyn and Bacon, Inc.: Boston, MA, USA, 1966.
11. Singal, M.K.; Mathur, A. On nearly-compact spaces. *Boll. Unione Mat. Ital.* **1969**, *6*, 702–710.
12. Thompson, T. S-closed spaces. *Proc. Am. Math. Soc.* **1976**, *60*, 335–338.

mathematics

MDPI

Article

Ricci Vector Fields

Hanan Alohali and Sharief Deshmukh *

Department of Mathematics, College of Science, King Saud University, P.O. Box 2455, Riyadh 11451, Saudi Arabia; halohali@ksu.edu.sa

* Correspondence: shariefd@ksu.edu.sa

Abstract: We introduce a special vector field ω on a Riemannian manifold (N^m, g), such that the Lie derivative of the metric g with respect to ω is equal to ρRic, where Ric is the Ricci tensor of (N^m, g) and ρ is a smooth function on N^m. We call this vector field a ρ-Ricci vector field. We use the ρ-Ricci vector field on a Riemannian manifold (N^m, g) and find two characterizations of the m-sphere $S^m(\alpha)$. In the first result, we show that an m-dimensional compact and connected Riemannian manifold (N^m, g) with nonzero scalar curvature admits a ρ-Ricci vector field ω such that ρ is a nonconstant function and the integral of $Ric(\omega, \omega)$ has a suitable lower bound that is necessary and sufficient for (N^m, g) to be isometric to m-sphere $S^m(\alpha)$. In the second result, we show that an m-dimensional complete and simply connected Riemannian manifold (N^m, g) of positive scalar curvature admits a ρ-Ricci vector field ω such that ρ is a nontrivial solution of the Fischer–Marsden equation and the squared length of the covariant derivative of ω has an appropriate upper bound, if and only if (N^m, g) is isometric to m-sphere $S^m(\alpha)$.

Keywords: ρ-Ricci vector fields; Fischer–Marsden equation; m-sphere; Ricci curvature

MSC: 53C20; 53C21; 53B50

1. Introduction

An m-dimensional complete simply connected Riemannian manifold of constant curvature α is isometric to one of the following spaces: the m-sphere $S^m(\alpha)$, the Euclidean space R^m, or the hyperbolic space $H^m(\alpha)$, referred to as $\alpha > 0$, $\alpha = 0$, or $\alpha < 0$, respectively (cf. [1]). Because of this classification, there has been an interest in obtaining necessary and sufficient conditions on complete Riemannian manifolds so that they are isometric to one of the three model spaces $S^m(\alpha)$, R^m, and $H^m(\alpha)$, respectively. One of most sought questions is about obtaining different characterizations of spheres $S^m(\alpha)$ among complete Riemannian manifolds. In obtaining these characterizations, most of the time, the conformal and Killing vector fields are used on an m-dimensional complete Riemannian manifold (N^m, g) (cf. [2–11]). A vector field $\mathbf{u}$ on m-Riemannian manifold (N^m, g) is a conformal vector field if the Lie derivative $£_{\mathbf{u}} g$ has the expression

$$£_{\mathbf{u}} g = 2fg,$$

where f is a smooth function called the conformal factor. If $f = 0$ in the above definition, then $\mathbf{u}$ is called a Killing vector field.

In this paper, we are interested in a vector field ω on an m-dimensional Riemannian manifold (N^m, g) that satisfies

$$\frac{1}{2} £_{\omega} g = \rho Ric, \tag{1}$$

where $£_{\omega} g$ is the Lie-derivative of the metric g with respect to ω, ρ is a smooth function, and Ric is the Ricci tensor of (N^m, g). We call ω satisfying Equation (1) a ρ-Ricci vector field on (N^m, g). Naturally, if (N^m, g) is an Einstein manifold, then a ρ-Ricci vector field

Citation: Alohali, H.; Deshmukh, S. Ricci Vector Fields. *Mathematics* **2023**, *11*, 4622. https://doi.org/10.3390/math11224622

Academic Editor: Daniele Ettore Otera

Received: 25 October 2023
Revised: 9 November 2023
Accepted: 10 November 2023
Published: 12 November 2023

ω is a conformal vector field on (N^m, g) (cf. [3,4]). If, in Equation (1), we take $\rho = 0$, then the 0-Ricci vector field ω on (N^m, g) is a Killing vector field on (N^m, g) (cf. [12]). A ρ-Ricci vector field on (N^m, g) is also a particular form of a potential field of a generalized soliton (cf. [12]), with $\alpha = -\rho$ and $\beta = \gamma = 0$.

We could also approach to Equation (1) in another context (cf. [13]). On the m-dimensional Riemannian manifold (N^m, g), take a smooth function ρ and consider a 1-parameter family of metrics $g(t)$ satisfying the generalized Ricci flow (or ρ-Ricci flow) equation

$$\partial_t g = 2\rho Ric, \quad g(0) = g. \tag{2}$$

To reach a solution of above flow, we take a 1-parameter family of diffeomorphisms $\varphi_t : N^m \to N^m$ generated by the family of vector fields $\mathbf{W}(t)$ and let $\sigma(t)$ be a scale factor. Then, we are interested in a solution of flow (2) of the form

$$g(t) = \sigma(t)\varphi_t^*(g).$$

Differentiating the above equation with respect to t and substituting $t = 0$, while assuming $\sigma(0) = 1, \dot{\sigma}(0) = 0, \mathbf{W}(0) = \omega$, and using $\varphi_0 = id$, we obtain

$$\pounds_\omega g - 2\rho Ric = 0,$$

which is Equation (1). Thus, a ρ-Ricci vector field ω on (N^m, g) can be considered as stable solution of the flow (2).

We see that as a trivial example on the Euclidean space R^m, a constant vector field $\mathbf{a}$ is a ρ-Ricci vector field for any smooth function ρ on R^m. Similarly on the complex Euclidean space C^m with complex structure J and the vector field

$$\xi = \sum_{i=1}^{m} z^i \frac{\partial}{\partial z^i},$$

where $z^1, \ldots, z^m$ are Euclidean coordinates, the vector field $\omega = J\xi$ is a ρ-Ricci vector field for any smooth function ρ on C^m.

Next, we show that on the sphere $S^m(\alpha)$ of constant curvature α, there are many ρ-Ricci vector fields. With the embedding $i : S^m(\alpha) \to R^{m+1}$ and unit normal ξ and shape operator $-\sqrt{\alpha}I$, upon taking a nonzero constant vector field $\mathbf{b}$ on the Euclidean space R^{m+1}, we have $\mathbf{b} = \omega + f\xi$, where $f = \langle \mathbf{b}, \xi \rangle$ and ω is the tangential component of $\mathbf{b}$ to the sphere $S^m(\alpha)$. We denote the induced metric on the sphere $S^m(\alpha)$ by g and the Riemannian connection by D. Then, differentiating the above equation with respect to the vector field X on $S^m(\alpha)$, we have

$$D_X\omega = -\sqrt{\alpha} f X, \quad \nabla f = \sqrt{\alpha}\omega, \tag{3}$$

where ∇f is the gradient of f. Using the first equation in (3), it follows that

$$\pounds_\omega g = -2\sqrt{\alpha} f g$$

and the Ricci tensor of the sphere $S^m(\alpha)$ is given by

$$Ric = (m-1)\alpha g.$$

Thus, we see that the vector field ω on the sphere $S^m(\alpha)$ satisfies

$$\frac{1}{2}\pounds_\omega g = \rho Ric, \quad \rho = -\frac{1}{(m-1)\sqrt{\alpha}} f, \tag{4}$$

that is, ω is a ρ-Ricci vector field on the sphere $S^m(\alpha)$. Indeed, for each nonzero constant vector field on the Euclidean space R^{m+1}, there is a ρ-Ricci vector field on the sphere $S^m(\alpha)$.

The above example naturally leads to a question: Under what conditions is a compact and connected m-dimensional Riemannian manifold (N^m, g) admitting a ρ-Ricci vector field ω isometric to a m-sphere $S^m(\alpha)$?

There are two well-known differential equations on a Riemannian manifold (N^m, g). The first is Obata's differential equation, namely (cf. [6,7]),

$$Hess(\sigma) = -\alpha\sigma g, \tag{5}$$

where σ is a non-constant smooth function, α is a positive constant, and $Hess(\sigma)$ is the Hessian of σ defined by

$$Hess(\sigma)(X, Y) = g(D_X \nabla\sigma, Y),$$

for smooth vector fields X, Y on N^m. Obata proved that a necessary and sufficient condition for a complete and simply connected Riemannian manifold (N^m, g) to admit a nontrivial solution of differential Equation (5) is that (N^m, g) is isometric to the sphere $S^m(\alpha)$ (cf. [6,7]). The other differential equation on (N^m, g) is the Fischer–Marsden equation (cf. [14–19])

$$(\Delta\sigma)g + \sigma Ric = Hess(\sigma), \tag{6}$$

where σ is a smooth function on N^m and $\Delta\sigma = div(\nabla\sigma)$ is the Laplacian of σ. We shall abbreviate the above Fischer–Marsden equation as FM-equation. Taking trace in the FM-Equation (6), we obtain

$$\Delta\sigma = -\frac{\tau}{m-1}\sigma, \tag{7}$$

where $\tau = TrRic$ is the scalar curvature of the Riemannian manifold (N^m, g). It is known that if (N^m, g) admits a nontrivial solution to the FM-equation, then the scalar curvature τ is necessarily constant (cf. [14]).

Note that by Equation (3), the smooth function f on the sphere $S^m(\alpha)$ has the Hessian

$$Hess(f)(X, Y) = g(D_X \nabla f, Y) = \sqrt{\alpha} g(D_X\omega, Y) = -\alpha f g(X, Y),$$

the Laplacian $\Delta f = div(\sqrt{\alpha}\omega) = -m\alpha f$, and $Ric = (m-1)\alpha g$. Consequently, on $S^m(\alpha)$, we see that

$$(\Delta f)g + f Ric = Hess(f), \tag{8}$$

that is, f is a solution of the FM-equation on the sphere $S^m(\alpha)$. If we combine the two, namely a Riemannian manifold (N^m, g) admits a ρ-Ricci vector field ω such that ρ is a nontrivial solution of the FM-equation on (N^m, g), and seek an additional condition under which (N^m, g) is isometric to $S^m(\alpha)$, we can notice that the ρ-Ricci vector field ω on the sphere $S^m(\alpha)$ is a closed vector field. Therefore, in this paper, we use the closed ρ-Ricci vector field ω on a Riemannian manifold (N^m, g) and answer these two question in Section 3, where we find two characterizations of the sphere $S^m(\alpha)$.

In respect to first question raised above, in Section 3, we show that if a closed ρ-Ricci vector field ω on an m-dimensional compact and connected Riemannian manifold (N^m, g), $m > 2$ with scalar curvature $\tau \neq 0$, and nonzero nonconstant function ρ satisfies

$$\int_M Ric(\omega, \omega) \geq \frac{m-1}{m} \int_M (div\omega)^2,$$

then the scalar curvature τ is a positive constant $\tau = m(m-1)\alpha$, and (N^m, g) is isometric to $S^m(\alpha)$ (cf. Theorem 1). Also, the converse holds. Moreover, in respect to the second question raised above, we prove that if an m-dimensional complete and simply connected Riemannian manifold (N^m, g) with scalar curvature $\tau > 0$ admits a closed ρ-Ricci vector field ω such that the function ρ is a nontrivial solution of the FM-equation and the length of covariant derivative of ω satisfies

$$\|\nabla\omega\|^2 \leq \frac{1}{m}\tau^2\rho^2,$$

then τ is a positive constant $\tau = m(m-1)\alpha$ and (N^m, g) is isometric to $S^m(\alpha)$ (cf. Theorem 2), and the converse also holds.

2. Preliminaries

Let ω be a closed ρ-Ricci vector field on an m-dimensional Riemannian manifold (N^m, g). If β is the 1-form dual to ω, that is,

$$\beta(X) = g(\omega, X), \quad X \in \Theta(TN^m), \tag{9}$$

where $\Theta(TN^m)$ is the space of smooth sections of the tangent bundle TN^m, then we have $d\beta = 0$. We denote by ∇_X the covariant derivative operator with respect to the Riemannian connection on (N^m, g) and notice that for the closed ρ-Ricci vector field ω, we have

$$\begin{aligned} 2g(\nabla_X \omega, Y) &= g(\nabla_X \omega, Y) + g(\nabla_Y \omega, X) + g(\nabla_X \omega, Y) - g(\nabla_Y \omega, X) \\ &= (\pounds_\omega g)(X, Y) + d\beta(X, Y) = 2\rho Ric(X, Y). \end{aligned}$$

Thus, for a closed ρ-Ricci vector field ω, we have

$$\nabla_X \omega = \rho T X, \quad X \in \Theta(TN^m), \tag{10}$$

where T is a symmetric operator called the Ricci operator given by

$$Ric(X, Y) = g(TX, Y).$$

Using the expression for the curvature tensor field R of (N^m, g)

$$R(X, Y)Z = [\nabla_X, \nabla_Y]Z - \nabla_{[X,Y]}Z, \quad X, Y, Z \in \Theta(TN^m),$$

and Equation (10), we obtain

$$R(X, Y)\omega = X(\rho)TY - Y(\rho)TX + \rho((\nabla_X T)(Y) - (\nabla_Y T)(X)), \tag{11}$$

$X, Y \in \Theta(TN^m)$, where $(\nabla_X T)(Y) = \nabla_X TY - T(\nabla_X Y)$. The scalar curvature τ of (N^m, g) is given by $\tau = TrT$, where TrT is the trace of the symmetric operator T. Choosing a local frame $\{F_1, \ldots, F_m\}$ and using the definition of the Ricci tensor Ric

$$Ric(X, Y) = \sum_{j=1}^{m} g(R(F_j, X)Y, F_j),$$

together with Equation (3), we conclude that

$$Ric(Y, \omega) = Ric(Y, \nabla\rho) - \tau Y(\rho) + \rho g\left(Y, \sum_{j=1}^{m}\left(\nabla_{F_j} T\right)(F_j)\right) - \rho Y(\tau), \tag{12}$$

where $\nabla\rho$ is the gradient of ρ. It is known that the gradient of scalar curvature τ satisfies (cf. [1])

$$\frac{1}{2}\nabla\tau = \sum_{j=1}^{m}\left(\nabla_{F_j} T\right)(F_j). \tag{13}$$

Consequently, Equation (12) takes the form

$$Ric(Y, \omega) = Ric(Y, \nabla\rho) - \tau Y(\rho) - \frac{1}{2}\rho Y(\tau) \tag{14}$$

and we have

$$T(\omega) = T(\nabla\rho) - \tau\nabla\rho - \frac{1}{2}\rho\nabla\tau. \tag{15}$$

3. Characterizing Spheres via ρ-Ricci Fields

Let ω be a closed ρ-Ricci vector field on an m-dimensional Riemannian manifold (N^m, g). We shall use ρ-Ricci vector field and find two characterizations of m-sphere $\mathbf{S}^m(\alpha)$. In our first result, we prove the following result:

Theorem 1. *A closed ρ-Ricci vector field ω on an m-dimensional compact and connected Riemannian manifold (N^m, g), $m > 2$ with scalar curvature $\tau \neq 0$ and nonzero nonconstant function ρ satisfies*

$$\int_M Ric(\omega, \omega) \geq \frac{m-1}{m} \int_M (div\omega)^2,$$

if and only if, τ is a positive constant $m(m-1)\alpha$, and (N^m, g) is isometric to $S^m(\alpha)$.

Proof. Let (N^m, g) be an m-dimensional compact and connected Riemannian manifold, $m > 2$ with scalar curvature $\tau \neq 0$ and ω be a closed ρ-Ricci vector field defined on (N^m, g) with nonzero and nonconstant function ρ satisfying

$$\int_M Ric(\omega, \omega) \geq \frac{m-1}{m} \int_M (div\omega)^2. \tag{16}$$

Then using Equation (10), we have

$$div\omega = \rho\tau. \tag{17}$$

Choosing a local orthonormal frame $\{F_1, \dots, F_m\}$ and using

$$\|T\|^2 = \sum_{j=1}^{m} g(TF_j, TF_j)$$

and an outcome of Equation (10) as

$$(\pounds_\omega g)(X, Y) = 2\rho g(TX, Y), \quad X, Y \in \Theta(TN^m),$$

we conclude

$$\frac{1}{2}|\pounds_\omega g|^2 = 2\rho^2 \|T\|^2. \tag{18}$$

Note that, we have

$$\begin{aligned} \left\|T - \frac{\tau}{m} I\right\|^2 &= \sum_{j=1}^{m} g\left(\left(TE_j - \frac{\tau}{m} E_j\right), \left(TE_j - \frac{\tau}{m} E_j\right)\right) \\ &= \|T\|^2 + \frac{1}{m}\tau^2 - 2\sum_{j=1}^{m} g\left(TE_j, \frac{\tau}{m} E_j\right), \end{aligned}$$

that is,

$$\left\|T - \frac{\tau}{m} I\right\|^2 = \|T\|^2 - \frac{1}{m}\tau^2. \tag{19}$$

Now, using Equation (10), we have

$$\rho\left(TX - \frac{\tau}{m} X\right) = \left(\nabla_X \omega - \frac{\tau}{m} \rho X\right),$$

which in view of a local frame $\{F_1, \ldots, F_m\}$ on (N^m, g) implies

$$\begin{aligned}\rho^2\left\|T - \frac{\tau}{m}I\right\|^2 &= \sum_{j=1}^{m} g\left(\rho\left(TE_j - \frac{\tau}{m}E_j\right), \rho\left(TE_j - \frac{\tau}{m}E_j\right)\right) \\ &= \sum_{j=1}^{m} g\left(\nabla_{E_j}\omega - \frac{\tau}{m}\rho E_j, \nabla_{E_j}\omega - \frac{\tau}{m}\rho E_j\right) \\ &= \|\nabla\omega\|^2 + \frac{1}{m}\tau^2\rho^2 - \frac{2}{m}\tau\rho div\omega.\end{aligned}$$

Using (17), in above equation, yields

$$\rho^2\left\|T - \frac{\tau}{m}I\right\|^2 = \|\nabla\omega\|^2 - \frac{1}{m}\tau^2\rho^2,$$

which upon integration gives

$$\int_{N^m} \rho^2\left\|T - \frac{\tau}{m}I\right\|^2 = \int_{N^m}\left(\|\nabla\omega\|^2 - \frac{1}{m}\tau^2\rho^2\right). \tag{20}$$

Next, we recall the following integral formula (cf. [20])

$$\int_{N^m}\left(Ric(\omega,\omega) + \frac{1}{2}|\pounds_\omega g|^2 - \|\nabla\omega\|^2 - (div\omega)^2\right) = 0,$$

and employing it in Equation (20), we conclude

$$\int_{N^m} \rho^2\left\|T - \frac{\tau}{m}I\right\|^2 = \int_{N^m}\left(Ric(\omega,\omega) + \frac{1}{2}|\pounds_\omega g|^2 - (div\omega)^2 - \frac{1}{m}\tau^2\rho^2\right).$$

Using Equations (17) and (18) in the above equation yields

$$\int_{N^m} \rho^2\left\|T - \frac{\tau}{m}I\right\|^2 = \int_{N^m}\left(Ric(\omega,\omega) + 2\rho^2\|T\|^2 - \tau^2\rho^2 - \frac{1}{m}\tau^2\rho^2\right),$$

that is,

$$\int_{N^m} \rho^2\left\|T - \frac{\tau}{m}I\right\|^2 = \int_{N^m}\left(Ric(\omega,\omega) + 2\rho^2\left(\|T\|^2 - \frac{1}{m}\tau^2\rho^2\right) - \tau^2\rho^2 + \frac{1}{m}\tau^2\rho^2\right).$$

In view of Equation (19), the above equation implies

$$\int_{N^m} \rho^2\left\|T - \frac{\tau}{m}I\right\|^2 = \int_{N^m}\left(\frac{m-1}{m}\tau^2\rho^2 - Ric(\omega,\omega)\right)$$

and substituting from Equation (17), it yields

$$\int_{N^m} \rho^2\left\|T - \frac{\tau}{m}I\right\|^2 = \frac{m-1}{m}\int_{N^m}(div\omega)^2 - \int_{N^m} Ric(\omega,\omega).$$

Employing inequality (16) in the above equation, we conclude

$$\rho^2\left\|T - \frac{\tau}{m}I\right\|^2 = 0.$$

However, $\rho \neq 0$ on connected N^m, gives

$$T = \frac{\tau}{m}I. \tag{21}$$

Taking the covariant derivative in above equation, we have

$$(\nabla_X T)(Y) = \frac{1}{m} X(\tau) Y$$

and using a frame $\{F_1, \ldots, F_m\}$ on (N^m, g) in above equation, we have

$$\sum_{j=1}^{m} \left(\nabla_{E_j} T\right)(E_j) = \frac{1}{m} \nabla \tau.$$

Using Equation (13) in this equation, we arrive at

$$\frac{1}{2} \nabla \tau = \frac{1}{m} \nabla \tau$$

and as $m > 2$, we conclude $\nabla \tau = 0$. Hence, the scalar curvature τ is a constant, and it is a nonzero constant. Now, Equations (15) and (21) imply

$$\frac{\tau}{m} \omega = \frac{\tau}{m} \nabla \rho - \tau \nabla \rho,$$

that is,

$$\omega = -(m-1) \nabla \rho \tag{22}$$

and it gives $div\omega = -(m-1)\Delta\rho$, which, in view of Equation (17), implies $\tau\rho = -(m-1)\Delta\rho$, that is,

$$-(m-1)\rho\Delta\rho = \tau\rho^2.$$

Integrating the above equation by parts, we arrive at

$$(m-1) \int_{N^m} \|\nabla \rho\|^2 = \tau \int_{N^m} \rho^2.$$

Since ρ is a nonconstant, from the above equation, we conclude the constant $\tau > 0$. We put $\tau = m(m-1)\alpha$ for a positive constant α. Now, differentiating Equation (22) and using Equations (10) and (21), we conclude

$$\nabla_X \nabla \rho = -\alpha \rho X, \quad X \in \Theta(TN^m),$$

where ρ is a nonconstant function and $\alpha > 0$ is a constant. Hence, $Hess(\rho) = -\alpha\rho g$; that is, (N^m, g) is isometric to the sphere $S^m(\alpha)$ (cf. [6,7]).

Conversely, suppose that (N^m, g) is isometric to the sphere $S^m(\alpha)$. Then, we know that a nonzero constant vector field $\mathbf{b}$ on the ambient Euclidean space R^{m+1} induces a vector field ω on the sphere $S^m(\alpha)$, which, according to Equation (4), is a ρ-Ricci vector field. Clearly, the scalar curvature of $S^m(\alpha)$ is given by $\tau = m(m-1)\alpha \neq 0$. We claim that the function ρ is nonzero and nonconstant. If $\rho = 0$, then by Equation (4), we have $f = 0$, which, in view of Equation (3), implies $\omega = 0$, and this in turn will imply that the constant vector field $\mathbf{b} = 0$. This is contrary to the assumption that $\mathbf{b}$ is a nonzero constant vector field. Hence, $\rho \neq 0$. Now, suppose ρ is a constant; then, by Equation (4), f is a constant, and by Equation (3), we have $div\omega = -m\sqrt{\alpha} f$, which, by Stokes's Theorem on compact $S^m(\alpha)$, would imply $f = 0$. This in turn, by virtue of Equation (4), implies $\rho = 0$, which is a contradiction, as seen above. Hence, the function ρ is nonzero and nonconstant.

Next, using Equations (3) and (4), we have

$$div\omega = m(m-1)\alpha\rho \tag{23}$$

and it gives

$$\int_{S^m(\alpha)} (div\omega)^2 = m^2(m-1)^2\alpha^2 \int_{S^m(\alpha)} \rho^2. \tag{24}$$

Now, using Equation (4), we have

$$\nabla\rho = -\frac{1}{(m-1)\sqrt{\alpha}}\nabla f, \tag{25}$$

which, on using Equation (3), gives

$$\nabla\rho = -\frac{1}{m-1}\omega.$$

Taking divergence in the above equation and using Equation (23), we conclude $\Delta\rho = -m\alpha\rho$, that is, $\rho\Delta\rho = -m\alpha\rho^2$. Integrating this equation by parts, we conclude

$$\int_{S^m(\alpha)}\|\nabla\rho\|^2 = m\alpha\int_{S^m(\alpha)}\rho^2.$$

Treating this equation with Equation (24), we conclude

$$\int_{S^m(\alpha)}(div\omega)^2 = m(m-1)^2\alpha\int_{S^m(\alpha)}\|\nabla\rho\|^2. \tag{26}$$

Also, using Equations (3) and (25), we have

$$\omega = -(m-1)\nabla\rho$$

and it changes Equation (26) to

$$\int_{S^m(\alpha)}(div\omega)^2 = m\alpha\int_{S^m(\alpha)}\|\omega\|^2.$$

Finally, using $Ric(\omega,\omega) = (m-1)\|\omega\|^2$ in the above equation, we conclude

$$\int_{S^m(\alpha)}Ric(\omega,\omega) = \frac{m-1}{m}\int_{S^m(\alpha)}(div\omega)^2$$

and this finishes the proof. □

Next, we consider a closed ρ-Ricci vector field on a compact and connected Riemannian manifold (N^m, g) such that the smooth function ρ is a nontrivial solution of the FM-equation and find yet another characterization of the sphere $S^m(\alpha)$. Indeed we prove the following theorem.

Theorem 2. *An m-dimensional complete and simply connected Riemannian manifold (N^m, g) with scalar curvature $\tau > 0$ admits a closed ρ-Ricci vector field ω such that the function ρ is a nontrivial solution of the FM-equation and the length of covariant derivative of ω satisfies*

$$\|\nabla\omega\|^2 \leq \frac{1}{m}\tau^2\rho^2,$$

if and only if τ is a positive constant $\tau = m(m-1)\alpha$ and (N^m, g) is isometric to $S^m(\alpha)$.

Proof. Suppose (N^m, g) is an m-dimensional complete and simply connected Riemannian manifold with scalar curvature $\tau > 0$, and it admits a closed ρ-Ricci vector field ω, where ρ is a nontrivial solution of the FM-Equation (6) and the length of covariant derivative of ω satisfies

$$\|\nabla\omega\|^2 \leq \frac{1}{m}\tau^2\rho^2. \tag{27}$$

For ρ, we define the operator B_ρ by

$$B_\rho X = \nabla_X \nabla \rho, \quad X \in \Theta(TN^m),$$

then B_ρ is a symmetric operator related to $Hess(\rho)$ by

$$Hess(\rho)(X,Y) = g(B_\rho X, Y), \quad X, Y \in \Theta(TN^m). \tag{28}$$

As ρ is a nontrivial solution of the FM-equation, using Equations (6) and (28), we have

$$\rho T X = B_\rho X - (\Delta \rho) X,$$

which, in view of Equation (7), becomes

$$B_\rho X = \rho T X - \frac{\tau}{m-1} \rho X. \tag{29}$$

Note that owing to the fact that ρ is a nontrivial solution of the FM-equation on (N^m, g), the scalar curvature τ is a constant and we put $\tau = m(m-1)\alpha$ for a constant α. Using Equation (29), we have

$$B_\rho X + \alpha \rho X = \rho T X - (m-1)\alpha \rho X, \quad X \in \Theta(TN^m).$$

Now, using Equation (10) in the above equation, we have

$$B_\rho X + \alpha \rho X = \nabla_X \omega - (m-1)\alpha \rho X, \quad X \in \Theta(TN^m).$$

Taking a local frame $\{F_1, \ldots, F_m\}$ on (N^m, g), by the above equation, we conclude

$$\begin{aligned} \|B_\rho + \alpha \rho I\|^2 &= \sum_{j=1}^m g(B_\rho F_j + \alpha \rho F_j, B_\rho F_j + \alpha \rho F_j) \\ &= \sum_{j=1}^m g\Big(\nabla_{F_j} \omega - (m-1)\alpha \rho F_j, \nabla_{F_j} \omega - (m-1)\alpha \rho F_j\Big) \\ &= \|\nabla \omega\|^2 + m(m-1)^2 \alpha^2 \rho^2 - 2(m-1)\alpha \rho (div \omega). \end{aligned}$$

Now, using Equation (10), we have $div \omega = \tau \rho = m(m-1)\alpha \rho$, and inserting it in the above equation, we arrive at

$$\|B_\rho + \alpha \rho I\|^2 = \|\nabla \omega\|^2 - m(m-1)^2 \alpha^2 \rho^2,$$

that is,

$$\|B_\rho + \alpha \rho I\|^2 = \|\nabla \omega\|^2 - \frac{1}{m} \tau^2 \rho^2.$$

Using inequality (27) in the above equation results in

$$B_\rho = -\alpha \rho I,$$

that is,

$$Hess(\rho) = -\alpha \rho g. \tag{30}$$

Note that as $\tau > 0$, the constant $\alpha > 0$, and ρ is a nontrivial solution, ρ is a nonconstant function. Hence, by Equation (30), the complete and simply connected Riemannian manifold (N^m, g) is isometric to the sphere $S^m(\alpha)$ (cf. [6,7]).

Conversely, suppose that (N^m, g) is isometric to the sphere $S^m(\alpha)$. Then, by Equation (7), the function f is a solution of FM-equation on the sphere $S^m(\alpha)$, which has a closed ρ-Ricci vector field ω. The solution f of the FM-equation is related to ρ by Equation (4), that is,

$$f = -(m-1)\sqrt{\alpha}\rho. \tag{31}$$

In the proof of Theorem 1, we have seen that ρ is a nonconstant function on $S^m(\alpha)$. Moreover, using Equation (31), we have

$$\Delta f = -(m-1)\sqrt{\alpha}\Delta\rho, \quad Hess(f) = -(m-1)\sqrt{\alpha}Hess(\rho)$$

and the Equation (7) takes the form

$$-(m-1)\sqrt{\alpha}(\Delta\rho)g + fRic = -(m-1)\sqrt{\alpha}Hess(\rho),$$

which, in view of Equation (31), changes to

$$(\Delta\rho)g + \rho Ric = Hess(\rho).$$

Hence, ρ is a nontrivial solution of the FM-equation on the sphere $S^m(\alpha)$. Now, the Ricci operator T of the sphere $S^m(\alpha)$ is given by $T = (m-1)\alpha I$ and, therefore, Equation (10) on $S^m(\alpha)$ is

$$\nabla_X\omega = (m-1)\alpha\rho X, \quad X \in \Theta(TS^m(\alpha)).$$

Using the expression for the scalar curvature $\tau = m(m-1)\alpha$ for the sphere $S^m(\alpha)$, we have

$$\nabla_X\omega = \frac{\tau}{m}\rho X, \quad X \in \Theta(TS^m(\alpha)).$$

This proves

$$\|\nabla\omega\|^2 = \frac{1}{m}\tau^2\rho^2$$

and completes the proof. □

4. Conclusions

In the previous section, we used a closed ρ-Ricci vector field ω on an m-dimensional Riemannian manifold (N^m, g) to find two different characterizations of an m-sphere $S^m(\alpha)$. The scope of studying ρ-Ricci vector fields on a Riemannian manifold is quite modest. We observe that, in the previous section, we restricted the ρ-Ricci vector field ω to be closed, which simplified the expression for the covariant derivative of ω. It will be interesting to investigate whether we could achieve similar results after removing the restriction that the ρ-Ricci vector field ω is closed. It will be an interesting future topic to study the geometry of an m-dimensional Riemannian manifold (N^m, g) that admits a ρ-Ricci vector field ω, which needs not be closed. In order to simplify the findings on an m-dimensional Riemannian manifold (N^m, g) admitting a ρ-Ricci vector field ω which is not necessarily closed, we could impose the restriction on the Ricci operator T of (N^m, g) to be a Codazzi-type tensor, such that it satisfies

$$(\nabla_X T)(Y) = (\nabla_Y T)(X), \quad X, Y \in \Theta(TN^m).$$

Note that above restriction on (N^m, g) is slightly stronger than demanding the scalar curvature be a constant.

Author Contributions: Writing—original draft preparation, S.D.; writing—review and editing, H.A. All authors have read and agreed to the published version of the manuscript.

Funding: This research received no external funding.

Data Availability Statement: No new data were created or analyzed in this study. Data sharing is not applicable to this article.

Acknowledgments: The authors would like to extend their sincere appreciations to Supporting project number (RSPD2023R860) King Saud University, Riyadh, Saudi Arabia.

Conflicts of Interest: The authors declare no conflict of interest.

References

1. Besse, A.L. *Einstein Manifolds*; Springer: Berlin/Heidelberg, Germany, 1987.
2. Al-Dayel, I.; Deshmukh, S.; Belova, O. A remarkable property of concircular vector fields on a Riemannian manifold. *Mathematics* **2020**, *8*, 469. [CrossRef]
3. Chen, B.Y. Some results on concircular vector fields and their applications to Ricci solitons. *Bull. Korean Math. Soc.* **2015**, *52*, 1535–1547. [CrossRef]
4. Deshmukh, S. Characterizing spheres and Euclidean spaces by conformal vector field. *Ann. Mat. Pura Appl.* **2017**, *196*, 2135–2145. [CrossRef]
5. Fialkow, A. Conformal geodesics. *Trans. Amer. Math. Soc.* **1939**, *45*, 443–473. [CrossRef]
6. Obata, M. Conformal transformations of Riemannian manifolds. *J. Diff. Geom.* **1970**, *4*, 311–333. [CrossRef]
7. Obata, M. The conjectures about conformal transformations. *J. Diff. Geom.* **1971**, *6*, 247–258.
8. Berestovskii, V.; Nikonorov, Y. Killing vector fields of constant length on Riemannian manifolds. *Sib. Math. J.* **2008**, *49*, 395–407. [CrossRef]
9. Lynge, W.C. Sufficient conditions for periodicity of a Killing vector field. *Proc. Am. Math. Soc.* **1973**, *38*, 614–616. [CrossRef]
10. Rong, X. Positive curvature, local and global symmetry, and fundamental groups. *Am. J. Math.* **1999**, *121*, 931–943. [CrossRef]
11. Yorozu, S. Killing vector fields on complete Riemannian manifolds. *Proc. Am. Math. Soc.* **1982**, *84*, 115–120. [CrossRef]
12. Ishan, A.; Deshmukh, S. A Note on Generalized Solitons. *Symmetry* **2023**, *15*, 954. [CrossRef]
13. Chow, B.; Lu, P.; Lei Ni. Hamilton's Ricci flow, volume 77 of Graduate Studies in Mathematics. *Am. Math. Soc. Provid. RI* **2006**, *24*, 109–148.
14. Fischer, A.E.; Marsden, J.E. Manifolds of Riemannian metrics with prescribed scalar curvature. *Bull. Am. Math. Soc.* **1974**, *80*, 479–484. [CrossRef]
15. Kobayashi, O. A dierential equation arising from scalar curvature function. *J. Math. Soc. Jpn.* **1982**, *34*, 665–675. [CrossRef]
16. Geng, X.; Hou, S. Gradient estimates for the Fisher-KPP equation on Riemannian manifolds. *Bound. Value Probl.* **2018**, *2018*, 25. [CrossRef]
17. Countinho, F.; Diógenes, R.; Leandro, B.; Ribeiro, E., Jr. Static perfect fluid space-time on compact manifolds. *Class. Quantum Grav.* **2020**, *37*, 015003. [CrossRef]
18. Shen, Y. A note on Fischer-Marsden's conjecture. *Proc. Am. Math. Soc.* **1997**, *125*, 901–905. [CrossRef]
19. Wang, Y.-Z.; Zhang, X. The log entropy formula and entropy power for p-heat equation on Riemannian manifolds. *Nonlinear Anal.* **2021**, *209*, 112360. [CrossRef]
20. Yano, K. *Integral Formulas in Riemannian Geometry*; Marcel Dekker Inc.: New York, NY, USA, 1970.

mathematics

MDPI

Article

On the Space of G-Permutation Degree of Some Classes of Topological Spaces

Ljubiša D. R. Kočinac [1,2,*], Farkhod G. Mukhamadiev [3] and Anvar K. Sadullaev [4]

1 Faculty of Sciences and Mathematics, University of Niš, 18000 Niš, Serbia
2 Department of Mathematics, State University of Novi Pazar, 36300 Novi Pazar, Serbia
3 Faculty of Mathematics, National University of Uzbekistan Named after Mirzo Ulugbek, Str. University 4, Tashkent 100174, Uzbekistan; farhod8717@mail.ru
4 Department of Exact Sciences, Yeoju Technical Institute in Tashkent, Str. Usman Nasyr 156, Tashkent 100121, Uzbekistan; anvars1997@mail.ru
* Correspondence: lkocinac@gmail.com

Abstract: In this paper, we study the space of G-permutation degree of some classes of topological spaces and the properties of the functor SP^n_G of G-permutation degree. In particular, we prove: (a) If a topological space X is developable, then so is $\mathrm{SP}^n_G X$; (b) If X is a Moore space, then so is $\mathrm{SP}^n_G X$; (c) If a topological space X is an M_1-space, then so is $\mathrm{SP}^n_G X$; (d) If a topological space X is an M_2-space, then so is $\mathrm{SP}^n_G X$.

Keywords: functor of permutation degree; developable space; Moore space; M_1-space; M_2-space; Nagata space

MSC: 18F60; 54B30; 54E99

Citation: Kočinac, L.D.R.; Mukhamadiev, F.G.; Sadullaev, A.K. On the Space of G-Permutation Degree of Some Classes of Topological Spaces. *Mathematics* **2023**, *11*, 4624. https://doi.org/10.3390/math11224624

Academic Editor: Daniele Ettore Otera

Received: 24 October 2023
Revised: 9 November 2023
Accepted: 10 November 2023
Published: 12 November 2023

1. Introduction

Let F be a covariant functor acting on a class of topological spaces. The following natural general problem in the theory of covariant functors was posed by V. V. Fedorchuk at the Prague Topological Symposium in 1981 (see [1]).

Let $\mathcal{P}$ be a topological property and F a covariant functor. If a topological space X has the property $\mathcal{P}$, then whether $\mathrm{F}(X)$ has the same property, and vice versa, if $\mathrm{F}(X)$ has the property $\mathcal{P}$, does the space X also have the property $\mathcal{P}$?

This paper deals with such questions.

Let G be a subgroup of the symmetric group S_n, $n \in \mathbb{N}$, of all permutations of the set $\{1,2,\ldots,n\}$, and let X be a topological space. On the space X^n, define the following equivalence relation r_G: for elements $\mathbf{x} = (x_1, x_2, \ldots, x_n)$ and $\mathbf{y} = (y_1, y_2, \ldots, y_n)$ in X^n

$$\mathbf{x}\, r_G\, \mathbf{y} \Leftrightarrow \text{ there is } \sigma \in G \text{ with } y_i = x_{\sigma(i)}, 1 \le i \le n.$$

The relation r_G is called the *G-symmetric equivalence relation*. The equivalence class of an element $\mathbf{x} \in X^n$ is denoted by $[\mathbf{x}]_G$ or $[(x_1, x_2, \ldots, x_n)]_G$. The quotient space X^n/r_G (equipped with the quotient topology of the topology on X^n) is called the *space of G-permutation degree of* X and is denoted by $\mathrm{SP}^n_G X$. The quotient mapping of X^n to this space is denoted by $\pi^s_{n,G}$; when $G = S_n$, one writes π^s_G.

Let $f: X \to Y$ be a continuous mapping. Define the mapping $\mathrm{SP}^n_G : \mathrm{SP}^n_G X \to \mathrm{SP}^n_G Y$ by

$$\mathrm{SP}^n_G f([\mathbf{x}]_G) = [(f(x_1), f(x_2), \ldots, f(x_n))]_G, \ [\mathbf{x}]_G \in \mathrm{SP}^n_G X.$$

It is easy to verify that SP^n_G as defined is a functor in the category of compacta. This functor is called the *functor of G-permutation degree*.

In [1,2], V. V. Fedorchuk and V. V. Filippov investigated the functor of G-permutation degree, and it was proved that this functor is a normal functor in the category of compact spaces and their continuous mappings.

In recent years, a number of studies have investigated various covariant functors, in particular the functor of G-permutation degree, and their influence on some topological properties (see, for instance, [3–6]). In [3,4], the index of boundedness, uniform connectedness, and homotopy properties of the space of G-permutation degree have been studied, and it was shown in [4] that the functor SP^n_G preserves the homotopy and the retraction of topological spaces. References [5,6] deal with certain tightness-type properties and Lindelöf-type properties of the space of G-permutation degree.

The current paper is devoted to the investigation of some classes of topological spaces (such as developable spaces, Moore spaces, M_1-spaces, M_2-spaces, Lašnev's and Nagata's spaces) in the space of G-permutation degree.

Throughout the paper, all spaces are assumed to be T_1.

Observe that the space $\mathrm{SP}^n_G X$ is related to the space $\exp_n X$ of nonempty $\leq n$-element subsets of X equipped with the Vietoris topology whose base form the sets of the form

$$O\langle U_1, U_2, \ldots, U_k\rangle = \{F \in \exp_n X : F \subset \cup_{i=1}^k U_i,\ F \cap U_i \neq \emptyset,\ i = 1, \ldots, k\}$$

where $U_1, U_2, \ldots, U_k$ are open subsets of X [2].

Observe that the mapping $\pi^h_{n,G} : \mathrm{SP}^n_G X \to \exp_n X$ assigning to each G-symmetric equivalence class $[(x_1, x_2, \ldots, x_n)]_G$ the hypersymmetric equivalence class $[(x_1, x_2, \ldots, x_n)]^{hc}$ containing it represents the functor $\exp_n$ as the factor functor of the functor SP^n_G [1,2].

Also, the spaces $\mathrm{SP}^2_G X$ and $\exp_2 X$ are homeomorphic, while it is not the case for $n > 2$ [2].

2. Results

In this section, we present the results obtained in this study.

For an open cover γ of a space X and a subset A of X, *the star of A with respect to γ* is defined by $\mathrm{St}(A, \gamma) = \bigcup\{U \in \gamma : U \cap A \neq \emptyset\}$.

Let γ be an open cover of X. Obviously, $\mathrm{SP}^n_G \gamma = \{\pi^s_{n,G}(U_1 \times \ldots \times U_n) = [U_1 \times \ldots \times U_n]_G : U_1, \ldots, U_n \in \gamma\}$ is an open cover of $\mathrm{SP}^n_G X$.

Proposition 1. *Let $\mathrm{SP}^n_G \gamma$ be an open cover of $\mathrm{SP}^n_G X$. For each $[(x_1, \ldots, x_n)]_G \in \mathrm{SP}^n_G X$, we have*

$$\mathrm{St}([(x_1, \ldots, x_n)]_G, \mathrm{SP}^n_G \gamma) \subset [\mathrm{St}(x_1, \gamma) \times \ldots \times \mathrm{St}(x_n, \gamma)]_G.$$

Proof. Let $[(y_1, \ldots, y_n)]_G \in \mathrm{St}([(x_1, \ldots, x_n)]_G, \mathrm{SP}^n_G \gamma)$. Then, there exists $[U_1 \times \ldots \times U_n]_G \in \mathrm{SP}^n_G \gamma$ such that $[(y_1, \ldots, y_n)]_G \in [U_1 \times \ldots \times U_n]_G$. On the other hand, $[U_1 \times \ldots \times U_n]_G \subset [V_1 \times \ldots \times V_n]_G$ if and only if $\bigcup_{i=1}^n U_i \subset \bigcup_{i=1}^n V_i$ and for every V_i, $i = 1, 2, \ldots, n$, there exists a permutation $\sigma \in G$ such that $U_{\sigma(i)} \subset V_i$. Hence, we obtain that $[(y_1, \ldots, y_n)]_G \in [U_1 \times \ldots \times U_n]_G \subset [\mathrm{St}(x_1, \gamma) \times \ldots \times \mathrm{St}(x_n, \gamma)]_G$. This means that $\mathrm{St}([(x_1, \ldots, x_n)]_G, \mathrm{SP}^n_G \gamma) \subset [\mathrm{St}(x_1, \gamma) \times \ldots \times \mathrm{St}(x_n, \gamma)]_G$. □

Lemma 1. *Let $x_1, x_2, \ldots, x_n$ be points of X. For each $i = 1, 2, \ldots, n$, let $\{U_{im}\}_{m=1}^\infty$ be a decreasing sequence of nonempty subsets of X such that $\bigcap_{m=1}^\infty U_{im} = \{x_i\}$. Then,*

$$\bigcap_{m=1}^{\infty} [U_{1m} \times U_{2m} \times \ldots \times U_{nm}]_G = \{[(x_1, x_2, \ldots, x_n)]_G\}.$$

Proof. Let $i = 1, 2, \ldots, n$, and assume that $[y_1, y_2, \ldots, y_n]_G \in \bigcap_{m=1}^\infty [U_{1m} \times U_{2m} \times \ldots \times U_{nm}]_G$. Then, for each positive integer m, $[y_1, y_2, \ldots, y_n]_G \in [U_{1m} \times U_{2m} \times \ldots \times U_{nm}]_G$. This means that there exists a permutation $\sigma \in G$ such that $y_i \in U_{\sigma(i)m}$ for all $i = 1, 2, \ldots, n$. In addition, $y_i \in \bigcap_{m=1}^\infty U_{\sigma(i)m} = \{x_{\sigma(i)}\}$ for all $i = 1, 2, \ldots, n$. Consequently, it follows that $y_i = x_{\sigma(i)}$. This means that $[(y_1, y_2, \ldots, y_n)]_G = [(x_1, x_2, \ldots, x_n)]_G$. □

Proposition 2. *Let X be a space, and let $x_1, x_2, \ldots, x_n$ be points of X. For each $i = \overline{1,n}$, let $\mathcal{U}_i = \{\mathcal{U}_{im}\}_{m\in\mathbb{N}}$ be a local base of X at x_i. Then, $\mathrm{SP}^n_G\mathcal{U} = \{[\mathcal{U}_{1m} \times \mathcal{U}_{2m} \times \ldots \times \mathcal{U}_{nm}]_G : \mathcal{U}_{im} \in \mathcal{U}_i, i = \overline{1,n}\}_{m\in\mathbb{N}}$ is a local base of $\mathrm{SP}^n_G X$ at $[(x_1, x_2, \ldots, x_n)]_G$.*

Proof. Without loss of the generality, suppose that $\mathcal{U}_{im+1} \subset \mathcal{U}_{im}$ for every positive integer m. Let $\mathrm{SP}^n_G V$ be an open subset of $\mathrm{SP}^n_G X$ which contains $[(x_1, x_2, \ldots, x_n)]_G$. Then, there exist open subsets $V_1, V_2, \ldots, V_n$ of X such that $[(x_1, x_2, \ldots, x_n)]_G \in [V_1 \times V_2 \times \ldots \times V_n]_G \subset \mathrm{SP}^n_G V$. Put $V_{x_i} = \cap\{V \in \{V_1, V_2, \ldots, V_n\} : x_i \in V\}$ for every $i = \overline{1,n}$. Then, $V_{x_1}, \ldots, V_{x_n}$ are open subsets of X such that $[(x_1, x_2, \ldots, x_n)]_G \in [V_{x_1} \times V_{x_2} \times \ldots \times V_{x_n}]_G \subset [V_1 \times V_2 \times \ldots \times V_n]_G \subset \mathrm{SP}^n_G V$. Since $\mathcal{U}_i$ is a local base at x_i, there exists a positive integer m_i such that $x_i \in \mathcal{U}_{m_i i} \subset V_{x_i}$. Let $m = \max\{m_1, \ldots, m_n\}$. Then, $x_i \in \mathcal{U}_{mi} \subset V_{x_i}$. Consequently, $[\mathcal{U}_{1m} \times \mathcal{U}_{2m} \times \ldots \times \mathcal{U}_{nm}]_G \in \mathrm{SP}^n_G\mathcal{U}$ and $[(x_1, x_2, \ldots, x_n)]_G \in [\mathcal{U}_{1m} \times \mathcal{U}_{2m} \times \ldots \times \mathcal{U}_{nm}]_G \subset [V_{x_1} \times V_{x_2} \times \ldots \times V_{x_n}] \subset \mathrm{SP}^n_G V$. Therefore, $\mathrm{SP}^n_G\mathcal{U}$ is a local base of $\mathrm{SP}^n_G X$ at $[(x_1, x_2, \ldots, x_n)]_G$. □

A space X is *developable* [7,8] if there exists a sequence $\{\gamma_m : m \in \mathbb{N}\}$ of open covers of X such that, for each $x \in X$, $\{\mathrm{St}(x, \gamma_m) : m \in \mathbb{N}\}$ is a local base at x. Such a sequence of covers is called a *development* for X. It is well known that every metrizable space is developable, and every developable space is clearly first countable.

Remark 1. *Clearly, the above definition of the developable space is equivalent to the following:*

(a) For each $x \in X$ and for each positive integer m such that $\mathrm{St}(x, \gamma_m) \neq \emptyset$, $\mathrm{St}(x, \gamma_m)$ is a neighborhood of the point x, and

(b) For each $x \in X$ and for each open U containing x, there exists a positive integer m such that $x \in \mathrm{St}(x, \gamma_m) \subset U$.

Theorem 1. *If X is a developable space, then so is $\mathrm{SP}^n_G X$.*

Proof. Assume that X is a developable space and $\{\mu_m : m \in \mathbb{N}\}$ is a development for X. For every $m \in \mathbb{N}$, let

$$\gamma_m = \left\{\bigcap_{j=1}^{m} V_j : V_j \in \mu_j, j = \overline{1,n}\right\}.$$

Then, $\{\gamma_m\}_{m\in\mathbb{N}}$ is also a development for X such that $\mathrm{St}(x, \gamma_{m+1}) \subset \mathrm{St}(x, \gamma_m)$ for all $x \in X$ and every $m \in \mathbb{N}$. Put

$$\mathrm{SP}^n_G\gamma_m = \{[U_{m1} \times \ldots \times U_{mn}]_G : U_{m1}, \ldots, U_{mn} \in \gamma_m\}.$$

It can be easily checked that $\mathrm{SP}^n_G\gamma_m$ is an open cover of $\mathrm{SP}^n_G X$ for every $m \in \mathbb{N}$.

Now, we will prove that for each $[(x_1, x_2, \ldots, x_n)]_G \in \mathrm{SP}^n_G X$, $\{\mathrm{St}([(x_1, x_2, \ldots, x_n)]_G, \mathrm{SP}^n_G\gamma_m)\}_{m\in\mathbb{N}}$ is a local base at $[(x_1, x_2, \ldots, x_n)]_G$. Let $\mathrm{SP}^n_G U$ be an open subset of $\mathrm{SP}^n_G X$ such that $[(x_1, x_2, \ldots, x_n)]_G \in \mathrm{SP}^n_G U$. Then, there exist open subsets $U_1, U_2, \ldots, U_n$ of X such that $[(x_1, x_2, \ldots, x_n)]_G \in [U_1 \times U_2 \times \ldots \times U_n]_G \subset \mathrm{SP}^n_G U$. Since $\{\mathrm{St}(x_i, \gamma_m)\}_{m\in\mathbb{N}}$ is a local base at x_i for any $i = \overline{1,n}$, there exists a positive integer m_i such that $\mathrm{St}(x_i, \gamma_{m_i}) \subset U_{x_i} = \bigcap\{U_j : x_i \in U_j, j = \overline{1,n}\}$. Then ,there exists $m \geq \max\{m_1, m_2, \ldots, m_n\}$ such that $\mathrm{St}(x_i, \gamma_m) \subset \mathrm{St}(x_i, \gamma_{m_i})$ for all $i = \overline{1,n}$. By Proposition 1, we have

$$\begin{aligned} [(x_1, x_2, \ldots, x_n)]_G &\in \mathrm{St}([(x_1, x_2, \ldots, x_n)]_G, \mathrm{SP}^n_G\gamma_m) \\ &\subset [\mathrm{St}(x_1, \gamma_{m_1}) \times \ldots \times \mathrm{St}(x_n, \gamma_{m_n})]_G \\ &\subset [U_{x_1} \times \ldots \times U_{x_n}]_G \subset [U_1 \times \ldots \times U_n]_G \subset \mathrm{SP}^n_G U. \end{aligned}$$

By Statement (b) of Remark 1, it means that $\mathrm{SP}^n_G X$ is a developable space. □

A regular developable space is a *Moore space* [7,8].

Proposition 3. *If X is a Moore space, then so is $\mathrm{SP}^n_G X$.*

Proof. By Theorem 1, if X is a developable space, then the space $\mathrm{SP}^n_G X$ is also developable. On the other hand, it is well known from [9] that regularity is preserved under the closed-and-open mapping and Cartesian product. Therefore, if X is a regular space, then the space $\mathrm{SP}^n_G X$ is also regular. □

A family $\mathcal{U} = \{U_\alpha\}_{\alpha\in\mathcal{A}}$ of subsets of a topological space is *closure preserving* [7,9] if $\overline{\bigcup_{\alpha\in\mathcal{A}_0} U_\alpha} = \bigcup_{\alpha\in\mathcal{A}_0} \overline{U_\alpha}$ for every $\mathcal{A}_0 \subset \mathcal{A}$.

Theorem 2. *If $\mathcal{U}$ is a closure-preserving family of subsets of X, then $\mathrm{SP}^n_G\mathcal{U} = \{[U_1 \times U_2 \times \ldots \times U_n]_G : U_1, U_2, \ldots, U_n \in \mathcal{U}\}$ is a closure-preserving family of subsets of $\mathrm{SP}^n_G X$.*

Proof. Let $\mathrm{SP}^n_G\mathcal{U}_0$ be a subfamily of $\mathrm{SP}^n_G\mathcal{U}$ and $[(x_1, x_2, \ldots, x_n)]_G \in \mathrm{SP}^n_G X \setminus \bigcup\{\overline{\mathrm{SP}^n_G W} : \mathrm{SP}^n_G W \in \mathrm{SP}^n_G\mathcal{U}_0\}$. Let $V_i = X \setminus \bigcup\{\overline{U} : x_i \in X \setminus \overline{U}, U \in \mathcal{U}\}$. Since $\mathcal{U}$ is a closure preserving family of subsets of X, we have that $V_i = X \setminus \overline{\bigcup\{U : x_i \in X \setminus \overline{U}, U \in \mathcal{U}\}}$. This means that V_i is an open subset of X and $x_i \in V_i$ for all $i = 1, 2, \ldots, n$. Let $\mathrm{SP}^n_G V = [V_1 \times V_2 \times \ldots \times V_n]_G$. Then, $\mathrm{SP}^n_G V$ is open subset of $\mathrm{SP}^n_G X$, $[(x_1, x_2, \ldots, x_n)]_G \in \mathrm{SP}^n_G V$ and $\mathrm{SP}^n_G V \bigcap \mathrm{SP}^n_G W = \emptyset$ for all $\mathrm{SP}^n_G W \in \mathrm{SP}^n_G\mathcal{U}_0$. Therefore, $[(x_1, x_2, \ldots, x_n)]_G \in \mathrm{SP}^n_G V \subset \mathrm{SP}^n_G X \setminus \overline{\bigcup\{\mathrm{SP}^n_G W : \mathrm{SP}^n_G W \in \mathrm{SP}^n_G\mathcal{U}_0\}}$. It shows that $[(x_1, x_2, \ldots, x_n)]_G \in \mathrm{SP}^n_G X \setminus \overline{\bigcup\{\mathrm{SP}^n_G W : \mathrm{SP}^n_G W \in \mathrm{SP}^n_G\mathcal{U}_0\}}$. Hence, $\mathrm{SP}^n_G\mathcal{U}$ is a closure preserving family of subsets of $\mathrm{SP}^n_G X$. □

A family $\mathcal{U}$ is called *σ-closure preserving* [7] if it is represented as a union of countably many closure preserving subfamilies.

An *M_1-space* [7,8] is a regular space having a σ-closure preserving base.

Example 1. *Let $\mathbb{Q}$ denote the set of rational numbers. For $x \in \mathbb{R}$, put $L_x = \{(x, y) : (x, y) \in \mathbb{R}^2, y > 0\}$ and $X = \mathbb{R} \cup (\bigcup\{L_x : x \in \mathbb{R}\})$. Define a base for a topology on X as follows: for any $s, t \in \mathbb{Q}$ and $z = (x, w) \in L_x$ such that $0 < s < w < t$, we put $\mathcal{U}^x_{s,t}(z) = \{(x, y) : s < y < t\}$, and let $\mathcal{U}$ be the set of all such $\mathcal{U}^x_{s,t}(z)$. For all $r, s, t \in \mathbb{Q}$ and $z \in \mathbb{R}$ such that $s < z < t$ and $r > 0$, we put*

$$\mathcal{V}_{r,s,t}(z) = (s, t) \cup (\bigcup\{(w, y) : 0 < y < r, w \in (s, t) \setminus \{z\}\})$$

, and let $\mathcal{V}$ be the set of all $V_{r,s,t}(z)$. Now, put $\mathcal{B} = \mathcal{U} \cup \mathcal{V}$. Then one can check that $\mathcal{B}$ is a σ-closure preserving base for X. It shows that X is an M_1-space. Moreover, the space X is a first countable, but non-metrizable space.

Theorem 3. *If X is an M_1-space, then so is $\mathrm{SP}^n_G X$.*

Proof. Let X be an M_1-space and $\mathcal{U} = \bigcup_{i=1}^{\infty} \mathcal{U}_i$ be a σ-closure preserving base in X. Since the union of two closure preserving family of subsets of X is also closure preserving, we assume that $\mathcal{U}_i \subset \mathcal{U}_{i+1}$ for each i. For every positive integer i, set $\mathrm{SP}^n_G\mathcal{U}_i = \{[U_1 \times U_2 \times \ldots \times U_n]_G : U_1, U_2, \ldots, U_n \in \mathcal{U}_i\}$. Obviously, $\mathrm{SP}^n_G\mathcal{U}_i \subset \mathrm{SP}^n_G\mathcal{U}_{i+1}$ for all positive integers i. By Theorem 2, $\mathcal{U}_i$ is a closure preserving family of subsets of $\mathrm{SP}^n_G X$, and at the same time $\mathcal{U}_i$ is a family of open subsets of $\mathrm{SP}^n_G X$. Therefore, $\mathrm{SP}^n_G\mathcal{U} = \bigcup_{i=1}^{\infty} \mathrm{SP}^n_G\mathcal{U}_i$ is a σ-closure preserving family of open subsets of $\mathrm{SP}^n_G X$.

Now, we will show that $\mathrm{SP}^n_G\mathcal{U}$ is a base for $\mathrm{SP}^n_G X$. Let $[(x_1, x_2, \ldots, x_n)]_G$ be an arbitrary element of $\mathrm{SP}^n_G X$ and $\mathrm{SP}^n_G U$ be an open subset of $\mathrm{SP}^n_G X$ such that $[(x_1, x_2, \ldots, x_n)]_G \in \mathrm{SP}^n_G U$. Since $\mathcal{U}$ is a base for X, there exist $U_1, U_2, \ldots, U_n \in \mathcal{U}$ such that $[(x_1, x_2, \ldots, x_n)]_G \in [U_1 \times U_2 \times \ldots \times U_n]_G \subset \mathrm{SP}^n_G U$. Since $\mathcal{U}_i \subset \mathcal{U}_{i+1}$ for each positive integer i, there exists i_0 such that $U_1, U_2, \ldots, U_n \in \mathcal{U}_{i_0}$. Then it follows that $[U_1 \times U_2 \times \ldots \times U_n]_G \in \mathrm{SP}^n_G\mathcal{U}_{i_0}$. Therefore, $\mathrm{SP}^n_G\mathcal{U}$ is a base for $\mathrm{SP}^n_G X$. This means that $\mathrm{SP}^n_G X$ is an M_1-space. □

A collection $\mathcal{B}$ of (not necessarily open) subsets of a regular space X is a *quasi-base* in X [7] if whenever $x \in X$ and U is a neighborhood of x, there exists a $B \in \mathcal{B}$ such that $x \in \mathrm{Int}B \subset B \subset U$.

An M_2-*space* [7,8] is a regular space having a σ-closure preserving quasi-base.

Theorem 4. *If X is an M_2-space, then so is $\mathrm{SP}^n_G X$.*

Proof. Suppose that X is an M_2-space and $\mathcal{B} = \bigcup_{i=1}^{\infty} \mathcal{B}_i$ is a σ-closure preserving quasi-base. Since the union of two closure-preserving family of subsets of X is also closure preserving, we assume that $\mathcal{B}_i \subset \mathcal{B}_{i+1}$ for each i. For each positive integer i, put $\mathrm{SP}^n_G \mathcal{B}_i = \{[B_1 \times B_2 \times \ldots \times B_n]_G : B_1, B_2, \ldots, B_n \in \mathcal{B}_i\}$. Obviously, $\mathrm{SP}^n_G \mathcal{B}_i \subset \mathrm{SP}^n_G \mathcal{B}_{i+1}$ for all i. By Theorem 2, $\mathcal{B}_i$ is a closure preserving family of subsets of $\mathrm{SP}^n_G X$. Therefore, $\mathrm{SP}^n_G \mathcal{B} = \bigcup_{i=1}^{\infty} \mathrm{SP}^n_G \mathcal{B}_i$ is a σ-closure preserving family of subsets of $\mathrm{SP}^n_G X$.

Now, we will prove that $\mathrm{SP}^n_G \mathcal{B}$ is a quasi-base for $\mathrm{SP}^n_G X$. Let $[(x_1, x_2, \ldots, x_n)]_G$ be an arbitrary element of $\mathrm{SP}^n_G X$ and $\mathrm{SP}^n_G V$ be an open subset of $\mathrm{SP}^n_G X$ such that $[(x_1, x_2, \ldots, x_n)]_G \in \mathrm{SP}^n_G V$. Consequently, there exist open subsets $V_1, V_2, \ldots, V_n$ of X such that $[(x_1, x_2, \ldots, x_n)]_G \in [V_1 \times V_2 \times \ldots \times V_n]_G \subset \mathrm{SP}^n_G V$. Since $\mathcal{B}$ is a quasi-base for X, there exist a permutation $\sigma \in G$ and $B_{\sigma(j)} \in \mathcal{B}_i$ such that $x_j \in \mathrm{Int} B_{\sigma(j)} \subset V_{\sigma(j)}$, where $j = 1, 2, \ldots, n$. Note that $[(x_1, x_2, \ldots, x_n)]_G \in [\mathrm{Int} B_1 \times \mathrm{Int} B_2 \times \ldots \times \mathrm{Int} B_n]_G \subset \mathrm{Int}([B_1 \times B_2 \times \ldots \times B_n]_G) \subset [B_1 \times B_2 \times \ldots \times B_n]_G \subset [V_1 \times V_2 \times \ldots \times V_n]_G \subset \mathrm{SP}^n_G V$. It shows that $\mathrm{SP}^n_G \mathcal{B}$ is a quasi-base for $\mathrm{SP}^n_G X$. □

Recall now that a space X is said to be stratifiable if f for every closed subset $F \subset X$ there is a sequence of open subsets $(U(F,k))_{k \in \mathbb{N}}$ such that (i) $F = \bigcap_{k \in \mathbb{N}} U(F,k) = \bigcap_{k \in \mathbb{N}} \overline{U(F,k)}$, and (ii) if $F_1 \subset F_2$, then $U(F_1, k) \subset U(F_2, k)$ for each $k \in \mathbb{N}$. In the paper [10] it was proved that a space is stratifiable if and only if it is M_2. Therefore, we obtain the following:

Corollary 1. *If a space X is stratifiable, then so is $\mathrm{SP}^n_G X$.*

A space X is a *Lašnev space* [7,8] if there exist a metric space Z and a continuous closed mapping from Z onto X. Lašnev spaces are known to be M_1-spaces.

Theorem 5. *Let X be a space, and let n be a positive integer. If X^n is a Lašnev space, then so is $\mathrm{SP}^n_G X$.*

Proof. Suppose that X^n is a Lašnev space. Then, there exist a metric space Z and a continuous closed mapping $g : Z \to X^n$. Since $\pi^s_{n,G} : X^n \to \mathrm{SP}^n_G X$ is a closed, onto mapping, we obtain that the mapping $\pi^s_{n,G} \circ g : Z \to \mathrm{SP}^n_G X$ is also a closed mapping from the metric space Z onto the space $\mathrm{SP}^n_G X$. This means that the space $\mathrm{SP}^n_G X$ is a Lašnev space. □

Theorem 6 ([8])**.** *Let X be a space. Then, X^2 is a Lašnev space if and only if $\exp_2 X$ is a Lašnev space.*

As we said in the Introduction, in Reference [2], it was shown that the spaces $\mathrm{SP}^2 X$ and $\exp_2 X$ are homeomorphic. Hence, we obtain the following corollary.

Corollary 2. *Let X be a space. Then, X^2 is a Lašnev space if and only if $\mathrm{SP}^2 X$ is a Lašnev space.*

A space X is a *Nagata space* [11] provided that for each $x \in X$, there exist sequences $\{U_m(x)\}_{m \in \mathbb{N}}$ and $\{V_m(x)\}_{m \in \mathbb{N}}$ of open neighborhoods of x such that for all $x, y \in X$:

(1) $\{U_m(x)\}_{m \in \mathbb{N}}$ is a local base at x;
(2) if $y \notin U_m(x)$, then $V_m(x) \cap V_m(y) = \varnothing$ (or equivalently, if $V_m(x) \cap V_m(y) \neq \varnothing$, then $x \in U_m(y)$).

The definition of the Nagata space is equivalent to the following [11,12]: a Nagata space is a first countable stratifiable space.

Corollary 3. *Let X be a space, and let n be a positive integer. If X is a Nagata space, then so is* $\mathsf{SP}^{\mathsf{n}}_{\mathsf{G}}X$.

3. Conclusions

This work is related to the following important question. Let F be a covariant functor and $\mathcal{P}$ a topological property. If a space X has the property $\mathcal{P}$, whether $\mathsf{F}(X)$ has the same or some other property. We studied the preservation of certain classes of spaces (developable spaces, Moore space, M_1- and M_2-spaces, Nagata spaces) under the influence of the functor $\mathsf{SP}^{\mathsf{n}}_{\mathsf{G}}$ of G-permutation degree. We proved that this functor preserves each mentioned class of spaces. It would be interesting to study the preservation of these and some other properties under the influence of other important functors.

Author Contributions: Conceptualization, L.D.R.K.; Investigation, L.D.R.K., F.G.M. and A.K.S. All authors have read and agreed to the published version of the manuscript.

Funding: This research received no external funding.

Data Availability Statement: The data presented in this study are available on request from the corresponding author.

Conflicts of Interest: The authors declare no conflict of interest.

References

1. Fedorchuk, V.V. Covariant functors in the category of compacta absolute retracts and Q-manifolds. *Russ. Math. Surv.* **1981**, *36*, 211–233. [CrossRef]
2. Fedorchuk, V.V.; Filippov, V.V. *Topology of Hyperspaces and Its Applications*; Znanie: Moscow, Russia, 1989. (In Russian)
3. Beshimov, R.B.; Georgiou, D.N.; Zhuraev, R.M. Index boundedness and uniform connectedness of space of the G-permutation degree. *Appl. Gen. Topol.* **2021**, *22*, 447–459. [CrossRef]
4. Kočinac, LD.R.; Mukhamadiev, F.G.; Sadullaev, A.K. Some cardinal and geometric properties of the space of permutation degree. *Axioms* **2022**, *11*, 290. [CrossRef]
5. Kočinac, LD.R.; Mukhamadiev, F.G.; Sadullaev, A.K. Tightness-type properties of the space of permutation degree. *Mathematics* **2022**, *10*, 3341. [CrossRef]
6. Kočinac, LD.R.; Mukhamadiev, F.G.; Sadullaev, A.K. Some topological and cardinal properties of the space of permutation degree. *Filomat* **2022**, *36*, 7059–7066. [CrossRef]
7. Hart, K.P.; Nagata, J.I.; Vaughan, J.E. *Encyclopedia of General Topology*; Elsevier Science Ltd.: Amsterdam, The Netherlands, 2004.
8. Good, C.; Macias, S. Symmetric products of generalized metric spaces. *Topol. Appl.* **2016**, *206*, 93–114. [CrossRef]
9. Engelking, R. *General Topology*; Heldermann Verlag: Berlin, Germany, 1989.
10. Gruenhage, G. Stratifiable spaces are M_2. *Topol. Proc.* **1976**, *1*, 221–226.
11. Junnila, H.; Ziqiu, Y. On Nagata spaces. *Topol. Proc.* **2000**, *25*, 553–561.
12. Ceder, J.G. Some generalizations of metric spaces. *Pac. J. Math.* **1961**, *11*, 105–125. [CrossRef]

mathematics MDPI

Review

On the Geometry and Topology of Discrete Groups: An Overview

Renata Grimaldi

Dipartimento di Ingegneria, Universita Degli Studi di Palermo, Piazza Marina n. 61, 90133 Palermo, Italy; renata.grimaldi@unipa.it

Abstract: In this paper, we provide a brief introduction to the main notions of geometric group theory and of asymptotic topology of finitely generated groups. We will start by presenting the basis of discrete groups and of the topology at infinity, then we will state some of the main theorems in these fields. Our aim is to give a sample of how the presence of a group action may affect the geometry of the underlying space and how in many cases topological methods may help the determine solutions of algebraic problems which may appear unrelated.

Keywords: discrete groups; Cayley graph; quasi-isometry; ends; simple connectivity at infinity; Universal Covering Conjecture; topological filtrations; inverse representations

MSC: 20F65; 20F69; 57M10

1. Introduction

The central idea of the branch of mathematics called geometric group theory (briefly GGT) is to study group theory from a geometrical viewpoint by means of geometric and topological methods, for example with the notions of the fundamental group and covering space (see [1] for an introduction to the subject).

Geometric group theory focuses in particular on those global geometric and topological invariants which detect the shape at infinity of all universal covers of compact spaces having the same fundamental group.

This research field has its origin in the work of Dehn from the beginning of the last century. With his combinatorial approach, he initiated the study of two closely related research areas: 3-manifolds in topology and infinite groups given by presentations in algebra. His ability to use simple combinatorial diagrams to illustrate the synergy between algebra, geometry and topology has made it clear that most of the topological properties of covering spaces are related to the fundamental group and do not depend on its presentation (and hence on the choice of the space one may associate with the group) (see [2]).

More recently, the field of geometric group theory has undergone impressive development due to the work of Gromov [3–5]. The main novelty he introduced is that, instead of studying groups algebraically, GGT uses both topological and geometric methods, since one can consider group theory as "contained" in the vast area of geometry via the notions of word metric and quasi-isometry.

The underlying idea is that, once a group is chosen, the class of all topological models constructed from it should have some common global geometric conditions (at infinity).

For instance, let us consider the following construction. Start with a finitely generated group Γ. For any such group, there exists a topological space X with $\pi_1(X) = \Gamma$. The group Γ acts effectively on the universal cover $\tilde{X}$ of X, and the quotient space for this action is X itself (i.e., $\tilde{X}/\Gamma = X$). The space X can also be chosen to be a 2-complex, and, if the group is finitely presented, X is compact.

Of course, both X and $\tilde{X}$ are not unique. On the other hand, some of the algebraic properties of the group Γ are transferred into geometric/topological conditions of the space

Citation: Grimaldi, R. On the Geometry and Topology of Discrete Groups: An Overview. *Mathematics* **2024**, *12*, 766. https://doi.org/10.3390/math12050766

Academic Editors: Daniele Ettore Otera and Fu-Gui Shi

Received: 19 November 2023
Revised: 22 February 2024
Accepted: 2 March 2024
Published: 4 March 2024

$\tilde{X}$ (or X), and one can refer to them as asymptotic (or geometric) properties. Vice versa, there are also properties of $\tilde{X}$ (or of X) which depend only on Γ.

One of the first examples that comes to mind when thinking of a topological demonstration of an algebraic result is the well known theorem of Schreier, stating that any subgroup H of a free group F_l on l generators ($l \geq 1$ integer) is itself free (see [1,6]).

Here, we have a pure algebraic problem in a pure algebraic setting. The algebraic proof of this fact involves a meticulous and tedious sequence of special transformations on the subgroup's generating set that reduces its length. On the other hand, the process is made more straightforward with a change in perspective and method. More precisely, consider the free group F_l as the fundamental group of a wedge of circles X_l and the covering space associated with the subgroup H, namely $p : \overline{X} \to X_l$, where $\pi_1(\overline{X}) = H$. The space $\overline{X}$ is actually a graph (since it is a cover of a graph), and hence, by contracting a maximal tree T of $\overline{X}$, one obtains another wedge of circles X_m which is homotopically equivalent to $\overline{X}/T$. Finally, by the van Kampen theorem, one obtains that $H \cong \pi_1(\overline{X}) \cong \pi_1(\overline{X}/T) \cong \pi_1(X_m) \cong F_m$, namely a free group.

This example shows how the use of geometry and topology can help to elucidate and visualize the problem and how this can effectively reduce the length and the difficulties of its solution.

In the next sections, we will provide some basic definitions of geometric group theory and of asymptotic topology of groups in order to depict the strong interplay of geometry and topology with group theory, in the spirit of this Special Issue.

2. Discrete Groups and Associated Spaces

For a *discrete group*, we simply mean a countable group with the discrete topology.

Definition 1. *A discrete group Γ is said to be **finitely generated** if there is a finite set S of generators (which means that any element $g \in \Gamma$ is a product of finitely many powers of some of the generators $s \in S$).*

*The group Γ is said to be **finitely presented**, $\Gamma = \langle S \mid \mathcal{R} \rangle$, if, additionally, it possesses a finite number of relators $r \in \mathcal{R}$ (i.e., words, made of elements of S, that are equal to the identity e).*

Now, to any finitely generated group Γ with a generating set S, one can define a somehow "natural" metric on it, which is called **the word metric** (for more details, see [1]).

Definition 2. *Given a finitely generated group Γ and its generating set S, the length $l_S(g)$ of any element g of Γ is the smallest integer n such that there exists a sequence $(s_1, s_2, \cdots, s_n)$ of generators in S for which $g = s_1 s_2 \ldots s_n$. The distance of two elements a, b of Γ is*

$$d_S(a,b) = l_S(a^{-1}b).$$

Due to this definition, the pair (Γ, d_S), i.e., the group together with the word metric, becomes a metric space. So, the geometry and topology are already known to some extent (even if the so-defined space is discrete).

However, we can do better. To any finitely generated group Γ, we may associate a graph, called the **Cayley graph** of Γ (denoted $Cay(\Gamma, S)$), which depends on the generating set S.

Definition 3. *The vertex set of $Cay(\Gamma, S)$ is Γ. Two vertices g, h are connected by an edge iff $d_S(g,h) = 1$, namely if and only if $h = gs$ or gs^{-1}, for some $s \in S$. Or, equivalently, any vertex g is joined by an edge with all the vertices of the form gs, for $s \in S$.*

Since the group Γ is finitely generated, this graph is locally finite. By construction it is directed and labeled. Moreover, since S generates Γ, the Cayley graph is connected. Finally, one can also define a "natural metric", denoted also by d_S, on $Cay(\Gamma; S)$, as follows:

- One declares any edge to be of length 1;

- The distance $d(x;y)$ of any two points of the Cayley graph can be defined as the length of the shortest path going from x to y.

In this way, the Cayley graph $Cay(\Gamma;S)$ becomes a connected metric space containing (isometrically) Γ. Obviously, it is finite/infinite if and only if Γ is. Furthermore, when restricting this metric to $\Gamma \subset Cay(\Gamma;S)$, one recovers just the word metric of Γ.

If the group Γ is finitely presented, it is possible to improve the construction of the above in order to obtain a locally finite 2-dimensional space associated with it.

Let $\langle S \mid \mathcal{R}\rangle$ be a finite presentation for a finitely presented group Γ.

Definition 4. *The* ***Cayley 2-complex*** *of* $\Gamma = \langle S \mid \mathcal{R}\rangle$ *is obtained by gluing a disk (i.e., a 2-cell) to all the (closed) paths of the Cayley graph which are labeled by relators* $r \in \mathcal{R}$.

Remark 1. *Obviously, the Cayley 2-complex is simply connected, because all closed paths in the Cayley graph are labeled by words which are equal to 1 in* Γ*, and, by definition, the set of relators* $\mathcal{R}$ *generates all the relations.*

In most cases, the constructions described above are the most useful ones, but there may be other situations where more of the topology must be determined, and, actually, there is a second, different way to construct the Cayley graph and Cayley 2-complex in a topological vein (see also [2]).

Consider the **standard 2-complex** $X_{\mathcal{P}}$ associated with the presentation $\mathcal{P} = \langle S \mid \mathcal{R}\rangle$ as follows: Start with a bouquet of loops, i.e., the graph with just one vertex v and with $\sharp S$-edge loops at v (one for each $s \in S$), labeled by s. Now, for each relator $r \in \mathcal{R}$ one attaches, along r, a 2-cell with $l(r)$ sides (where $l(g)$ is the length of g) to the bouquet of circles. Obviously, according to the van Kampen theorem, $\pi_1(X_{\mathcal{P}}) = \Gamma$, and its universal covering space $\widetilde{X}_{\mathcal{P}}$ is simply the Cayley 2-complex of Γ, whereas the 1-skeleton of $\widetilde{X}_{\mathcal{P}}$ is the Cayley graph of Γ.

Large-Scale Equivalence

The aforementioned constructions depend on the presentation but not at a "large scale". This is the viewpoint of Gromov [4,5]. If spaces are similar (seen from a long distance), then they should share some common properties that depend on the group that acts on them.

In fact, the word metrics, Cayley graphs and Cayley 2-complexes constructed from distinct presentations of the same group Γ are actually **quasi-isometric** (i.e., geometrically and metrically "similar" in a rough sense).

Definition 5. *A* ***quasi-isometry*** *between two metric spaces* (X, d_X) *and* (Y, d_Y) *is a map* $f : X \to Y$ *such that, for constants* C *and* λ*:*

$$\lambda^{-1} d_X(x_1, x_2) - C \leq d_Y(f(x_1), f(x_2)) \leq \lambda d_X(x_1, x_2) + C$$

$$\text{and }, \forall y \in Y,\ d_Y(y, f(X)) \leq C.$$

Roughly speaking, this means that the images of two points which are close (or very far from each others) remain close (or very far), and any point of the target space is uniformly close to the image of some point of the domain. Quasi-isometries do not distinguish small details of the space but rather detect the global geometric behavior.

Since it turns out that an algebraic classification of the class of finitely presented groups is not possible (because the word problem is undecidable), the main goal of geometric group theory is to classify them "geometrically", that is, **up to quasi-isometries**.

From this perspective, one is interested in properties of groups which are quasi-isometry invariants (in fact called *geometric* or *asymptotic* properties).

Remark 2.

- *A quasi-isometry is not necessarily continuous. For instance, real numbers $\mathbb{R}$ and integers $\mathbb{Z}$ are quasi-isometric.*
- *Any finitely generated group Γ (with finite generating set S) is quasi-isometric to its Cayley graph $Cay(\Gamma, S)$ (because the inclusion $(\Gamma, d_S) \hookrightarrow Cay(\Gamma, d_S)$ is a quasi-isometry).*
- *If S and T are two generating sets for the same group G, then the (distinct) metric spaces (G, d_S) and (G, d_T) are quasi-isometric.*
- *As a consequence, given a finitely generated group, one can consider* **the** *word metric and* **the** *Cayley graph (in the sense that they are well-defined, up to quasi-isometries).*

Let us analyze some basic examples that can elucidate the geometric meaning of quasi-isometries (see [1] for details).

- A metric space is quasi-isometric to a point if and only if it has a finite diameter.
- The group G is finite if and only if its Cayley graph is quasi-isometric to a point. Thus, the *quasi-isometry class* of the trivial group coincides with the set of finite groups. This is why GGT studies only infinite groups.
- The free abelian groups $\mathbb{Z}^n$ and $\mathbb{Z}^m$ are quasi-isometric if and only if $n = m$ (i.e., they have the same rank).
- The free group of rank 2, F_2, is quasi-isometric to F_k, for any $k \geq 2$.

Now, the obvious question is the following one: when are two groups quasi-isometric? For a far more complete answer, see [1,5].

Definition 6. *A geodesic in a metric space X is a map $f : [a; b] \to X$ s.t. $\forall s; t \in [a, b]$,*

$$d(f(s); f(t)) = |s - t|.$$

A space X is called a geodesic space if any 2 points can be joined by a geodesic. This is equivalent to saying that the distance between any 2 points is the length of the shortest path which joins them.

The space X is said a proper metric space if any closed ball is compact.

An isometric action of a group Γ on a metric space X is said discrete if for any $x \in X$ and $M \in [0; \infty)$, the set $\{g \in \Gamma | d(gx; x) < M\}$ is finite.

The action is said co-compact if the quotient X/Γ is a compact space.

In what follows, and until the end of this section, we will refer to [1,2,5] for terminology.

Lemma 1. *If X, Y are two proper geodesic metric spaces with Γ-actions which are discrete, cocompact and by isometries, then Γ is finitely generated and the spaces X and Y are quasi-isometric. (Consequently, X and Y are quasi-isometric to $Cay(\Gamma; S)$).*

Corollary 1. *The fundamental group of a closed Riemannian manifold is quasi-isometric to its universal covering space.*

Hence, we can deduce that [1]:

- If $H \subset \Gamma$ is a subgroup of a finite index, then H and Γ are quasi-isometric.
- The fundamental group of a closed orientable surface of genus $g \geq 2$ is quasi-isometric to the hyperbolic plane $\mathbb{H}^2$.
- The circle $S^1 = \mathbb{R}/\mathbb{Z}$ has $\pi_1 S^1 = \mathbb{Z}$, and so $\mathbb{Z}$ is quasi-isometric to $\mathbb{R}$.
- The torus $T^n = \mathbb{R}^n/\mathbb{Z}^n$ has $\pi_1 T^n = \mathbb{Z}^n$, and so $\mathbb{Z}^n$ is quasi-isometric to $\mathbb{R}^n$.
- The Euclidean space $\mathbb{R}^n$ is quasi-isometric to $\mathbb{R}^m$ if and only if $n = m$.
- The hyperbolic space $\mathbb{H}^n$ is quasi-isometric to $\mathbb{H}^m$ if and only if $n = m$.
- The hyperbolic space $\mathbb{H}^n$ and the Euclidean space $\mathbb{R}^n$ are not quasi-isometric.

Theorem 1 (Gromov [3], Pansu [7]). *A group is quasi-isometric to $\mathbb{R}^n$ if and only if it contains a finite index subgroup isomorphic to $\mathbb{Z}^n$.*

Theorem 2 (Gromov [5], Stallings [8]). *If a group is quasi-isometric to the free group in two generators, then it acts properly on some locally finite tree, and hence it is virtually free.*

3. The Topology at Infinity

In this section, we will focus on a more topological aspect of GGT; in particular, we will consider those topological properties of non-compact spaces which depend on some group actions (for an accurate introduction to the subject, see [2]).

The topology at infinity may be defined as the study of global topological properties of complements of compact subsets in open topological spaces. The topological behavior "close to infinity" of non-compact spaces, especially open manifolds, in the presence of a group action, is under study. The idea is to take a space X together with a *filtration* by compact subsets $C_i \subset X$, such that $C_i \subset C_{i+1}$ and $X = \cup_i C_i$, and to look at the topology of $X - C_i$ as i goes to infinity.

3.1. Ends

The simplest topological property at infinity is the condition of being ***one-ended*** (or *connected at infinity*). In other words, being one-ended is equivalent to say that, outside very large compacts, there is only one "way to go to infinity" (for more details, see [1,2,9]).

In fact, with any topological space X, one can associate the so-called **space of ends** (that corresponds, intuitively, to the different ways to go to infinity): it is the set of unbounded connected component of $X - K$ for large compact subspaces K of X.

The next results represent probably the very beginning of geometric group theory.

Theorem 3 (Hopf [10]). *Let K be a finite simplicial complex. The number of ends of the universal covering space $\widetilde{K}$ of K depends only on $\pi_1(K)$.*

Hence, it is possible to define the number of ends for a finitely generated group:

Definition 7. *The* ***number of ends*** *$e(G)$* ***of a group*** *G is the number of ends of the universal covering space $\widetilde{K}$ of some (equivalently any) finite complex X having G as the fundamental group.*

Remark 3. *The number of ends of the finitely generated group G may also be defined as the number of ends of (one of) its Cayley graph.*

Theorem 4 (Hopf [10]). *The number of ends of a group belongs to the set $\{0, 1, 2, \infty\}$.*

Actually, if we have 3 ends, we may consider a compact subset $C \subset \widetilde{K}$, outside of which starts the three different ways to go to infinity e_1, e_2, e_3. Hence, when a non-trivial element of the group $G = \pi_1(X)$ translates C within $\widetilde{K}$, it will belong to only one of these directions, say, e_1. However, outside gC, we must again have three directions to go to infinity. In this new configuration, $\widetilde{K} - gC$, the two directions e_2, e_3 represent the same direction to infinity. However, since $e(G) = 3$ and this number must be homogeneous outside any large compact subset, the direction e_1 should split in two different directions, thus creating a new different end e_4. Using this simple idea, one can prove that, in fact, if $e(G) > 2$, then $e(G)$ must be infinite (see [1,2]).

In the latter result, we have seen how the presence of a group, and hence of a group action, puts very strong constraints on the topological behavior at infinity.

Theorem 5 (Gromov [5]). *The number of ends of a group is a quasi-isometry invariant.*

Remark 4.

- *The two last theorems are not true for general open manifolds.*
- *A group has* 0 *ends if and only if it is finite.*
- *The number of ends of* $\mathbb{Z}$ *is* 2*, while* $e(\mathbb{Z}^n)$*, for* $n \geq 2$*, is* 1.
- *The free group of rank* 2 *has infinitely many ends.*

At this point, one may wonder whether it is possible to catch some algebraic condition as from the topological notion of number of ends. This is the key problem in geometric group theory: relating geometric properties of a group and its algebraic structure.

Theorem 6 (Hopf [10])**.** *A group has* 2 *ends if and only if it has an infinite cyclic subgroup (i.e.,* $\mathbb{Z}$*) of finite index.*

This result was then generalized by Stallings in the 1970s [8] (but see also [6]). He provided a structure theorem for infinitely ended groups, and, as a result, Dunwoody in [11] was able to prove the famous Wall's Conjecture [12] for finitely presented groups by giving a complete characterization of them starting from finite groups and one-ended groups via a finite number of natural operations (called amalgamated free products and HNN extensions over finite subgroups).

Theorem 7 (Stallings [8])**.** *Let G be a finitely generated group with infinitely many ends.*

- *If G is torsion-free, then G is a non-trivial free product;*
- *Or G is a non-trivial free product with amalgamation, with finite amalgamated subgroup.*

3.2. The Simple Connectivity at Infinity

Having in mind Stallings' theorem and the fact that one-ended groups are the basic pieces for constructing all discrete groups [11], one is led to the study of groups with one end. Furthermore, the first topological notion needed in order to obtain a well-behaved topology is the simple connectivity. Hence, one usually focuses on the behavior at infinity of manifolds and groups with "simply connected ends". Furthermore, for one-ended spaces, the easiest and strongest topological "tameness" condition at infinity is the so-called **simple connectivity at infinity** (see [2,9]). The simple connectivity at infinity tells us approximately that loops which are very far away (i.e., "at infinity") should bound disks which are at a sufficient distance (i.e., "near the infinity").

Definition 8. *A connected, locally compact, topological space X with* $\pi_1(X) = 0$ *is* **simply connected at infinity** *(SCI) if for any compact* $k \subseteq X$ *there exists a larger compact* $k \subseteq K \subseteq X$ *such that any closed loop in* $X - K$ *is null homotopic in* $X - k$*.*

Why is this condition so interesting and powerful? Because it turns out that, for $n \geq 3$, the simple connectivity at infinity just features Euclidean spaces $\mathbb{R}^n$ among open contractible n-manifolds, as proven by the following theorem (that is actually a sum of several extensive results of different authors).

Theorem 8 (Stallings [13]; Freedman [14]; Perelman [15])**.**

1. *In dimension* $n \geq 5$*, any differential manifold which is open, contractible and simply connected at infinity is diffeomorphic to the Euclidean space* $\mathbb{R}^n$*.*
2. *In dimension* $n = 4$*, the result is true only for topological manifolds.*
3. *Finally, in dimension* $n = 3$*, the same result holds for both topological and differential manifolds.*

Remark 5.

- *As a corollary, one obtains that Euclidean space* $\mathbb{R}^n$*, for* $n \neq 4$*, admits a unique differential structure.*

- *On the other hand, $\mathbb{R}^4$ supports infinitely many different differential structures (Donaldson [16]).*

Now, what can we say about discrete groups?

Definition 9. *A finitely presented group Γ is simply connected at infinity if the universal covering space $\tilde{X}$ of some compact complex X, having Γ as fundamental group, is* SCI.

Theorem 9.

- *The simple connectivity at infinity is a well-defined property for finitely presented groups (in the sense that it does not depend on the presentation) [17].*
- *The simple connectivity at infinity is also a quasi-isometry invariant of finitely presented groups [18].*

3.3. The Universal Covering Conjecture

Another interesting implication of the simple connectivity at infinity comes from its connection with the so-called *Universal Covering Conjecture*. Since the 1960s, topologists have studied the behavior at infinity of contractible universal covering spaces of closed 3-manifolds and proposed the following problem/conjecture (for a more historical panoramic view, see [9,19]):

Conjecture 1 (Universal Covering Conjecture). *The universal covering space of a (connected, orientable) closed, aspherical (i.e., with a contractible universal cover) 3-manifold is simply connected at infinity. If the manifold is also irreducible, then the universal cover is $\mathbb{R}^3$.*

- This conjecture is now a theorem due to Perelman's recent proof of Thurston *Geometrization Conjecture* [15].
- On the other hand, the Universal Covering Conjecture fails in a higher dimension, as proved by Davis in the 1980s.

Theorem 10 (Davis [20]). *For any $n \geq 4$, there exist closed, aspherical n-manifolds whose universal covers are not homeomorphic to Euclidean spaces (in particular, they are not SCI).*

So we are left with the following natural, interesting and difficult question:

Question 1. *Are there topological conditions which characterize the class of contractible universal covering spaces of closed manifolds?*

3.4. Topological Filtrations

In the 1980s, Poénaru partially solved the Universal Covering Conjecture, for those 3-manifolds whose fundamental groups satisfy some geometric or topological conditions (see, e.g., [21]), by "approximating" the universal cover with a filtration of compact and simply connected 3-manifolds.

Definition 10. *A topological space X is **weakly geometrically simply connected** (briefly* WGSC *[22]) if it can be written as an ascending union of compact, connected and simply connected subspaces. Namely, X is* WGSC *if it admits a **filtration**, $X = \cup_i K_i$, with $K_i \subset K_{i+1}$ and such that K_i are compact, connected and with $\pi_1 K_i = 0$.*

Definition 11. *A simply connected complex X is* **quasi-simply filtered** (QSF) *if for any compact sub-complex $C \subset X$ there exists a simply connected compact complex K and a PL-map $f : K \to X$ so that $C \subset f(K)$ and $f|_{f^{-1}(C)} : f^{-1}(C) \to C$ is a PL-homeomorphism.*

The latter condition simply means that every compact subset C of X can be included (homeomorphically) inside of the image of an abstract compact and simply connected complex that is equipped with a simplicial map into X, whose set of double points lies outside the compact C we started with. In other words, a topological space is QSF if it admits a **quasi-simple filtration**, i.e., a filtration which can be "approximated" by finite, simply connected complexes.

This topological notion has interesting group-theoretical ramifications, as testified by the next results:

Theorem 11 (Brick–Mihalik [23]; Funar–Otera [22]).

- *If K_1, K_2 are two presentation complexes for the same finitely presented group Γ, then $\tilde{K}_1$ is QSF $\iff$ $\tilde{K}_2$ is QSF. (Ths implies the that QSF property is well-defined fro finitely presented groups).*
- *Many finitely presented groups are* QSF *(see Remark 7).*

The main reason for using this notion lies in the fact that, since for open 3-manifolds, being simply connected at infinity is equivalent to being WGSC, in order to prove the Universal Covering Conjecture, one simply needs a method which yields a filtration of the universal cover of a closed 3-manifold.

Theorem 12 (Poénaru [24]). *An open* QSF *3-manifold is* WGSC *and hence simply connected at infinity.*

Remark 6. *Thus, in order to verify the simple connectivity at infinity of the universal cover of a closed 3-manifold, it suffices to construct a quasi-filtration of it (and this is much easier than obtaining a whole* WGSC *filtration).*

Theorem 13 (Poénaru [21]). *Let M^3 be a closed 3-manifold, and assume that $\Gamma = \pi_1(M^3)$ satisfies some "nice geometric condition", then $\widetilde{M}^3$ is* QSF *(and hence simply connected at infinity).*

Remark 7. *The set of "nice geometric conditions" includes: Gromov hyperbolicity, Cannon almost-convexity, automaticity and combability (in the sense of Thurston), geometric simple connectivity, etc. In particular, the class of groups with a "nice geometry" is quite large (see, e.g., [9,25,26]).*

4. Inverse Representations

The main tool for proving the last theorems of the previous section was the following notion, invented and developed by Poénaru in [27] and thereafter utilized in his scientific work (see [28] but also [19,26,29]):

Definition 12. *Let M^3 be a 3-manifold. A topological* ***inverse representation*** *for M^3 is a non-degenerate simplicial map*

$$f : X^2 \longrightarrow M^3 \text{ such that:}$$

- *X^2 is a simplicial 2-complex, which is* QSF;
- *The map f is "essentially surjective", which means that M^3 can be obtained from the closure $\overline{f(X^2)}$ with the addition of cells of dimensions $\lambda = 2$ and $\lambda = 3$;*
- *The map f is "zippable" (one can pass from X^2 to $f(X^2)$ by an infinite sequence of "simple" quotient maps f_i of very special type, and this has a strong control over the singularities of f).*

This exotic notion seems to be suited for the world of 3-manifolds, but it turns out that it can be used very well for discrete groups too. The necessary adjustment is to look at groups as 3-dimensional objects. However, of course, not all groups are 3-manifold groups; hence, one has to allow manifolds to have singularities.

Lemma 2. *Any finitely presented group $G = \langle S | R \rangle$ can be seen as the fundamental group of a compact but singular 3-manifold $M^3(G)$ associated with G.*

This is proved in [26,30]. Here, we can simply state that $M^3(G)$ is obtained by attaching $|R|$ handles of index 2 to a handlebody of genus $|S|$.

Definition 13. *A topological inverse representation for a finitely presented group G is a topological inverse representation of the 3-manifold* $\widetilde{M}^3(G)$.

In general, the image

$$\mathrm{Im}(f) \subset M^3$$

and the set of double points of f,

$$M_2(f) = \{x \in X^2 \mid \sharp\{f^{-1}(f(x))\} > 1\} \subset X^2,$$

are not closed subsets, and this is one of the main difficulties when dealing with inverse representations [28]. Furthermore, as a result, the following definitions arise naturally:

Definition 14. *A topological inverse representation is* ***easy*** *if* $f(X^2)$ *and* $M_2(f)$ *are closed.*

Definition 15. *An* ***easy group*** *is a finitely presented group G admitting an easy inverse-representation; this is a non-degenerate, zippable, quasi-surjective, simplicial map* $f : X^2 \to \widetilde{M}^3(G)$, *from a* QSF *complex* X^2, *for which* $f(X^2)$ *and* $M_2(f)$ *are closed subsets.*

Here, below, we summarize the recent developments concerning this interesting property of groups and manifolds.

Theorem 14 (Otera–Poénaru [30])**.** *Easy groups are* QSF.

Theorem 15 (Otera–Poénaru, [25])**.** *Groups admitting Lipschitz and tame 0-combings are easy.*

Theorem 16 (Otera–Poénaru, [31])**.** *Given a finitely presented* QSF *group* Γ, *one can construct a 2-dimensional* WGSC *topological inverse representation, which is both easy and equivariant.*

Conjecture 2 (Poénaru)**.** *All finitely presented groups are easy.*

5. Conclusions

In this short essay, we intended to give an elementary idea of the close basic connections between geometry, topology and group theory, following the underlying idea of this Special Issue. In particular, we have focused on two aspects, one quite geometric (geometric group theory) and the other more topological (asymptotic topology).

Funding: This research received no external funding.

Institutional Review Board Statement: Not applicable.

Informed Consent Statement: Not applicable.

Data Availability Statement: Not applicable.

Conflicts of Interest: The author declares no conflicts of interest.

References

1. de la Harpe, P. *Topics in Geometric Group Theory;* Chicago Lectures in Mathematics; Chicago University Press: Chicago, IL, USA, 2000.
2. Geoghegan, R. *Topological Methods in Group Theory;* Graduate Texts in Mathematics 243; Springer: Berlin/Heidelberg, Germany, 2008.
3. Gromov, M. Groups of polynomial growth and expanding maps. *Publ. Math. Inst. Hautes Etud. Sci.* **1981**, *53*, 53–73. [CrossRef]
4. Gromov, M. Hyperbolic groups. In *Essays in Group Theory;* Mathematical Sciences Research Institute Publications; Springer: New York, NY, USA, 1987; Volume 8, pp. 75–263.

5. Gromov, M. Asymptotic invariants of infinite groups. In *Geometric Group Theory, Volume 2;* London Mathematical Society Lecture Note Series 182; Cambridge University Press: Cambridge, UK, 1993; pp. 1–295.
6. Serre, J.P. *Trees;* Springer Monographs in Mathematics; Springer: Berlin/Heidelberg, Germany, 2022.
7. Pansu, P. Croissance des boules et des géodésiques fermées dans les nilvariétés. *Ergod. Theory Dynam. Syst.* **1983**, *3*, 415–445. [CrossRef]
8. Stallings, J.R. On torsion-free groups with infinitely many ends. *Ann. Math.* **1968**, *88*, 312–334. [CrossRef]
9. Otera, D.E. Topological tameness conditions of groups. Results and developments. *Lith. Math. J.* **2016**, *3*, 357–376. [CrossRef]
10. Hopf, H. Enden offener räume und unendliche diskontinuierliche gruppen. *Comment. Math. Helv.* **1944**, *16*, 81–100. [CrossRef]
11. Dunwoody, M.J. The accessibility of finitely presented groups. *Invent. Math.* **1985**, *81*, 449–457. [CrossRef]
12. Wall, C.T.C. Pairs of relative cohomological dimension one. *J. Pure Appl. Algebra* **1971**, *1*, 141–154. [CrossRef]
13. Stallings, J.R. The piece-wise linear structure of Euclidean spaces. *Proc. Cambr. Math. Soc.* **1962**, *58*, 481–488. [CrossRef]
14. Freedman, M. The Topology of four-dimensional manifolds. *J. Diff. Geom.* **1983**, *17*, 279–315. [CrossRef]
15. Kleiner, B.; Lott, J. Notes on Perelman's papers. *Geom. Topol.* **2008**, *12*, 2587–2855. [CrossRef]
16. Donaldson, S.K. An application of gauge theory to four-dimensional topology. *J. DIff. Geom.* **1983**, *18*, 278–315. [CrossRef]
17. Tanasi, C. Sui gruppi semplicemente connessi all'infinito. *Rend. Ist. Mat. Univ. Trieste* **1999**, *31*, 61–78.
18. Funar, L.; Otera, D.E. A refinement of the simple connectivity at infinity of groups. *Arch. Math.* **2003**, *81*, 360–368. [CrossRef]
19. Otera, D.E. On simplicial resolutions of groups. *Rev. Real Acad. Cienc. Exactas Fis. Nat. Ser. A-Mat.* **2022**, *16*, 138. [CrossRef]
20. Davis, M.W. Groups generated by reflections and aspherical manifolds not covered by Euclidean spaces. *Ann. Math.* **1983**, *117*, 293–324. [CrossRef]
21. Poénaru, V. Almost convex groups, Lipschitz combing, and π_1^∞ for universal covering spaces of closed 3-manifolds. *J. Diff. Geom.* **1992**, *35*, 103–130.
22. Funar, L.; Otera, D.E. On the WGSC and QSF tameness conditions for finitely presented groups. *Groups Geom. Dyn.* **2010**, *4*, 549–596. [CrossRef]
23. Brick, S.G.; Mihalik, M.L. The QSF property for groups and spaces. *Math. Z.* **1995**, *220*, 207–217. [CrossRef]
24. Poénaru, V. Killing handles of index one stably and π_1^∞. *Duke Math. J.* **1991**, *63*, 431–447. [CrossRef]
25. Otera, D.E.; Poénaru, V. Tame combings and easy groups. *Forum Math.* **2017**, *29*, 665–680. [CrossRef]
26. Otera, D.E.; Poénaru, V. Topics in Geometric Group Theory, Part I. In *Handbook of Group Actions, Volume V, Advanced Lectures in Mathematics Volume 48;* International Press of Boston, Inc.: Boston, MA, USA, 2020; pp. 307–353.
27. Poénaru, V. The collapsible pseudo-spine representation theorem. *Topology* **1992**, *31*, 625–636. [CrossRef]
28. Poénaru, V. Topics in Geometric Group Theory, Part II. In *Handbook of Group Actions, Volume V, Advanced Lectures in Mathematics Volume 48;* International Press of Boston, Inc.: Boston, MA, USA, 2020; pp. 347–398.
29. Otera, D.E. On Poénaru's inverse representations. *Quaes. Math.* **2017**, *40*, 277–293. [CrossRef]
30. Otera, D.E.; Poénaru, V. "Easy" Representations and the QSF property for groups. *Bull. Belgian Math. Soc.-Simon Stevin* **2012**, *19*, 385–398. [CrossRef]
31. Otera, D.E.; Poénaru, V. Finitely presented groups and the Whitehead nightmare. *Groups Geom. Dyn.* **2017**, *11*, 291–310. [CrossRef]

mathematics MDPI

Article

A Characterization of Procyclic Groups via Complete Exterior Degree

Bernardo G. Rodrigues [1] **and Francesco G. Russo** [2,3,*]

[1] Department of Mathematics and Applied Mathematics, University of Pretoria, Hatfield, Pretoria 0028, South Africa; bernardo.rodrigues@up.ac.za
[2] Department of Mathematics and Applied Mathematics, University of Cape Town, Private Bag X1, Rondebosch, Cape Town 7701, South Africa
[3] Department of Mathematics and Applied Mathematics, University of the Western Cape, New CAMS Building, Private Bag X17, Bellville 7535, South Africa
* Correspondence: francescog.russo@yahoo.com

Abstract: We describe the nonabelian exterior square $G\widehat{\wedge}G$ of a pro-p-group G (with p arbitrary prime) in terms of quotients of free pro-p-groups, providing a new method of construction of $G\widehat{\wedge}G$ and new structural results for $G\widehat{\wedge}G$. Then, we investigate a generalization of the probability that two randomly chosen elements of G commute: this notion is known as the "complete exterior degree" of a pro-p-group and we will use it to characterize procyclic groups. Among other things, we present a new formula, which simplifies the numerical aspects which are connected with the evaluation of the complete exterior degree.

Keywords: nonabelian exterior square; pro-p-groups; Schur multiplier; free profinite groups

MSC: 20P05; 20J05; 20E10; 20J06

Citation: Rodrigues, B.G.; Russo, F.G. A Characterization of Procyclic Groups via Complete Exterior Degree. *Mathematics* **2024**, *12*, 1018. https://doi.org/10.3390/math12071018

Academic Editor: Mario Gionfriddo

Received: 22 February 2024
Revised: 25 March 2024
Accepted: 25 March 2024
Published: 28 March 2024

1. Introduction and Formulation of the Main Results

In the present paper we deal only with topological Hausdorff groups. Topological groups with a discrete topology are called *discrete groups* or *abstract groups*. Topological groups with a compact topology are called *compact groups*. Of course, finite groups are examples of discrete compact groups but the additive group $\mathbb{Z}_p$ of the p-adic integers (p prime) is an example of an infinite nondiscrete compact group, see Example 1.28 (i) and Exercise E1.10 in [1]. The usual notion of an *abelian tensor product* of two abstract abelian groups, which is described by Propositions A1.44, A1.45 and A1.46 of [1], has been adapted to the context of profinite groups in §5.4 and §5.5 of [2], introducing the *complete abelian tensor product* of two profinite abelian groups. Usually, one formulates a universal property and then provides an explicit construction, as indicated in Lemma 5.5.1, Lemma 5.5.2 and Proposition 5.5.4 of [2]. Brown and Loday [3,4] introduced the *nonabelian tensor product* of two abstract groups, which are not necessarily abelian. Adapting the notion of Brown and Loday to topological groups, the presence of a topology should be compatible with the algebraic structure of the tensor product and some difficulties can appear even if we consider compact groups.

Let us focus on a special class of compact groups. First of all, we mention from §1.1 of [2] that a topological space X, which arises as projective limit on a given (directed) set of indices J, can be written as

$$X = \varprojlim_{j \in J} X_j \quad \text{with } X_j \text{ finite space endowed with the discrete topology } \forall j \in J \qquad (1)$$

and X is called *profinite space*. Secondly, we may look at finite groups and a projective limit

$$G = \varprojlim_{j \in J} G_j \quad \text{with } G_j \text{ finite } p - \text{group } \forall j \in J \tag{2}$$

is called a *pro-p-group*, as indicated by Definition 1.27 of [1]. These are special types of *profinite groups*, that is, totally disconnected compact groups, which are described by Theorem 1.34 of [1]. Several results of classification of compact groups involve maximal closed subgroups which are pro-p-groups; just to give an idea, Corollaries 8.5, 8.6 and 8.8 of [1] classify compact abelian groups via their pro-p-subgroups; in particular Corollary 8.8 of [1] shows that any compact abelian group is totally disconnected if and only if it is the direct product of pro-p-groups.

Following §3.3 of [2], if X is a profinite space, $F_p(X)$ a pro-p-group and $\iota : X \to F_p(X)$ a continuous map such that $F_p(X) = \overline{\langle \iota(X) \rangle}$, we say that the pair $(F_p(X), \iota)$, or briefly $F_p(X)$, is a *free pro-p-group* on X, if the following universal property is satisfied

$$\begin{array}{ccc} X & \xrightarrow{\quad \iota \quad} & F_p(X) \\ {\scriptstyle \varphi}\downarrow & \swarrow {\scriptstyle \psi} & \\ G & & \end{array} \tag{3}$$

where $\varphi : X \to G$ is a continuous map into a pro-p-group G, $\varphi(X)$ *topologically generates* G (i.e., $\overline{\langle \varphi(X) \rangle} = G$) and $\psi : F_p(X) \to G$ is a continuous homomorphism such that (3) commutes (i.e., $\psi \circ \iota = \varphi$). Diagram (3) describes a universal property defining $F_p(X)$. The reader can look at Theorem A3.28 of [1] for a more general perspective on the definition of objects in a prescribed category by a universal property. Here, we assume that X is nonempty and $|X| \geq 2$ in order to avoid trivial examples. We also note that ι is an embedding by Lemma 3.3.1 of [2] and that for every profinite space X there exists a unique free pro-p-group $F_p(X)$ on X by Proposition 3.3.2 of [2].

We recall briefly the details of the construction of $F_p(X)$ here. For instance, if X is a profinite space, F a free abstract group on X and $N \triangleleft F$ (i.e., N is a normal subgroup of F), then one observes that

$$\mathcal{N}(F) = \{ N \triangleleft F \mid F/N \text{ finite } p\text{-group and } X \cap fN \text{ open in } X, \ \forall f \in F \} \tag{4}$$

is a filter basis which allows us to form the projective limit

$$\lim_{N \in \mathcal{N}(F)} F/N =: F_p(X). \tag{5}$$

This is a concrete construction of the free pro-p-group on X and we may check that $F_p(X)$ satisfies the universal property expressed by (3), as illustrated by Proposition 3.3.2 and Exercise 3.3.3 of [2]. Note also that $F_p(X)$ possesses the topology induced by (4) and is compatible with the structure of the projective limit. The same logic applies to any filter basis and works in fact for free compact groups, but also for a free pro-$\mathcal{C}$-group with $\mathcal{C}$ an arbitrary class of finite groups closed under taking quotients and finite subdirect products (and containing groups of order two). The reader may refer to Chapter 11 of [1], to Chapter 3 of [2] and to [5] for more information on topological free groups.

We recall now that a *Cantor cube* is a topological space which is homeomorphic to a product space $\{0,1\}^{\aleph}$ for some infinite cardinal $\aleph$, see Definition A4.30 in [1]. A *dyadic space* is a continuous image of a Cantor cube. Our first main result provides a new approach to the notion of a *complete nonabelian tensor square* $G \widehat{\otimes} G$ of a pro-p-group G, originally studied in [6,7] for pro-p-groups, but introduced by Brown and Loday [3,4] for finite groups.

Theorem 1. *Let $G = \varprojlim_{j \in J} G_j$ be a pro-p-group with G_j finite p-groups for all $j \in J$.*

Then, there exists a profinite space Y such that the complete nonabelian tensor square $G\widehat{\otimes}G$ is the pro-p-group which is topologically isomorphic to the quotient group $F_p(Y)/K$ of the free pro-p-group $F_p(Y)$ on Y by the smallest closed normal subgroup K of $F_p(Y)$ containing the set

$$\{\iota(gz,h)\iota(g,h)^{-1}\iota(z^g,h^g)^{-1}, \iota(g,ht)\iota(g^h,t^h)^{-1}\iota(g,h)^{-1} \mid g,z,h,t \in G\}.$$

Moreover, ι embeds Y into $F_p(Y)$ and, if in addition $G\widehat{\otimes}G$ is metrizable, then $G\widehat{\otimes}G$ is a dyadic space.

We should mention that Theorem 1 has been recently proved for arbitrary compact groups in Theorem 1.4 of [8], involving the representation theory of compact groups. Here we do not use the representation theory and offer an argument, which involves only constructions via projective limits. The concrete description of Theorem 1 allows us to illustrate our second main result.

First of all, we consider $\widehat{\nabla}(G) = \overline{\langle x\widehat{\otimes}x \mid x \in G\rangle}$, which turns out to be a closed normal subgroup of $G\widehat{\otimes}G$, called a *diagonal subgroup* of $G\widehat{\otimes}G$, and then we form the quotient

$$(G\widehat{\otimes}G)/\widehat{\nabla}(G) = G\widehat{\wedge}G \tag{6}$$

which is called a *complete nonabelian exterior square* of the pro-p-group G. We mention that the set

$$\widehat{C}_G(x) = \{a \in G \mid a\widehat{\wedge}x = 1\} \tag{7}$$

is a closed subgroup of G, called a *complete exterior centralizer* of x in G (see [7,9]), and the Haar measure μ on G, whose properties are illustraed by Theorem 2.8 and Exercise E2.3 in [1], allows us to introduce the *complete exterior degree*

$$\widehat{\text{d}}(G) := \int_G \mu(\widehat{C}_G(x))d\mu \tag{8}$$

of the pro-p-group G. In particular, if G is finite and we consider the counting measure on G, then we find *the exterior degree of finite groups* in [10–12]. The *complete exterior center*

$$\widehat{Z}(G) = \bigcap_{x \in G} \widehat{C}_G(x) = \{a \in G \mid a\widehat{\wedge}x = 1, \forall x \in G\}, \tag{9}$$

plays a relevant role in [7,9] and is always a subgroup of the usual center $Z(G)$ of G.

Secondly, we note that the notion of the *FC-center* is well known (i.e., it is the set of elements with finite conjugacy classes) and investigated by Baer in 14.5.6 of [13] and by Neumann in 14.5.9 and 14.5.11 of [13]. In case of a pro-p-group G the *complete exterior FC-center* is more recent:

$$\widehat{FC}(G) := \{x \in G \mid |G : \widehat{C}_G(x)| \text{ is finite}\}. \tag{10}$$

This set turns out to be a closed normal subgroup of G by Lemma 3 of [9].

Thirdly, we recall that a pro-p-group P is *procyclic*, if it is topologically generated by a single element. As indicated by Proposition 2.7.1 of [2], a procyclic group P is either isomorphic to $\mathbb{Z}_p$ or to the cyclic group $\mathbb{Z}(p^n)$ of p-power order (with $n \geq 1$). Detecting procyclic groups among totally disconnected compact groups turns out to be relevant for several results of classification (for instance, they are involved in the theory of *near abelian compact groups*, whose structure is described by Theorems 6, 15, 26, 35 in Overview of [14]. In particular, some homological notions such as the notion of the *Schur multiplier* should be involved (see [2,14] and Definition 3 below). Our second main result is devoted to recognize procyclic groups through the complete exterior degree.

Theorem 2. *For a pro-p-group G, the following conditions are satisfied:*

(i). $\widehat{\mathrm{d}}(G) = 0$ *if and only if* $\widehat{FC}(G)$ *is not open in G;*
(ii). $\widehat{\mathrm{d}}(G) = 1$ *if and only if G is procyclic.*

In particular, if G is a nonprocyclic pro-p-group with $\widehat{Z}(G)$ *open in G, then there exists a finite p-group E with number of conjugacy classes k(E) such that*

$$\widehat{\mathrm{d}}(G) = \widehat{\mathrm{d}}(E) = \sum_{i=1}^{k(E)} \frac{|\widehat{C}_E(x_i)|}{|C_E(x_i)|}. \quad (11)$$

Note that Theorem 2 was inspired by a similar property, which was shown by Abdollahi and others [15] for *the probability* $\mathrm{d}(G)$ *that two randomly picked elements* x, y *commute* in a pro-p-group G. In fact, our third main result connects $\widehat{\mathrm{d}}(G)$ with $\mathrm{d}(G)$.

Theorem 3. *If G is a pro-p-group with a trivial Schur multiplier, then there exists a finite p-group H such that* $\mathrm{d}(G) = \widehat{\mathrm{d}}(G) = \widehat{\mathrm{d}}(H)/|G : \widehat{FC}(G)|^2$.

Section 2 proves Theorem 1 and gives a formal description of complete nonabelian tensor squares and complete nonabelian exterior squares in terms of quotients of free pro-p-groups. Section 3 recalls some facts of homological algebra and previous bounds on the exterior degree, setting the ground for the proofs of the remaining main theorems which are given in Section 4. Examples appear at the end, in order to support the main results. Notations and terminology are standard and follow [1,2,14,16].

2. The First Main Theorem and Its Proof

We say that a pro-p-group G acts *compatibly and continuously on itself by conjugation*, if the action $(a, b) \in G \times G \mapsto a^b \in G$ is continuous and the compatibility relations $x^{(y^z)} = x^{z^{-1}yz}$ and $t^{(z^y)} = t^{y^{-1}zy}$ are satisfied for all $x, y, z, t \in G$.

Definition 1 (Continuous Crossed Pairings of Pro-p-Groups). *Let A be a pro-p-group and G another pro-p-group acting compatibly and continuously on itself by conjugation. A map* $\varphi : G \times G \to A$ *is called a continuous crossed pairing if for all* $g, h, t, z \in G$ *we have*

$$\varphi(gz, h) = \varphi(z^g, h^g)\,\varphi(g, h) \;\; and \;\; \varphi(g, ht) = \varphi(g, h)\,\varphi\left(g^h, t^h\right) \quad (12)$$

If G and A are profinite abelian groups, Definition 1 gives the notion of a *bilinear continuous map*, or *middle linear continuous map*, according to §5.5 of [2]. It is possible to introduce categorically the complete nonabelian tensor square via an appropriate universal property.

Definition 2 (Universal Property of Complete nonabelian Tensor Squares). *Consider a pro-p-group A and pro-p-group G acting compatibly and continuously on itself by conjugation. The complete nonabelian tensor square of G is the pro-p-group* $G\widehat{\otimes}G$ *together with a continuous crossed pairing* $\widehat{\otimes} : (g, h) \in G \times G \mapsto g\widehat{\otimes}h \in G\widehat{\otimes}G$ *such that for any continuous crossed pairing* $\varphi : G \times G \to A$ *there is a unique homomorphism* $\widehat{\varphi} : G\widehat{\otimes}G \to A$ *of pro-p-groups making commutative the following diagram (i.e.,* $\widehat{\varphi} \circ \widehat{\otimes} = \varphi$*)*

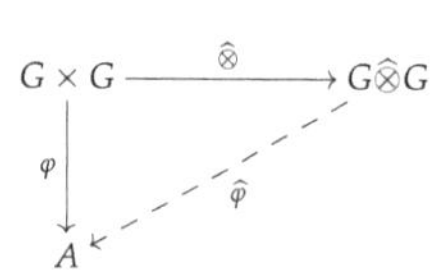

(13)

Note the universal property of complete abelian tensor products in §5.5 of [2]. It is also useful to compare Lemma 5.5.1, Lemma 5.5.2 and Proposition 5.4 of [2] with Theorems

2.1 and 3.1 of [6], in order to understand how we generalize the results on complete abelian tensor squares of profinite groups to complete nonabelian tensor squares of profinite groups. We now begin with the proof of our first main result.

Proof of Theorem 1. First of all, we note that $Y = G \times G$ is a profinite space since we have

$$Y = G \times G = \varprojlim_{i \in J} G_i \times \varprojlim_{j \in J} G_j = \varprojlim_{i,j \in J} (G_i \times G_j). \tag{14}$$

If $\varphi : (g,h) \in Y \mapsto \varphi(g,h) \in A$ is a continuous crossed pairing of pro-p-groups, then the universal property defining $F_p(Y)$ implies that there is a continuous homomorphism $\widehat{\varphi} : F_p(Y) \to A$, which is unique in making commutative the following diagram:

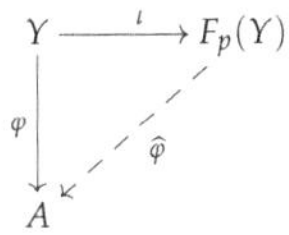

(15)

Here, ι is the embedding of Y into $F_p(Y)$. Let K be the smallest closed normal subgroup of $F_p(Y)$ that is topologically generated by the elements

$$\iota(gz,h)\iota(g,h)^{-1}\iota(z^g,h^g)^{-1} \text{ and } \iota(g,ht)\iota(g^h,t^h)^{-1}\iota(g,h)^{-1} \tag{16}$$

for all $g,z,h,t \in G$. Since φ is a crossed pairing,

$$\widehat{\varphi}\Big(\iota(gz,h)\iota(g,h)^{-1}\iota(z^g,h^g)^{-1}\Big) = \widehat{\varphi}(\iota(gz,h))\widehat{\varphi}\Big(\iota(g,h)^{-1}\Big)\widehat{\varphi}\Big(\iota(z^g,h^g)^{-1}\Big) \tag{17}$$

$$= \varphi(gz,h)\varphi(g,h)^{-1}\varphi(z^g,h^g)^{-1} = \varphi(z^g,h^g)\varphi(g,h)\varphi(g,h)^{-1}\varphi(z^g,h^g)^{-1} = 1.$$

We also have for the same reason

$$\widehat{\varphi}\Big(\iota(g,ht)\iota(g^h,t^h)^{-1}\iota(g,h)^{-1}\Big) = \widehat{\varphi}(\iota(g,ht)\widehat{\varphi}(\iota(g^h,t^h)^{-1})\widehat{\varphi}(\iota(g,h)^{-1}) \tag{18}$$

$$= \varphi(g,ht)\varphi(g^h,t^h)^{-1}\varphi(g,h)^{-1} = \varphi(g,h)\varphi(g^h,t^h)\varphi(g^h,t^h)^{-1}\varphi(g,h)^{-1} = 1.$$

Therefore, $K \subseteq \ker \widehat{\varphi}$ and $\widehat{\varphi}$ is a continuous homomorphism of pro-p-groups vanishing on the topological generators of K. Now, $\pi : F_p(Y) \to F_p(Y)/K$ is the quotient homomorphism, hence a surjective continuous homomorphism of pro-p-groups, and we may consider the composition $\pi \circ \iota : Y \to F_p(Y)/K$. In this situation, there is a continuous homomorphism of pro-p-groups $\widehat{\varphi}_K : F_p(Y)/K \to A$, which is unique in making commutative the following diagram

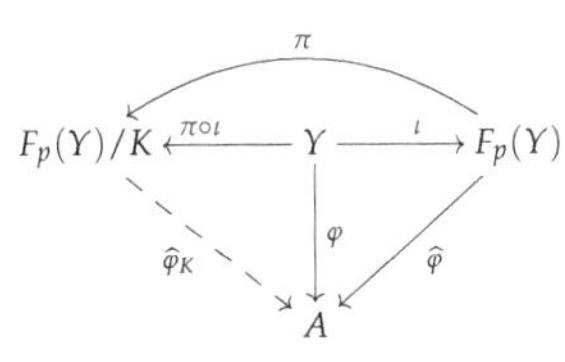

(19)

Setting $G\widehat{\otimes}G = F_p(Y)/K$ and $g\widehat{\otimes}h = \pi(\iota(g,h))$, Definition 2 is satisfied by the left portion of the diagram above. Of course, we may repeat the proof taking any pro-p-group which is topologically isomorphic to $F_p(Y)/K$ and we reach the same conclusions. The first part of Theorem 1 follows.

Concerning the remaining part of the theorem, we shall note that $G\widehat{\otimes}G$ is a pro-p-group and by a result of Alexandroff in Lemma A4.31 of [1], so it is a dyadic space, whenever it is metrizable. □

From Theorem A4.16 of [1], it can be useful to mention that first countable pro-p-groups are always metrizable. This happens for instance when pro-p-groups are topologically finitely generated. Therefore, one could also note from the proof above that if G is topologically finitely generated, then so is $G\widehat{\otimes}G$ and in this situation automatically $G\widehat{\otimes}G$ is metrizable, hence a dyadic space.

3. Some Observations on the Schur Multipliers

In the present section we report some results on the exterior degree in [2,7,9] but also some results of homological algebra in [1,2,16]. Here, $\overline{[G,G]}$ denotes the closure of the *commutator subgroup*

$$[G,G] = \langle [x,y] \mid x,y \in G\rangle = \langle x^{-1}y^{-1}xy \mid x,y \in G\rangle. \tag{20}$$

While in general $Z(G)$ is a closed subgroup of a pro-p-group G, it can easily be seen that this is not the case for $[G,G]$, and so we need to consider $\overline{[G,G]}$ if we want to preserve both its algebraic and topological structure in a pro-p-group, see [1].

Definition 3 (See [6,16]). *The Schur multiplier $M(G)$ of a pro-p-group G is defined to be the second homology group $H_2(G,\mathbb{Z}_p)$ with coefficients in the ring $\mathbb{Z}_p$ of the p-adic integers.*

The above notion is largely used in [7,16–18] but it is useful to recall how Definition 3 should be interpreted in case of a finite p-group. For instance, we may consider a pro-p-group on a countable set of indices, that is, $G = \varprojlim_{m\in\mathbb{N}} G_m$ with each G_m finite p-group. The situation does not change if $G = \varprojlim_{j\in J} G_j$ and J is an arbitrary set of indices, but take J being countable as a temporary assumption.

From Proposition 6.5.7 of [2], there is a continuous homomorphism of pro-p-groups such that

$$H_2(G,\mathbb{Z}_p) = H_2\left(\varprojlim_{m\in\mathbb{N}} G_m, \varprojlim_{m\in\mathbb{N}} \frac{\mathbb{Z}}{p^m\mathbb{Z}}\right) \simeq \varprojlim_{m\in\mathbb{N}} H_2\left(G_m, \frac{\mathbb{Z}}{p^m\mathbb{Z}}\right), \tag{21}$$

where $\mathbb{Z}/p^m\mathbb{Z} = \mathbb{Z}(p^m)$ denotes the cyclic group of order p^m as per Example 1.28 (i) of [1]. Let us carefully examine the construction of the above homology groups with coefficients in $\mathbb{Z}_p$. Consider a *free homogeneous Bar resolution* (with each L_n free profinite $\mathbb{Z}_p$-modules on the profinite space $\{(1,x_1,\ldots,x_n) \mid x_i \in G\}$) according to §6.2 in [2]

$$\ldots \longrightarrow L_n \xrightarrow{\partial_n} L_{n-1} \longrightarrow \ldots L_1 \longrightarrow L_0 \xrightarrow{\epsilon} \mathbb{Z}_p \longrightarrow 0, \tag{22}$$

where ∂_n is the *boundary map* defined by

$$\partial_n(x_0,x_1,\ldots,x_n) = \sum_{i=0}^{n} (-1)^i \, (x_0,x_1,\ldots x_{i-1},x_{i+i},\ldots,x_n), \tag{23}$$

and ϵ is the *augmentation map* defined by

$$\epsilon : x \in L_0 \mapsto \epsilon(x) = 1 \in \mathbb{Z}_p. \tag{24}$$

Both (23) and (24) are continuous homomorphisms of pro-p-groups. Now, G is a pro-p-group, $\mathbb{Z}_p$ is a commutative pro-p-ring and we may consider B which is a pro-p right $[[\mathbb{Z}_pG]]$-module, that is, a pro-p-module on the complete group algebra $[[\mathbb{Z}_pG]]$. See §5.1, §5.2 and §5.3 of [2] for definitions and details. In this situation, $\mathrm{Tor}_n^{[[\mathbb{Z}_pG]]}(B,\mathbb{Z}_p)$ is the n-th left derived functor of the complete abelian tensor product, $\widehat{\otimes}_{[[\mathbb{Z}_pG]]}\ \mathbb{Z}_p$, as noted in [2] (§6.3), and so we have

$$\ldots \longrightarrow B\widehat{\otimes}_{[[\mathbb{Z}_pG]]}L_n \xrightarrow{\partial_n} B\widehat{\otimes}_{[[\mathbb{Z}_pG]]}L_{n-1} \longrightarrow \ldots \xrightarrow{\partial_2} B\widehat{\otimes}_{[[\mathbb{Z}_pG]]}L_1 \xrightarrow{\partial_1} B\widehat{\otimes}_{[[\mathbb{Z}_pG]]}L_0 \xrightarrow{\epsilon} \mathbb{Z}_p \longrightarrow 0. \tag{25}$$

Since $u\widehat{\otimes}(x_0, x_1, \ldots, x_n) \in B\widehat{\otimes}_{[[\mathbb{Z}_pG]]}L_n \mapsto u\widehat{\otimes}\partial_n(x_0, x_1, \ldots, x_n) \in B\widehat{\otimes}_{[[\mathbb{Z}_pG]]}L_{n-1}$, we may use the symbol ∂_n in (23) also in (25), because it is induced by (23). In particular, $B = \mathbb{Z}_p$ can be regarded as a pro-p-module on $[[\mathbb{Z}_pG]]$ and so we have

$$H_2(G, \mathbb{Z}_p) = \mathrm{Tor}_2^{[[\mathbb{Z}_pG]]}(\mathbb{Z}_p, \mathbb{Z}_p) = \frac{\ker \partial_2}{\mathrm{im}\ \partial_3}. \tag{26}$$

A careful examination of §6.8 of [2] suggests that we have a short exact sequence

$$0 \longrightarrow \mathbb{Z}_p \xrightarrow{p} \mathbb{Z}_p \xrightarrow{q} \frac{\mathbb{Z}}{p\mathbb{Z}} \longrightarrow 0 \tag{27}$$

where p denotes the multiplication by p in $\mathbb{Z}_p$ and q the limit map from $\mathbb{Z}_p$ to $\mathbb{Z}/p\mathbb{Z}$ arising from the structure of the projective limit of $\mathbb{Z}_p$, and so there is a long exact sequence of abelian pro-p-groups

$$\begin{array}{llllllll} \ldots & \longrightarrow & H_2(G,\mathbb{Z}_p) & \xrightarrow{p_2} & H_2(G,\mathbb{Z}_p) & \xrightarrow{q_2} & H_2(G,\mathbb{Z}/p\mathbb{Z}) & \xrightarrow{\delta_2} \\ & \xrightarrow{\delta_2} & H_1(G,\mathbb{Z}_p) & \xrightarrow{p_1} & H_1(G,\mathbb{Z}_p) & \xrightarrow{q_1} & H_1(G,\mathbb{Z}/p\mathbb{Z}) & \xrightarrow{\delta_1} \\ & \xrightarrow{\delta_1} & H_0(G,\mathbb{Z}_p) & \xrightarrow{p_0} & H_0(G,\mathbb{Z}_p) & \xrightarrow{q_0} & H_0(G,\mathbb{Z}/p\mathbb{Z}) & \end{array} \tag{28}$$

where p_1 and p_2 are induced by p, q_1 and q_2 by q, and δ_1 and δ_2 are connecting continuous homomorphisms. Since $H_0(G,\mathbb{Z}_p) \xrightarrow{p_0} H_0(G,\mathbb{Z}_p) = \mathbb{Z}_p \xrightarrow{p} \mathbb{Z}_p$ is a monomorphism, we have

$$H_1(G,\mathbb{Z}_p) \xrightarrow{p_1} H_1(G,\mathbb{Z}_p) \longrightarrow H_1(G,\mathbb{Z}/p\mathbb{Z}) \longrightarrow 0 \tag{29}$$

and so (28) becomes

$$\begin{array}{llllllll} \ldots & \longrightarrow & H_2(G,\mathbb{Z}_p) & \xrightarrow{p_2} & H_2(G,\mathbb{Z}_p) & \xrightarrow{q_2} & H_2(G,\mathbb{Z}/p\mathbb{Z}) & \xrightarrow{\delta_2} \\ & \xrightarrow{\delta_2} & H_1(G,\mathbb{Z}_p) & \xrightarrow{p_1} & H_1(G,\mathbb{Z}_p) & \xrightarrow{q_1} & H_1(G,\mathbb{Z}/p\mathbb{Z}) & \longrightarrow 0 \end{array} \tag{30}$$

On the other hand, Lemma 6.8.6 of [2] allows us to conclude that $H_1(G,\mathbb{Z}/p\mathbb{Z}) \simeq G/G^p\overline{[G,G]}$ and $H_1(G,\mathbb{Z}_p) \simeq G/\overline{[G,G]}$; hence, (23) becomes (up to isomorphisms of abelian pro-p-groups) the following long exact sequence of abelian pro-p-groups

$$\begin{array}{llllllll} \ldots & \longrightarrow & H_2(G,\mathbb{Z}_p) & \xrightarrow{p_2} & H_2(G,\mathbb{Z}_p) & \xrightarrow{q_2} & H_2(G,\mathbb{Z}/p\mathbb{Z}) & \xrightarrow{\delta_2} \\ & \xrightarrow{\delta_2} & G/\overline{[G,G]} & \xrightarrow{p_1} & G/\overline{[G,G]} & \xrightarrow{q_1} & G/G^p\overline{[G,G]} & \longrightarrow 0 \end{array} \tag{31}$$

We make two observations on the basis of the homological algebra, which was used.

Remark 1. Assume we start with $G = G_1$ finite p-group, that is, $G = G_1 = G_2 = G_3 = \ldots$ in the projective limit describing G. Then, there is a presentation $1 \to R \to F \to G \to 1$ for $G = F/R$ with F a free abstract group and R a normal subgroup of F. Applying Theorem 9.5.10 of [16], we obtain the isomorphism of finite abelian p-groups

$$H_2(G,\mathbb{Z}/p\mathbb{Z}) \simeq \frac{R \cap (F'F^p)}{[R,F]F^p}, \tag{32}$$

where $F^p = \langle a^p \mid a \in F \rangle$ denotes the subgroup of p-powers of F, $[F,F] = F'$ the commutator subgroup of F and $[R,F] = \langle [a,b] \mid a \in R, b \in F \rangle \subseteq F'$. In particular, the long exact sequence (31) becomes in this situation

$$\ldots \xrightarrow{q_2} R \cap (F'F^p)/[R,F]F^p \xrightarrow{\delta_2} G/[G,G] \xrightarrow{p_1} \tag{33}$$

$$G/[G,G] \xrightarrow{q_1} G/G^p[G,G] \longrightarrow 0$$

so we may concretely visualize Definition 3 in the case of finite p-groups.

Note that (32) modifies the *Hopf's Formula* for the Schur multiplier, which is available in Theorem 9.5.6 of [16] and usually formulated as

$$H_2(G,\mathbb{Z}) \simeq \frac{R \cap F'}{[R,F]}, \tag{34}$$

when $G = F/R$ is an arbitrary abstract group with presentation $1 \to R \to F \to G \to 1$, so not necessarily a finite p-group. Now, we make our second observation as a further description of Definition 3.

Remark 2. Comparing (34) with (32), we note that the terms F^p and $p\mathbb{Z}$ are significant in the case of finite p-groups and this justifies the construction of $H_2(G,\mathbb{Z}_p)$, which is designed for infinite pro-p-groups as large projective limits of finite p-groups. The temporary assumption of working with J countable facilitates the understanding of the functorial behavior in (21), where $H_2(G,\mathbb{Z}_p)$ preserves the structure of projective limit. This relevant observation and general versions of Hopf's Formula such as (32) allow us to consider $H_2(G,\mathbb{Z}_p)$ as a projective limit of smaller homology groups $H_2(G_m,\mathbb{Z}/p^m\mathbb{Z})$ when m tends to infinity. The reader can find in [19] details of a categorical nature on Hopf Formulas.

Now we remove the temporary assumption to have a countable J and consider a pro-p-group G which is a projective limit of G_j with an arbitrary set J of indices. Note that Theorem 1 involves the nonabelian tensor square $G\widehat{\otimes}G$ of an arbitrary pro-p-group G and one has the following maps

$$\widehat{\kappa} : x\widehat{\otimes}y \in G\widehat{\otimes}G \mapsto [x,y] \in \overline{[G,G]} \text{ and } \widehat{\kappa'} : x\widehat{\wedge}y \in G\widehat{\wedge}G \mapsto [x,y] \in \overline{[G,G]}, \tag{35}$$

which are continuous surjective homomorphisms of pro-p-groups such that

$$\widehat{J}_2(G) = \ker\widehat{\kappa} \supseteq \widehat{\nabla}(G) \text{ and } \ker\widehat{\kappa'} \simeq M(G). \tag{36}$$

We give a proof of the following result for convenience of the reader.

Lemma 1. *In a pro-p-group G, the maps $\widehat{\kappa}$ and $\widehat{\kappa'}$ in (35) are continuous surjective homomorphisms of pro-p-groups and the following diagram has rows which are central extensions of pro-p-groups*

$$\begin{array}{ccccccccc} 1 & \longrightarrow & \widehat{J}_2(G) & \longrightarrow & G\widehat{\otimes}G & \xrightarrow{\widehat{\kappa}} & \overline{[G,G]} & \longrightarrow & 1 \\ & & \downarrow{\scriptstyle \widehat{\varepsilon}_|} & & \downarrow{\scriptstyle \widehat{\varepsilon}} & & \| & & \\ 1 & \longrightarrow & M(G) & \longrightarrow & G\widehat{\wedge}G & \xrightarrow{\widehat{\kappa'}} & \overline{[G,G]} & \longrightarrow & 1. \end{array} \tag{37}$$

Moreover, we have $\ker\widehat{\kappa} \supseteq \widehat{\nabla}(G)$ *and there is a continuous isomorphism of pro-p-groups such that* $\ker\widehat{\kappa'} \simeq M(G)$.

Proof. From Definition 2, there are continuous crossed pairings $\widehat{\otimes} : (x,y) \in G \times G \mapsto x\widehat{\otimes}y \in G\widehat{\otimes}G$ and $\kappa : (x,y) \in G \times G \to [x,y] \in \overline{[G,G]}$ of pro-p-groups, inducing the map $\widehat{\kappa} : x\widehat{\otimes}y \in G\widehat{\otimes}G \mapsto [x,y] \in \overline{[G,G]}$, which is a continuous crossed pairing such that $\widehat{\kappa} \circ \widehat{\otimes} = \kappa$ and the upper part of the following diagram is commutative

$$\begin{array}{ccc} G \times G & \xrightarrow{\widehat{\otimes}} & G\widehat{\otimes}G \\ {\scriptstyle\kappa}\downarrow & \swarrow_{\widehat{\kappa}} & \downarrow{\scriptstyle\widehat{\varepsilon}} \\ \overline{[G,G]} & \xleftarrow{\widehat{\kappa'}} & G\widehat{\wedge}G \end{array} \tag{38}$$

This shows that $\widehat{\kappa}$ is a continuous homomorphism of pro-p-groups. Note that $\widehat{\kappa}$ is surjective, because $\widehat{\kappa} \circ \widehat{\otimes} = \kappa$ and κ is surjective by construction. Concerning $\widehat{\kappa'}$, we look at the lower part of the same diagram, where $\widehat{\varepsilon} : G\widehat{\otimes}G \to G\widehat{\wedge}G$ is the natural projection of $G\widehat{\otimes}G$ onto $G\widehat{\wedge}G$ with $\ker\widehat{\varepsilon} = \widehat{\nabla}(G)$. Then, $\widehat{\kappa'}$ is induced by $\widehat{\kappa}$ modulo $\widehat{\nabla}(G)$ and is a continuous homomorphism of pro-p-groups such that $\widehat{\kappa'} \circ \widehat{\varepsilon} = \widehat{\kappa}$. Of course, $\ker\widehat{\varepsilon} \subseteq \ker\widehat{\kappa}$ and, if $x\widehat{\otimes}x \in \ker\widehat{\varepsilon} = \widehat{\nabla}(G)$, then for all $y\widehat{\otimes}z \in G\widehat{\otimes}G$ we have

$$(x\widehat{\otimes}x)\,(y\widehat{\otimes}z)\,(x\widehat{\otimes}x)^{-1} = (y\widehat{\otimes}z)^{[x,x]} \implies (x\widehat{\otimes}x)\,(y\widehat{\otimes}z) = (y\widehat{\otimes}z)\,(x\widehat{\otimes}x) \tag{39}$$

showing that $\ker\widehat{\varepsilon} \subseteq Z(G\widehat{\otimes}G)$. Note that more generally the same argument applies to any element $a\widehat{\otimes}b \in \ker\widehat{\kappa}$, in fact

$$(a\widehat{\otimes}b)\,(y\widehat{\otimes}z)\,(a\widehat{\otimes}b)^{-1} = (y\widehat{\otimes}z)^{[a,b]} \implies (a\widehat{\otimes}b)\,(y\widehat{\otimes}z) = (y\widehat{\otimes}z)\,(a\widehat{\otimes}b) \tag{40}$$

hence, $\ker\widehat{\kappa} \subseteq Z(G\widehat{\otimes}G)$. We may conclude that both the sequence

$$1 \longrightarrow \widehat{J_2}(G) \longrightarrow G\widehat{\otimes}G \xrightarrow{\widehat{\kappa}} \overline{[G,G]} \longrightarrow 1 \tag{41}$$

and the sequence

$$1 \longrightarrow \ker\widehat{\kappa'} \longrightarrow G\widehat{\wedge}G \xrightarrow{\widehat{\kappa'}} \overline{[G,G]} \longrightarrow 1. \tag{42}$$

are short exact sequences, which describe central extensions of pro-p-groups. Considering the restriction $\widehat{\varepsilon}_|$ of $\widehat{\varepsilon}$ to $\widehat{J_2}(G)$ we may conclude that

$$\begin{array}{ccccccccc} 1 & \longrightarrow & \widehat{J_2}(G) & \longrightarrow & G\widehat{\otimes}G & \xrightarrow{\widehat{\kappa}} & \overline{[G,G]} & \longrightarrow & 1 \\ & & {\scriptstyle\widehat{\varepsilon}_|}\downarrow & & {\scriptstyle\widehat{\varepsilon}}\downarrow & & \| & & \\ 1 & \longrightarrow & \ker\widehat{\kappa'} & \longrightarrow & G\widehat{\wedge}G & \xrightarrow{\widehat{\kappa'}} & \overline{[G,G]} & \longrightarrow & 1. \end{array} \tag{43}$$

is a commutative diagram whose rows are central extensions of pro-p-groups. It remains to show that $\ker\widehat{\kappa'}$ is isomorphic as a pro-p-group to $M(G)$. This is proved in [6] (Proposition 2.2), so we omit the details here. The result follows. □

Even if in principle $\widehat{\nabla}(G)$ may be a proper subgroup of $\widehat{J_2}(G)$, the computations show that most of the time $\widehat{J_2}(G) = \widehat{\nabla}(G)$ in case of finite groups (see [3,4]) and so (37) becomes most of the time

$$\begin{array}{ccccccccc} 1 & \longrightarrow & \widehat{\nabla}(G) & \xrightarrow{\alpha} & G\widehat{\otimes}G & \xrightarrow{\widehat{\kappa}} & \overline{[G,G]} & \longrightarrow & 1 \\ & & {\scriptstyle\widehat{\varepsilon}_|}\downarrow & & {\scriptstyle\widehat{\varepsilon}}\downarrow & & \| & & \\ 1 & \longrightarrow & M(G) & \xrightarrow{\beta} & G\widehat{\wedge}G & \xrightarrow{\widehat{\kappa'}} & \overline{[G,G]} & \longrightarrow & 1 \end{array} \tag{44}$$

where α embeds $\widehat{\nabla}(G)$ into $G\widehat{\otimes}G$ and β is induced by α and by $\widehat{\varepsilon}_| : x\widehat{\otimes}x \in \widehat{\nabla}(G) \mapsto x\widehat{\wedge}x \in M(G)$. Of course, if $\widehat{J_2}(G) \neq \widehat{\nabla}(G)$, then Im $\alpha \subseteq \ker\widehat{\kappa}$ and Im $\beta \subseteq \ker\widehat{\kappa'}$, so we have inclusions and lose the exactness of the sequences, that is, the diagram (44) is no longer formed by central extensions as rows but it is still (44) a commutative diagram.

Remark 3. In a finite p-group G, the quotient $C_G(x)/\widehat{C}_G(x)$ is isomorphic to a subgroup of the abelian group $H_2(G,\mathbb{Z})$ by the results in [7,10]. In particular, groups with $H_2(G,\mathbb{Z}) = 1$ have $C_G(x) = \widehat{C}_G(x)$ for all $x \in G$ and $Z(G) = \widehat{Z}(G)$ as well.

We recall that the *commutativity degree* of a pro-p-group G is defined by the formula

$$\mathrm{d}(G) := \int_G \mu(C_G(x))d\mu, \tag{45}$$

where μ is the Haar measure on G. This notion has been studied extensively in [20–23] both in the finite case and in the infinite case. Of course, (45) represents for finite groups the probability that a randomly picked pair (x,y) of elements of $G \times G$ commutes, that is, satisfies the condition $[x,y] = 1$. Following the same notion at the level of elements for the operator of exterior degree, instead of commutator, we find the probability that the same randomly picked pair (x,y) of elements of $G \times G$ satisfies $x\widehat{\wedge}y = 1$ (instead of $[x,y] = 1$). The two notions are related by the following result:

Lemma 2 (See [7], Theorem 1.1). *A pro-p-group G satisfies the following inequality*

$$\widehat{\mathrm{d}}(G) \le \mathrm{d}(G) - \left(\frac{p-1}{p}\right)\Big(\mu(Z(G)) - \mu(\widehat{Z}(G))\Big).$$

Furthermore, if $M(G)$ is finite, then

$$\widehat{\mathrm{d}}(G) \ge \mu(\widehat{Z}(G)) + \frac{1}{|M(G)|}\Big(\mathrm{d}(G) - \mu(\widehat{Z}(G))\Big).$$

It is also useful to mention that the abelian pro-p-group $Z(G)/\widehat{Z}(G)$ can be embedded in the abelian pro-p-group $M(G)$, involving some numerical invariants such as *the rank* of a pro-p-group G

$$\mathrm{rk}(G) = \sup\{m(H) \mid H = \overline{H} \text{ subgroup of } G\}, \tag{46}$$

where $m(H)$ is the minimal number of elements which topologically generate H. If G is a torsion-free pro-p-group, $\mathrm{rk}(G) = \mathrm{tf}(G)$ is called the *torsion-free rank*, see [17].

Lemma 3 (See [7], Theorem 1.2). *Let G be a pro-p-group such that* $\mathrm{rk}(G/\widehat{Z}(G)) = a$, $\mathrm{rk}(M(G)) = b$ *and* $\mathrm{tf}(M(G)) = c$.

(i). *If $M(G)$ is finite, then $|Z(G)/\widehat{Z}(G)|$ divides $|M(G)|^a$.*
(ii). *If $M(G)$ is infinite, then* $\mathrm{rk}(Z(G)/\widehat{Z}(G)) \le b^a$. *In particular, if $M(G)$ is torsion-free, then* $\mathrm{tf}(Z(G)/\widehat{Z}(G)) \le c^a$.

Now, we recall a characterization for the extremal cases of exterior degree equal to zero, or equal to one, via the notions of the complete exterior center and complete exterior centralizer.

Lemma 4 (See [7], Proposition 3.3). *A pro-p-group G has $\widehat{\mathrm{d}}(G) = 1$ if and only if $\widehat{Z}(G) = G$.*

We report a result similar to that of Abdollahi and others [15] for compact groups. This was at the origin of our investigations.

Lemma 5 (See [15], Theorem 1.1). *In a pro-p-group G of* $\mathrm{d}(G) > 0$ *there exists a finite p-group H such that* $\mathrm{d}(G)$ *is proportional to* $\mathrm{d}(H)$ *via a constant $\alpha = |G : FC(G)|^{-2}$ depending only on the FC-center $FC(G) = \{g \in \mid |G : C_G(g)| \text{ is } finite\}$ of G. In particular,* $\mathrm{d}(G) = \alpha\, \mathrm{d}(H)$.

We note explicitly that the formulation above is designed for our present context. It is also useful to collect some bounds, which can be obtained in terms of subgroups and quotients.

Lemma 6 (See [7], Proposition 3.6 and Corollary 5.3)**.** *Assume that G is a pro-p-group.*

(i). *If N is a closed normal subgroup of G, then $\widehat{\mathrm{d}}(G) \leq \widehat{\mathrm{d}}(G/N)$ and the equality holds if $N \leq \widehat{Z}(G)$;*

(ii). *If G is abelian nonprocyclic, then*

$$\widehat{\mathrm{d}}(G) \leq \frac{p^2+p-1}{p^3}$$

and the equality holds if and only if $G/\widehat{Z}(G)$ is p-elementary abelian of rank two;

(iii). *If G is nonabelian and $\widehat{Z}(G)$ is a proper subgroup of $Z(G)$, then*

$$\widehat{\mathrm{d}}(G) \leq \frac{p^3+p-1}{p^4}.$$

While the upper bounds on $\widehat{\mathrm{d}}(G)$ are useful to measure how far we are from the extremal case $\widehat{\mathrm{d}}(G) = 1$ in $[0,1]$, the lower bounds on $\widehat{\mathrm{d}}(G)$ may reveal the presence of quotients, which are small enough.

Remark 4. From Lemma 2, a pro-p-group G always has $\widehat{\mathrm{d}}(G) \leq \mathrm{d}(G)$, and, if $M(G)$ is finite, $\mu(\widehat{Z}(G))$ is finite and $\mu(\widehat{Z}(G)) \neq \mathrm{d}(G)$, then $\mathrm{d}(G)$ is nontrivially bounded from below. Note that nontrivial lower bounds for $\mathrm{d}(G)$ imply that G is virtually abelian by [22].

4. Proofs of the Main Theorems

With the results of the previous section at hand, we show Theorem 2.

Proof of Theorem 2. (i). The normalized Haar measure μ on the pro-p-group G is a left invariant Borel probability measure which respects the closed subgroups of G (see [22] for terminology); hence, for any closed subgroup M of G and $k \geq 1$, we have

$$\mu(M) = \begin{cases} \frac{1}{p^k}, & \text{if} \quad |G:M| = p^k \\ 0, & \text{if} \quad |G:M| = \infty. \end{cases} \tag{47}$$

Consider

$$\widehat{\mathrm{d}}(G) = \int_G \mu(\widehat{C}_G(x))d\mu(x). \tag{48}$$

We have from (47) that $\mu(\widehat{C}_G(x)) > 0$ iff $\widehat{C}_G(x)$ has p-power index in G, that is, $\mu(\widehat{C}_G(x)) = 0$ iff $\widehat{C}_G(x)$ has infinite index in G iff $x \notin \widehat{FC}(G)$. Since μ is a nonnegative normalized Haar measure on G, we have

$$0 = \widehat{\mathrm{d}}(G) = \int_G \mu(\widehat{C}_G(x))d\mu(x) \iff \mu(\widehat{C}_G(x)) = 0, \ \forall x \in G \tag{49}$$

iff $x \notin \widehat{FC}(G)$ for all $x \in G$ iff there are no elements in the interior $\widehat{FC}(G)$, i.e., $\widehat{FC}(G)^\circ = \emptyset$ but we know that (any set so in particular) $\widehat{FC}(G)$ is open iff $\widehat{FC}(G)^\circ = \widehat{FC}(G)$. This cannot happen since $1 \in \widehat{FC}(G)$ and $\widehat{FC}(G) \neq \emptyset$. Therefore, $\widehat{\mathrm{d}}(G) = 0$ happens iff $\widehat{FC}(G)^\circ = \emptyset$ iff $\widehat{FC}(G)$ is not open.

(ii). Assume that G is procyclic. If $G \simeq \mathbb{Z}(p^n)$ or $G \simeq \mathbb{Z}_p$, then $M(G)$ is trivial. Hence, $\widehat{Z}(G) = Z(G)$ by Lemma 3 and so $\widehat{Z}(G) = Z(G) = G$ is abelian. The bounds of Lemma 2 imply $\widehat{\mathrm{d}}(G) = 1$. Conversely, assume that G is a pro-p-group with $\widehat{\mathrm{d}}(G) = 1$.

From Lemma 4, $\widehat{\mathrm{d}}(G) = 1$ if and only if $\widehat{Z}(G) = G$. Hence, G is abelian. Therefore, we are assuming that G is an abelian pro-p-group of $\widehat{\mathrm{d}}(G) = 1$. Either G is procyclic or G is nonprocyclic. In the first case, the result follows. In the second case, Lemma 6 (ii) implies $p^3 \leq p^2 + p - 1$, which is a contradiction. Then, G must be necessarily procyclic.

(iii). Of course, $\widehat{\mathrm{d}}(G) \in [0,1]$. From (ii) above $\widehat{\mathrm{d}}(G) \neq 1$ iff G is nonprocyclic. On the other hand, (i) above shows that $\widehat{\mathrm{d}}(G) = 0$ iff $\widehat{FC}(G)^\circ = \emptyset$. Since $\widehat{Z}(G) \subseteq \widehat{FC}(G)$ and $\widehat{Z}(G)$ is open in G, we have $\widehat{Z}(G)^\circ \subseteq \widehat{FC}(G)^\circ$ hence $\widehat{FC}(G)^\circ \neq \emptyset$. This implies that $\widehat{\mathrm{d}}(G) > 0$. Therefore, a nonprocyclic pro-p-group G with $\widehat{Z}(G)$ open in G automatically has $\widehat{\mathrm{d}}(G) \in (0,1)$ and we may proceed with the proof of the formula for the computation of the complete exterior degree. Consider Lemma 6 (i) and that $\widehat{Z}(G)$ is also closed in G by Proposition A4.25 (ii) of [1] (in fact any open subgroup is closed). It follows that $G/\widehat{Z}(G) \simeq E$ is a finite p-group but also that

$$\widehat{\mathrm{d}}(G) = \widehat{\mathrm{d}}\left(\frac{G}{\widehat{Z}(G)}\right) = \widehat{\mathrm{d}}(E) = \sum_{i=1}^{k(E)} \frac{|\widehat{C}_E(x_i)|}{|C_E(x_i)|}, \tag{50}$$

where the last equality is due to [10] (Lemma 2.2). □

Now, we proceed to prove another main result.

Proof of Theorem 3. From Lemmas 2 and 3 we have $\mu(\widehat{Z}(G)) = \mu(Z(G))$ and $\mathrm{d}(G) = \widehat{\mathrm{d}}(G)$. Moreover, $\widehat{C}_G(x) = C_G(x)$ for all $x \in G$ in this situation; hence, $\widehat{FC}(G) = FC(G)$. From Lemma 5, we have a finite p-group H such that $\mathrm{d}(G) = \mathrm{d}(H)/|G : FC(G)|^2$, that is, $\widehat{\mathrm{d}}(G) = \widehat{\mathrm{d}}(H)/|G : \widehat{FC}(G)|^2$. □

As evidence of Theorem 2, we present the following construction.

Example 1. The present example appears in [9], so we report the main information only and a few new computations. Consider the elementary abelian p-group

$$A = \mathbb{Z}(p)^{(\mathbb{N})} \tag{51}$$

of countable rank, where $A_i = \langle a_i \rangle = \mathbb{Z}(p)$ is cyclic of order p and $i \in \mathbb{N}$. Then, consider

$$B = \mathbb{Z}(p)^n = A_1 \times \ldots \times A_n \tag{52}$$

elementary abelian p-subgroup of rank n of A. We have that

$$1 = \mathrm{d}(B) > \widehat{\mathrm{d}}(B) = \frac{p^n + p^{n-1} - 1}{p^{2n-1}} \quad \text{and} \quad 1 = \mathrm{d}(A) \geq \frac{p^2 + p - 1}{p^3} > \widehat{\mathrm{d}}(A). \tag{53}$$

Note that the complete exterior degree of abelian pro-p-groups is also described by Lemma 6 (ii). In fact, Theorem 2 shows that computations such as those in Lemma 6 are in general tedious, so that formulas of reduction are very useful. In addition to Example 1, we mention below a pro-p-group, whose structure is described in [17].

Example 2. Consider the infinite pro-2-group (with $r \geq 1$ arbitrary)

$$G = \overline{\langle a, t \mid a^{2^r} = 1, a^{-1}ta = t^{-1} \rangle} = \mathbb{Z}_2 \rtimes \mathbb{Z}(2^r), \tag{54}$$

which appears also in §1 of [18]. We have $M(G) = 1$ and so $Z(G) = \widehat{Z}(G) = 1$, but also $\widehat{\mathrm{d}}(G) = \mathrm{d}(G)$ and $\widehat{C}_G(x) = C_G(x)$ for all $x \in G$.

The following computations were carried out in Example 5.2 of [7] and are presented here for the convenience of the reader. First of all, we note that for $i = 0$ we have $\mu(\widehat{C}_G(t^i)) = 1$ but, for all $i \neq 0$, $\mu(\widehat{C}_G(t^i)) = 1/2^r$ and for all i and $1 \leq j \leq 2^r - 1$ instead $\mu(\widehat{C}_G(a^j t^i)) = 0$.

If $T = \overline{\langle t \rangle} = \mathbb{Z}_2$, then

$$\widehat{\mathrm{d}}(G) = \mu(\widehat{Z}(G)) + \int_{T-\widehat{Z}(G)} \mu(\widehat{C}_G(x))d\mu(x) + \int_{G-T} \mu(\widehat{C}_G(x))d\mu(x) \tag{55}$$

$$= \frac{1}{2^r}\mu(T - \{1\}) = \frac{1}{2^r}\mu(T) = \frac{1}{4^r}.$$

Theorem 2 cannot be used here and $FC(G) = \widehat{FC}(G) = T$ is closed and open in G.

Author Contributions: Methodology, B.G.R. and F.G.R.; Investigation, B.G.R. and F.G.R. All authors have read and agreed to the published version of the manuscript.

Funding: This research received no external funding.

Data Availability Statement: No new data were created or analyzed in this study. Data sharing is not applicable to this article.

Conflicts of Interest: The authors declare no conflicts of interest.

References

1. Hofmann, K.H.; Morris, S. *The Structure of Compact Groups*; de Gruyter: Berlin, Germany, 2006.
2. Ribes, L.; Zalesski, P. *Profinite Groups*; Springer: Berlin, Germany, 2009.
3. Brown, R.; Johnson, D.L.; Robertson, E.F. Some computations of non–abelian tensor products of groups. *J. Algebra* **1987**, *111*, 177–202. [CrossRef]
4. Brown, R.; Loday, J.-L. Van Kampen theorems for diagrams of spaces. *Topology* **1987**, *26*, 311–335. [CrossRef]
5. Sipacheva, O. The topology of free topological groups. *J. Math. Sci.* **2005**, *131*, 5765–5838. [CrossRef]
6. Moravec, P. On the Schur multipliers of finite p-groups of given coclass. *Israel J. Math.* **2011**, *185*, 189–205. [CrossRef]
7. Rezaei, R.; Russo, F.G. Commuting elements with respect to the operator $\wedge$ in infinite groups. *Bull. Korean Math. Soc.* **2016**, *53*, 1353–1362. [CrossRef]
8. Ramabulana, M.; Russo, F.G. Nonabelian tensor squares of compact groups via quotients of free compact groups. *J. Lie Theory* **2024**, *34*, 1–16.
9. Erwin, D.; Russo, F.G. The influence of the complete nonexterior square graph on some infinite groups. *Lith. Math. J.* **2016**, *56*, 492–502. [CrossRef]
10. Niroomand, P.; Rezaei, R. On the exterior degree of finite groups. *Comm. Algebra* **2011**, *39*, 335–343. [CrossRef]
11. Niroomand, P.; Rezaei, R.; Russo, F.G. Commuting powers and exterior degree of finite groups. *J. Korean Math. Soc.* **2012**, *49*, 855–865. [CrossRef]
12. Rodrigues, B.G.; Russo, F.G. Numerical bounds for the exterior degree of finite simple groups. *Comm. Algebra* **2021**, *49*, 2707–2721. [CrossRef]
13. Robinson, D.J. *An Introduction to the Theory of Groups*; Springer: Berlin, Germany, 1981.
14. Herfort, W.; Hofmann, K.H.; Russo, F.G. *Periodic Locally Compact Groups*; de Gruyter: Berlin, Germany, 2018.
15. Abdollahi, A.; Soleimani Malekan, M. Commuting probability of compact groups. *Bull. Austral. Math. Soc.* **2022**, *105*, 87–91. [CrossRef]
16. Leedham-Green, C.R.; McKay, S. *The Structure of Groups of Prime Power Order*; Oxford University Press: Oxford, UK, 2002.
17. Eick, B. Schur multiplicators of infinite pro-p-groups with finite coclass. *Israel J. Math.* **2008**, *166*, 147–156. [CrossRef]
18. Eick, B. Schur multiplicators of finite p-groups with fixed coclass. *Israel J. Math.* **2008**, *166*, 157–166. [CrossRef]
19. Everaert, T.; Gran, M.; van der Linden, T. Higher Hopf formulae for homology via Galois theory. *Adv. Math.* **2008**, *217*, 2231–2267. [CrossRef]
20. Erfanian, A.; Lescot, P.; Rezaei, R. On the relative commutativity degree of a subgroup of a finite group. *Comm. Algebra* **2007**, *35*, 4183–4197. [CrossRef]
21. Guralnick, R.M.; Robinson, G.R. On the commuting probability in finite groups. *J. Algebra* **2006**, *300*, 509–528. [CrossRef]
22. Hofmann, K.H.; Russo, F.G. The probability that x and y commute in a compact group. *Math. Proc. Cambridge Phil. Soc.* **2012**, *153*, 557–571. [CrossRef]
23. Lescot, P. Isoclinism classes and commutativity degrees of finite groups. *J. Algebra* **1995**, *177*, 847–869. [CrossRef]

mathematics MDPI

Article

Study of Random Walk Invariants for Spiro-Ring Network Based on Laplacian Matrices

Yasir Ahmad [1], Umar Ali [2], Daniele Ettore Otera [3,*] and Xiang-Feng Pan [1]

[1] School of Mathematical Sciences, Anhui University, Hefei 230601, China; yasirahmad6667@gmail.com (Y.A.); xfpan@ahu.edu.cn (X.-F.P.)
[2] Business School, University of Shanghai for Science and Technology, Shanghai 200093, China; umarali@usst.edu.cn or umarali.msc@gmail.com
[3] Institute of Data Science and Digital Technologies, Vilnius University, 08412 Vilnius, Lithuania
* Correspondence: daniele.otera@mif.vu.lt or daniele.otera@gmail.com

Abstract: The use of the global mean first-passage time (GMFPT) in random walks on networks has been widely explored in the field of statistical physics, both in theory and practical applications. The GMFPT is the estimated interval of time needed to reach a state j in a system from a starting state i. In contrast, there exists an intrinsic measure for a stochastic process, known as Kemeny's constant, which is independent of the initial state. In the literature, it has been used as a measure of network efficiency. This article deals with a graph-spectrum-based method for finding both the GMFPT and Kemeny's constant of random walks on spiro-ring networks (that are organic compounds with a particular graph structure). Furthermore, we calculate the Laplacian matrix for some specific spiro-ring networks using the decomposition theorem of Laplacian polynomials. Moreover, using the coefficients and roots of the resulting matrices, we establish some formulae for both GMFPT and Kemeny's constant in these spiro-ring networks.

Keywords: spiro-ring network; random walk; global mean first-passage time; Kemeny's constant

MSC: 05C50; 05C81; 05C92

Citation: Ahmad, Y.; Ali, U.; Otera, D.E.; Pan, X.-F. Study of Random Walk Invariants for Spiro-Ring Network Based on Laplacian Matrices. *Mathematics* **2024**, *12*, 1309. https://doi.org/10.3390/math12091309

Academic Editor: Andrea Scozzari

Received: 17 March 2024
Revised: 15 April 2024
Accepted: 23 April 2024
Published: 25 April 2024

1. Introduction

The empirical investigation of real-world networks has inspired many scientists to study complex chemical networks in detail. They have many useful applications in physics and biophysics, as well as in quantum chemistry for molecular modeling, in statistical mechanics for bulk matter properties, and in molecular dynamics simulations for the study of molecular behavior. These networks aid in the understanding of atomic and molecular structures, electronic properties, and fundamental physical origins in various physical contexts of materials science.

Recently, several scientific research fields have shown a particular interest in the study of random walks on complex networks. *Random walks* [1] are stochastic processes characterized by irregular fluctuations, where each step in the process is determined randomly, independently from past events. The mathematical theory of random walks has been widely applied in several domains, such as machine learning [2], optimization [3], artificial intelligence [4], engineering [5], biology [6], physics, and other disciplines [7,8].

In order to motivate our study, which concerns some specific chemical structures called *spiro compounds*, and to provide an explanation of the physical significance and justification behind the spreading processes on spiro-ring networks, we briefly highlight some practical implications and potential real-world applications of our findings, even if our main focus is more in chemistry than in physics. Random walks are often used as essential models in the field of physical systems to describe the probabilistic movement of particles or entities in different media, such as gases, liquids, or solids. To better understand the connections between the selected structures and physical processes, it is crucial to investigate the fundamental principles and behaviors which lie behind them. This involves exploring the geometric properties, topological arrangements, and dynamic aspects of these formations.

1.1. Global Mean First-Passage Time and the Kemeny Constant

Given a network, the so-called *first-passage time* (FPT) [9] is the estimated time needed by a random walker, starting from an initial point, to reach a particular target point. It represents a sort of metric, associated with a random walk, which helps the understanding of the physical system under observation. On the other hand, the *global mean first-passage time* (GMFPT), denoted also by $\langle T \rangle_g$ (where g stands for 'global'), is a related valuable tool for analyzing the behavior of random walks, since it describes the average of the FPT's obtained from all of the source points in the network.

The GMFPT measures the information propagation efficiency, discovery time, and predicted time for a random walker to visit a target node in a network. It is significant in order to measure the capability of transport operations between nodes in the context of a spiro-ring network. For instance, the GMFPT helps to indicate how quickly particles or information can travel between nodes in spiro-ring networks.

It is useful to emphasize the relevance of the GMFPT over other metrics used to analyze system dynamics. In fact, it presents a unique perspective by measuring the average time it takes for a message, particle, or entity to move from one place to another within the system. With this system-wide perspective, the GMFPT may measure the entire efficiency and dynamics of communication or particle movements, allowing research to find bottlenecks, inefficiencies, or preferred paths. Furthermore, its flexibility to varying system parameters, enables its use in a variety of scenarios, making it an effective tool for evaluating a wide range of systems, including networks, stochastic optimization [9], biological processes [10], finance [11], complex network analysis [12], and many others.

On the other hand, another important probabilistic notion directly associated with random walks in graphs and networks, is the *Kemeny constant* (also known as the Kemeny score), denoted by $\mathcal{K}$. It is a mathematical concept used to rank or order items based on preferences or pairwise comparisons. In the 1950s, Kemeny and Snell [13] established a model that represents the total time-scale associated with relaxation in a Markov chain or kinetic network. In one sentence, the Kemeny constant roughly measures the expected time it takes to go from a randomly chosen state of the network to another randomly chosen one. What is interesting here is that this quantity only depends on the network, and not on the chosen starting state!

The Kemeny constant can be thought of as an indicator of network effectiveness, since it represents the estimated minimum number of steps for a random walk on the network to attain a stationary distribution. It is a helpful statistic to differentiate networks on the basis of their traversal times. Furthermore, the analysis of random walk behavior on a spiro-ring network and the comparison of its characteristics with those of other networks requires the application of the Kemeny constant. It can be used to figure out how information spreads in a spiro-ring network.

The Kemeny constant has also sparked great attention in network research, graph theory, and data analysis. For instance, it is used to compute the Kirchhoff index of graphs, and it is offered as an objective function for optimization in graph clustering algorithms.

1.2. Notation and Definitions

All of the networks and graphs considered in this article are undirected and simple. Let $\mathcal{G}$ be an undirected graph with $|E_{\mathcal{G}}| = m$ and $|V_{\mathcal{G}}| = n$, where $E_{\mathcal{G}}$ and $V_{\mathcal{G}}$ are, respectively, the sets of edges and of vertices of $\mathcal{G}$. In this study, any standard notation and terminology that are not defined will be as defined in the classical literature, e.g., [14].

Let $D_{\mathcal{G}} = diag(d_1, \ldots, d_{|V_{\mathcal{G}}|})$ be the diagonal matrix representing the vertex degrees, where d_i indicates the degree of the vertex v_i in the graph $\mathcal{G}$; and denote by $A_{\mathcal{G}}$ the adjacency matrix, that is, the square matrix whose entry (i, j) is 1 if v_i is adjacent to v_j, and 0 otherwise. The standard matrix representation of a graph is given by its Laplacian matrix $L_{\mathcal{G}}$, which may be defined as $D_{\mathcal{G}} - A_{\mathcal{G}}$. The Laplacian matrix is positive semi-definite, and so its eigenvalues can be ordered in an ascending manner, and it turns out that a graph is connected if and only if the first eigenvalue of its Laplacian matrix is zero (see [14]).

In order to evaluate the spread of the signal network, one may use the first-passage time (FPT), that is, the time needed for a random walker to arrive at a target point starting from a given origin in a minimum number of steps. But also the mean first-passage time (MFPT), which is the average time it takes for a diffusing particle to reach a target position for the first time. One area of research investigates just the relationships between the distribution of the MFPT and the structural features of a network. This relationship can be used to improve search efficiency, but it requires prior knowledge of the target. Hence, in the absence of knowledge regarding the target node, the issue of search efficiency becomes a very difficult problem.

The average expected time across all point pairings of a graph $\mathcal{G}$, represented by $\langle T(\mathcal{G})\rangle_g$, is referred to as the global mean first-passage time (g stands for global), and it is defined as

$$\langle T(\mathcal{G})\rangle_g = \frac{1}{|V_{\mathcal{G}}|(|V_{\mathcal{G}}|-1)} \times \sum_{i \neq j} T_{ij}(\mathcal{G}), \quad (1)$$

where T_{ij} is the number of steps taken for a random walker between nodes i and j.

For a linked network $\mathcal{G}$ with n nodes, Zhu et al. [15] and Gutman and Mohar [16] have separately demonstrated that

$$n \sum_{i=2}^{n} \frac{1}{\gamma_i} = \sum_{i<j} r_{ij}, \quad (2)$$

where $0 = \gamma_1 < \gamma_2 \leq \gamma_3 \leq \ldots \leq \gamma_n$ are the eigenvalues of $L(\mathcal{G})$, and r_{ij} denotes the electric resistance distance between the vertices of the graph $\mathcal{G}$, namely, the resistance between the two respective vertices of an electrical network corresponding to $\mathcal{G}$, with the property that the resistance of each bond joining adjacent vertices is 1.

Chandra et al. [17] presented a novel method for a connected graph $\mathcal{G}$, discovering the following relationship between T_{ij} and r_{ij}:

$$T_{ij} + T_{ji} = 2|E_{\mathcal{G}}| \times r_{ij}. \quad (3)$$

Equation (3) implies, in particular, that $\sum_{i \neq j} T_{ij}(\mathcal{G}) = 2|E_{\mathcal{G}}| \times \sum_{i<j} r_{ij}$.

Therefore, by using all the equations above, we obtain formulae for MFPT:

$$\langle T(\mathcal{G})\rangle_g = \frac{2|E_{\mathcal{G}}|}{|V_{\mathcal{G}}|(|V_{\mathcal{G}}|-1)} \times \sum_{i<j} r_{ij} = \frac{2|E_{\mathcal{G}}|}{(|V_{\mathcal{G}}|-1)} \times \sum_{i=2}^{n} \frac{1}{\gamma_i} \quad (4)$$

On the other hand the Kemeny constant is given by the following formula (see [18]):

$$\mathcal{K}(\mathbb{SP}_n) = \sum_{j=2}^{n} \frac{1}{\gamma_j}, \quad \text{where, again, } \gamma_j \text{ are the eigenvalues of } L(\mathcal{G}). \quad (5)$$

Remark 1. *Note that in both formulae, the first eigenvalue (i.e., for $j = 1$) is zero due to the connectedness of the graph.*

In order to give an idea of the importance and use of the Laplacian matrix in practical applications, let us note that Xiao and Gutman [19] established the feasibility of calculating the resistance distance using the eigenvalues of the Laplacian matrix. In 2018, Zhang et al. [20] determined the GMFPT duration of random walks on Vicsek fractals by means of the Laplacian matrix eigenvalues. In [21], Zeman et al. determined the GMFPT and

Kemeny constant of a random walk of pentagonal networks. In 2021, Ali et al. [22,23] obtained the resistance-distance-based indices of linear pentagonal–quadrilateral networks. Topological indices for chemical graph products, carbon nanotubes, and generalized bridge molecular graphs were discussed by Zhang et al. [24]. Finally, the study conducted by Ullah et al. [25] determined degree-based topological indicators for molecular graphs.

In this article, motivated by previous works [26–28], we establish some explicit closed-form formulae for the GMFPT and Kemeny constant in the context of spiro-ring networks, using the Laplacian decomposition theorem. On the basis of the obtained results, comparative studies are carried out for them.

1.3. Spiro-Ring Networks

Spiro compounds represent a fundamental category of cycloalkanes within the field of organic chemistry. They are biologically active organic compounds with a particular structure, that can be found in a wide variety of natural products. More specifically, these compounds consist of two or more rings which have at least one common atom, represented by a cut-vertex in the corresponding molecular graph. A spiro-hexagonal chain $\mathbb{SP}_n$ is created when a spiro compound consists of hexagonal rings and every cut-vertex is shared by precisely two hexagons. The length of a spiro-hexagonal chain is defined as the number of hexagons it contains. There are different types of substances based on the number of spiro atoms (i.e., the common atoms) they contain, such as monospiro, dispiro, trispiro, and so on. Three straight polyspiro alicyclic hydrocarbons are shown in Figure 1. The basic idea and practical applications of modeling random paths on spiro-ring networks are related in particular to the representation of the structures of spiro compounds in chemistry.

In the present work, we will examine a subcategory of unbranched multispiro molecules whose corresponding graphs are referred to as spiro-hexagonal chains (or chain hexagonal cacti [29], or six-membered ring spiro chains [30]). In particular, these chains, denoted by $\mathbb{SP}_n$, consist of hexagonal rings, while the corresponding networks have $5n$ nodes and $6n$ edges (see Figure 2).

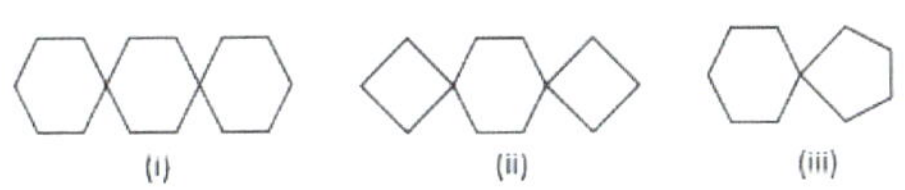

Figure 1. (**i**) Dispiro[5,2,5]hexadecane, (**ii**) spiro[4,5]decane, and (**iii**) dispiro[3,2,3,2]dodecane.

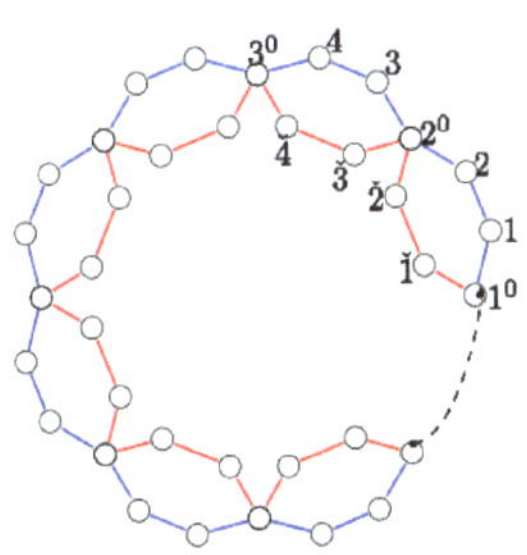

Figure 2. A spiro-ring network $\mathbb{SP}_n$.

The choice of spiro-ring networks as the subject for our study is inspired by their representation of spiro-compound structures in chemistry. Providing a better understanding of the physical principles underpinning the modeling of random walks on molecular structures gives valuable insights for the fundamental dynamics of molecular systems. Random walks are a key framework used to describe the stochastic movement of particles, explore structural distance, and study the kinetics of molecular interactions. By revealing the physical intuition and practical implications of modeling random walks on molecular structures, researchers may increase their knowledge of complex systems and propose novel ways for tackling contemporary issues.

Spreading processes, such as disease transmission or information propagation, are complicated phenomena impacted by multiple variables, including network structure, connection, and dynamics. Although spiro-ring-network-based theoretical models could provide insight into certain elements of spreading processes, their relevance to actual situations has to be carefully considered. Constructing physical spiro-ring networks and performing controlled tests to confirm theoretical predictions may offer considerable obstacles owing to the intricate architecture of these networks and the intricacy of spreading processes. Additionally, turning theoretical models into practical applications, such as creating efficient communication networks or forecasting disease outbreaks, needs exacting empirical evidence and validation from empirical data.

2. Main Lemmas

In the present context, and all through the paper, a square matrix B of order n will be represented by its characteristic polynomial $\varphi(B)$, defined as follows: $\varphi(B) = det(xI_n - B)$. Also, given a graph $\mathcal{G}$, an automorphism of it will be represented as a permutation π of $V_\mathcal{G}$ (the set of vertices of the graph), for which the following property holds: $v_i v_k \in E(\mathcal{G})$ if and only if $\pi(v_j)\pi(v_k)$ is a path in $\mathcal{G}$ (where $E(\mathcal{G})$ is the set of edges of the graph $\mathcal{G}$). Finally, from now on, we will use the notation $\langle T \rangle_g$ and $\mathcal{K}$ for the global mean first-passage time (GMFPT) and the Kemeny constant, respectively.

Based on the vertex labeling of the spiro-ring network $\mathbb{SP}_n$ shown in Figure 2, it is clear that $V_\mathcal{G}$ can be expressed as the union of three disjoint sets: $V_0 = \{1^0, 2^0, \ldots, n^0\}$, $V_1 = \{1, 2, \ldots, 2n\}$, and $V_2 = \{\check{1}, \check{2}, \ldots, \check{2n}\}$. This means that $|V_\mathcal{G}| = 5n$, while $|E_\mathcal{G}| = 6n$. It is also obvious that

$$\pi = (1^0)(2^0)\cdots(n^0)(1,\check{1})(2,\check{2})\cdots(2n,\check{2n}),$$

is an automorphism of $\mathbb{SP}_n$. Thus, the Laplacian matrix $L(\mathbb{SP}_n)$ can be represented in the form of the following block matrices:

$$L(\mathbb{SP}_n) = \begin{pmatrix} L_{V_{00}} & L_{V_{01}} & L_{V_{02}} \\ L_{V_{10}} & L_{V_{11}} & L_{V_{12}} \\ L_{V_{20}} & L_{V_{21}} & L_{V_{22}} \end{pmatrix},$$

where $L_{V_{ik}}$ represents the sub-matrix corresponding to the vertices of V_i and V_k, respectively, where $i, k \in \{0, 1, 2\}$. Further, $L_{V_{11}} = L_{V_{22}}$ thanks to the automorphism of $\mathcal{G}$ associated with π. Let

$$P = \begin{pmatrix} I_n & 0 & 0 \\ 0 & \frac{1}{\sqrt{2}} I_{2n} & \frac{1}{\sqrt{2}} I_{2n} \\ 0 & \frac{1}{\sqrt{2}} I_{2n} & -\frac{1}{\sqrt{2}} I_{2n} \end{pmatrix}$$

be the matrix of blocks whose dimensions are the same as those of the blocks in $L(\mathbb{SP}_n)$. Then, we have that

$$PL(\mathbb{SP}_n)P' = \begin{pmatrix} L_R(\mathbb{SP}_n) & 0 \\ 0 & L_S(\mathbb{SP}_n) \end{pmatrix},$$

where P' represents the transpose of P,

$$L_R(\mathbb{SP}_n) = \begin{pmatrix} L_{V_{00}} & \sqrt{2} L_{V_{01}} \\ \sqrt{2} L_{V_{10}} & L_{V_{11}} + L_{V_{12}} \end{pmatrix}, \text{ and } L_S(\mathbb{SP}_n) = L_{V_{11}} - L_{V_{12}}. \quad (6)$$

The Laplacian polynomial decomposition theorem is expressed by the following lemma:

Lemma 1 ([31]). *Assume that $L_R(\mathbb{SP}_n)$ and $L_S(\mathbb{SP}_n)$ are the matrices described above. Then,*

$$\varphi(L(\mathbb{SP}_n)) = \varphi(L_R(\mathbb{SP}_n)) \cdot \varphi(L_S(\mathbb{SP}_n)).$$

In accordance with Lemma 1, we initially determine the eigenvalues of the Laplacian for $\mathbb{SP}_n$. Subsequently, we will provide the formula for the summation of the reciprocal and products of the eigenvalues of the Laplacian. This formulation serves as the motivation for calculating $\mathcal{K}$ and $\langle T(\mathcal{G})\rangle_g$. According to the structure of Figure 2, we obtain that $L_{V_{00}} = 4I_n$ and $L_{V_{12}} = O_{2n\times 2n}$ So, $L_{V_{01}}$ and $L_{V_{11}}$ are matrices of sizes $n \times (2n)$ and $(2n) \times (2n)$, respectively, as shown below:

$$L_{V_{01}} = \begin{pmatrix} -1 & 0 & 0 & 0 & 0 & \cdots & -1 \\ 0 & -1 & -1 & 0 & 0 & \cdots & 0 \\ 0 & 0 & 0 & -1 & -1 & \cdots & 0 \\ \vdots & \vdots & \vdots & \vdots & \vdots & \ddots & \vdots \\ 0 & 0 & 0 & 0 & 0 & \cdots & 0 \end{pmatrix}, \text{ and } L_{V_{11}} = \begin{pmatrix} 2 & -1 & 0 & 0 & \cdots & 0 & 0 \\ -1 & 2 & 0 & 0 & \cdots & 0 & 0 \\ 0 & 0 & 2 & -1 & \cdots & 0 & 0 \\ 0 & 0 & -1 & 2 & \cdots & 0 & 0 \\ \vdots & \vdots & \vdots & \vdots & \ddots & \vdots & \vdots \\ 0 & 0 & 0 & 0 & \cdots & 2 & -1 \\ 0 & 0 & 0 & 0 & \cdots & -1 & 2 \end{pmatrix}_{2n\times 2n}.$$

Therefore,

$$L_R = \begin{pmatrix} 4 & 0 & 0 & \cdots & 0 & -\sqrt{2} & 0 & 0 & 0 & 0 & \cdots & -\sqrt{2} \\ 0 & 4 & 0 & \cdots & 0 & 0 & -\sqrt{2} & -\sqrt{2} & 0 & 0 & \cdots & 0 \\ 0 & 0 & 4 & \cdots & 0 & 0 & 0 & 0 & -\sqrt{2} & -\sqrt{2} & \cdots & 0 \\ \vdots & \vdots & \vdots & \ddots & \vdots & \vdots & \vdots & \vdots & \vdots & \vdots & \ddots & \vdots \\ 0 & 0 & 0 & \cdots & 4 & 0 & 0 & 0 & 0 & 0 & \cdots & 0 \\ -\sqrt{2} & 0 & 0 & \cdots & 0 & 2 & -1 & 0 & 0 & 0 & \cdots & 0 \\ 0 & -\sqrt{2} & 0 & & 0 & -1 & 2 & 0 & 0 & 0 & \cdots & 0 \\ 0 & -\sqrt{2} & 0 & \cdots & 0 & 0 & 0 & 2 & -1 & 0 & \cdots & 0 \\ 0 & 0 & -\sqrt{2} & \cdots & 0 & 0 & 0 & -1 & 2 & 0 & \cdots & 0 \\ 0 & 0 & -\sqrt{2} & \cdots & 0 & 0 & 0 & 0 & 0 & 2 & \cdots & 0 \\ \vdots & \vdots & \vdots & \ddots & \vdots & \vdots & \vdots & \vdots & \vdots & \vdots & \ddots & \vdots \\ -\sqrt{2} & 0 & 0 & \cdots & 0 & 0 & 0 & 0 & 0 & 0 & \cdots & 2 \end{pmatrix}_{3n\times 3n},$$

and $L_S = L_{V_{11}}$.

The matrix determinant lemma can be used in order to calculate the determinant of a square matrix of a rank-one perturbation.

Lemma 2 ([32]). *Let H_{11}, H_{12}, H_{21}, and H_{22} be matrices of orders $n \times m$, $n \times n$, $m \times n$, and $m \times m$, respectively. Assume that H_{22} is invertible. Then,*

$$\det\begin{pmatrix} H_{11} & H_{12} \\ H_{21} & H_{22} \end{pmatrix} = \det(H_{22}) \cdot \det(H_{11} - H_{12}H_{22}^{-1}H_{21}),$$

and $H_{11} - H_{12}H_{22}^{-1}H_{21}$ is called the Schur complement of H_{22}.

3. Kemeny's Constant and the GMFPT of Spiro-Ring Networks

Spiro-ring networks, known for their hexagonal configuration of interconnected nodes in a spiral pattern, are widely used in several fields due to their specific topology and features. Thanks to their distinctive topology, with a spiral arrangement of interconnected nodes, they have various applications. Researchers can use the implications of the GMFPT and the Kemeny constant to make informed choices that improve the reliability, efficiency, and scalability of spiro-ring networks in many areas, like telecommunications, transportation systems, and biological modeling. Furthermore, these observations provide new opportunities for the creation of innovative applications and technologies which employ the distinct characteristics of spiro-ring networks to tackle complex issues and propel progress in connectivity and communication.

One can easily apply Lemma 1 and Equation (5) in order to obtain the Laplacian spectrum of $\mathbb{SP}_n$ by adding the eigenvalues L_S and L_R. In particular, we obtain the following result.

Proposition 1. *Let $\mathbb{SP}_n$ be a spiro-ring network of length n. We have*

$$\mathcal{K}(\mathbb{SP}_n) = \sum_{j=2}^{3n} \frac{1}{\phi_j} + \sum_{k=1}^{2n} \frac{1}{\psi_k}, \quad n \geq 2$$

where ϕ_j, with $1 \leq j \leq 3n$, and ψ_k, with $1 \leq k \leq 2n$, represent the eigenvalues of L_R and L_S, respectively.

The following propositions give the formulae for $\sum_{k=1}^{2n} \frac{1}{\psi_k}$ and $\sum_{j=2}^{3n} \frac{1}{\phi_j}$ in accordance with the relationship between the roots and coefficients of L_S and L_R.

Proposition 2. *Assume that $0 = \psi_1 < \psi_2 \leq \cdots \leq \psi_{2n}$ are the eigenvalues of L_S. Then, $\sum_{j=1}^{2n} \frac{1}{\psi_j} = \frac{4n}{3}$, for $n \geq 2$.*

Proof. Let $\varphi(L_S) = x^{2n} + c_1 x^{2n-1} + \cdots + c_{2n-1}x^2 + c_{2n}$ be the characteristic polynomial. Now, we can precisely affirm that $\psi_1, \psi_2, \ldots, \psi_{2n}$ are actually the roots of the equation $x^{2n-1} + c_1 \cdot x^{2n-2} + \cdots + c_{2n-2} \cdot x + c_{2n-1} = 0$. By Vieta's theorem,

$$\sum_{j=1}^{2n} \frac{1}{\psi_j} = \frac{(-1)^{2n-1} c_{2n-1}}{(-1)^{2n} c_{2n}} = -\frac{c_{2n-1}}{\det(L_S)}. \tag{7}$$

□

Lemma 3. *The constant c_{2n-1} is equal to $-\frac{4}{3}n \cdot 3^n$.*

Proof. We know that

$$L_S = \begin{pmatrix} 2 & -1 & & & & & & \\ -1 & 2 & & & & & & \\ & & 2 & -1 & & & & \\ & & -1 & 2 & & & & \\ & & & & \ddots & & & \\ & & & & & & 2 & -1 \\ & & & & & & -1 & 2 \end{pmatrix}_{2n \times 2n}.$$

We have $\det(L_S(1)) = 3$, $\det(L_S(2)) = 9$ and $\det(L_S) = 3^n$, and so

$$\begin{aligned} c_{3n-1} &= \sum_{j=1}^{2n} \det(-L_S(\{j\}|\{j\})) = (-1)^{2n-1} \sum_{j=1}^{2n} \det(-L_S(\{j\}|\{j\})) \\ &= -\frac{2}{3} \sum_{j=1}^{2n} 3^n \\ &= -\frac{4}{3} n \cdot 3^n. \end{aligned}$$

□

As a result, we have proved Proposition 2.

Proposition 3. *Assume that* $0 = \phi_1 < \phi_2 \leq \cdots \leq \phi_{3n}$ *are the eigenvalues of* L_R. *Then, we have that* $\sum\limits_{j=2}^{3n} \frac{1}{\phi_j} = \frac{75n^2-11}{120}$.

Proof. As before, let $\varphi(L_R) = x^{3n} + b_1 x^{3n-1} + \cdots + b_{3n-2}x^2 + b_{3n-1}x$ be the characteristic polynomial. We can precisely determine $\phi_2, \phi_3, \ldots, \phi_{3n}$ as the roots of the equation: $x^{3n-1} + b_1 x^{3n-2} + \cdots + b_{3n-2}x + b_{3n-1} = 0$. From Vieta's formula, we have

$$\sum_{j=2}^{3n} \frac{1}{\phi_j} = -\frac{b_{3n-2}}{b_{3n-1}}. \tag{8}$$

□

The following two lemmas specify the expressions for b_{3n-2} and b_{3n-1}, respectively.

Lemma 4. $b_{3n-1} = (-1)^{n-1}\frac{15}{2} \cdot n^2 2^n$.

Proof. Refer to the Appendix A for the proof. □

Lemma 5. $b_{3n-2} = (-1)^n 2^n \frac{15(75n^4-11n^2)}{16}$.

Proof. Refer to the Appendix A for the proof. As a result, we have proved Proposition 3. □

Theorem 1. *Let* $\mathbb{SP}_n$ *be a spiro-ring network of length n (i.e., with n hexagons) and denote by* $\mathcal{K}$ *its Kemeny's constant. Then,*

$$\mathcal{K}(\mathbb{SP}_n) = \frac{75n^2 + 160n - 11}{120}.$$

Proof. Putting together Propositions 2 and 3 in the formula from Proposition 1, we obtain the desired result. □

Theorem 2. *Let* $\langle T(\mathbb{SP}_n)\rangle_g$ *represent the GMFPT of* $\mathbb{SP}_n$ *(a spiro-ring network of length n). Then,*

$$\langle T(\mathbb{SP}_n)\rangle_g = \frac{12}{5(5n-1)}\left(\frac{75n^2 + 160n - 11}{120}\right).$$

Proof. Putting together Propositions 2 and 3 in Equation (4), and noting that $|E_{\mathbb{SP}_n}| = 6n$, the desired result follows easily. □

In order to overcome any potential limitations of the graph spectrum method, we used the decomposition theorem of Laplacian polynomials to compute the Laplacian matrix, GMFPT, and Kemeny's constant for spiro-ring networks. This methodology enabled us to surpass the constraints of the graph spectrum method by integrating supplementary mathematical tools to obtain more precise analysis and outcomes.

Comparison

In this section, we present graphical representations of the relationship between Kemeny's constant $\mathcal{K}$ and GMFPT $\langle T\rangle_g$. The results obtained in Theorems 1 and 2 suggest that, within the network scales under consideration, there exists a linear and direct proportional connection between the quantities $\mathcal{K}(\mathbb{SP}_n)$ and $\langle T(\mathbb{SP}_n)\rangle_g$ as n varies. Our exact results are confirmed in Figure 3a,b, which indicate how $\mathcal{K}(\mathbb{SP}_n)$ and $\langle T(\mathbb{SP}_n)\rangle_g$ rises as the value of n increases. Similarly, in Figure 4, we just compare $\mathcal{K}(\mathbb{SP}_n)$ and $\langle T(\mathbb{SP}_n)\rangle_g$. Our analysis presents some fresh perspectives that make it simple to identify the structure of our network.

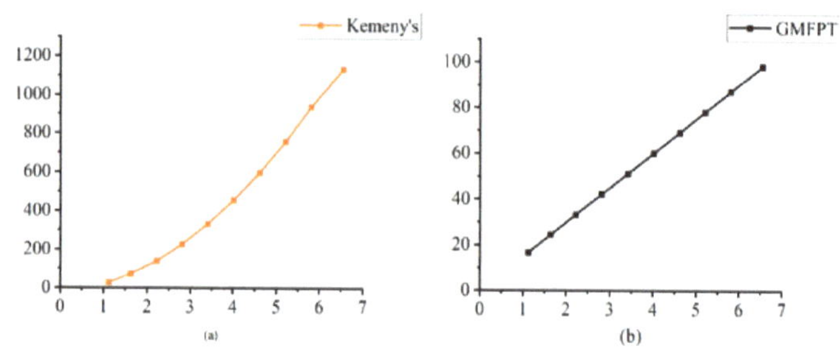

Figure 3. (**a**) Kemeny's constant $\mathcal{K}(\mathbb{SP}_n)$ and (**b**) GMFPT $\langle T(\mathbb{SP}_n)\rangle_g$.

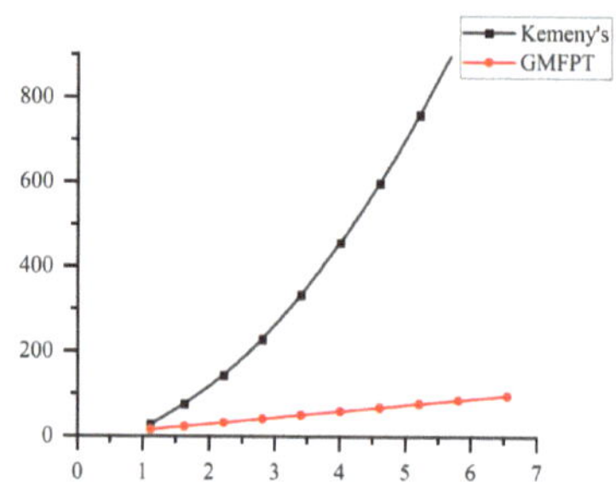

Figure 4. Comparison of $\mathcal{K}(\mathbb{SP}_n)$ and $\langle T(\mathbb{SP}_n)\rangle_g$.

The comparison study of Kemeny's constant and the GMFPT entails the examination of resulting metrics to evaluate the network efficiency, navigability, robustness, and scalability. The GMFPT gives insight into the average time it takes for objects to traverse the spiro-ring network, which is useful for assessing the overall network efficiency. Researchers can evaluate the impact of various network configurations or characteristics on the network efficiency and navigability by comparing the resulting matrices of the GMFPT and the Kemeny constant. These comparative studies offer useful insights into the efficiency and features of spiro-ring networks (see also Figure 5). They inform the design of networks, optimization methodologies, and decision-making processes to improve network efficacy in different applications.

Figure 5. Comparative graph with existing spiro techniques.

4. Conclusions

In the present study, we have dealt with the analysis of some important quantities for spiro-ring networks $\mathbb{SP}_n$ that are very relevant in network theory. For instance, the famous Kemeny constant $\mathcal{K}$ is a significant and valuable quantifier that finds several applications in a wide range of topics, particularly within the realm of Markov chains; whereas the GMFPT (global mean first-passage time) is the average of the mean first-passage times over the starting point of the walker, and it is considered as a quantitative indicator of the transport efficiency of a network.

In this paper, we emphasize the importance of employing the Laplacian matrix when analyzing graph structures, specifically when performing operations like partitioning a graph into communities or clusters. We demonstrate that the Laplacian matrix's eigenvalues provide useful insights into different elements of a graph, such as its connectivity qualities, spectrum, and the behavior of random walks inside the network. The Laplacian matrix is a powerful tool that may be utilized to analyze the intricate architecture of complex networks, such as social networks, transportation networks, and biological networks.

For instance, through the utilization of the spectra of the Laplacian of $\mathbb{SP}_n$, precise closed-form formulae have been established both for the GMFPT and $\mathcal{K}$ for $\mathbb{SP}_n$ networks. Finally, we performed a graphic comparison between them. The results derived from this study will be useful for further investigations in the field of network science.

Research in the field of deterministic structures is both relevant and intriguing due to the significant advancements in supramolecular experimental methods, which enable the chemical synthesis of a wide range of polymers with controlled molecular architectures, including molecular fractals. These models could assist in chemistry by providing insight into solvent effects, molecule binding, and reaction kinetics, which can then be used to develop novel materials or catalysts. Random walk models are used in biophysics to clarify the processes of molecular transport inside cells, the folding dynamics of proteins, and the building of biomolecular complexes. Furthermore, the ideas described in studies of spreading processes on spiro-ring networks could be applied to random graph models defined by blocked structures, such as the stochastic block model (SBM). The SBM is a widely used probabilistic model for modeling networks with a community structure, where nodes are divided into blocks or communities with dense connections inside blocks and sparser connections between blocks. Furthermore, expanding the research to blocked structures allows for the examination of other aspects that may affect spreading processes, such as the number and density of communities, the strength of inter-community linkages, and the existence of overlapping communities.

Author Contributions: Investigation, Y.A., U.A., D.E.O. and X.-F.P. All authors have read and agreed to the published version of the manuscript.

Funding: This research received no external funding.

Data Availability Statement: No new data were created or analyzed in this study. Data sharing is not applicable to this article.

Acknowledgments: We warmly thank the referees for the comments and the editor for the help.

Conflicts of Interest: The authors declare no conflicts of interest.

Appendix A

Lemma A1. *Let* $m \in \{1, 2, \ldots, 2n\}$ *and* $A_m = \begin{pmatrix} -\frac{3}{2} & 1 & & & & & \\ 1 & -\frac{3}{2} & \frac{1}{2} & & & & \\ & \frac{1}{2} & -\frac{3}{2} & 1 & & & \\ & & 1 & -\frac{3}{2} & & & \\ & & & & \ddots & & \\ & & & & & -\frac{3}{2} & 1 \\ & & & & & 1 & -\frac{3}{2} \end{pmatrix}_{m\times m}$.

Then, $\det(A_m) = \begin{cases} \left(\frac{1}{2}\right)^{\frac{m}{2}}\left(\frac{3m}{4}+1\right), & \text{when } m \text{ is even;} \\ -\left(\frac{1}{2}\right)^{\frac{m-1}{2}}\left(\frac{3m+3}{4}\right), & \text{when } m \text{ is odd.} \end{cases}$

Proof. When $m = 1, 2, 3, 4$, we have $\det(A_m) = -\frac{3}{2}, \frac{5}{4}, -\frac{3}{2}, 1$, respectively, and for $5 \le m \le 2n$, we possess the recurrence relationship $\det(A_m) = \det(A_{m-2}) - \frac{1}{4}\det(A_{m-4})$. When this relationship is resolved, we have

$$\det(A_m) = \begin{cases} \left(\frac{1}{2}\right)^{\frac{m}{2}}\left(\frac{3m}{4}+1\right), & \text{when } m \text{ is even;} \\ -\left(\frac{1}{2}\right)^{\frac{m-1}{2}}\left(\frac{3m+3}{4}\right), & \text{when } m \text{ is odd.} \end{cases}$$

□

Lemma A2. *Let* $m \in \{1, 2, \ldots, 2n\}$ *and* $D_m = \begin{pmatrix} -\frac{3}{2} & \frac{1}{2} & & & & & \\ \frac{1}{2} & -\frac{3}{2} & 1 & & & & \\ & 1 & -\frac{3}{2} & \frac{1}{2} & & & \\ & & \frac{1}{2} & -\frac{3}{2} & & & \\ & & & & \ddots & & \\ & & & & & -\frac{3}{2} & \frac{1}{2} \\ & & & & & \frac{1}{2} & -\frac{3}{2} \end{pmatrix}_{m\times m}$.

Then, $\det(D_m) = \left(\frac{1}{2}\right)^{\frac{m}{2}}\left(\frac{3m}{4}+1\right)$, *when* m *is even.*

Proof. It follows in the same vein as for the above Lemma A1. □

Lemma A3. *Let* $m \in \{1, 2, \ldots, 2n\}$ *and* $C_m = \begin{pmatrix} -2 & 1 & & & & & & \\ 1 & -\frac{3}{2} & \frac{1}{2} & & & & & \\ & \frac{1}{2} & -\frac{3}{2} & 1 & & & & \\ & & 1 & -\frac{3}{2} & & & & \\ & & & & \ddots & & & \\ & & & & & -\frac{3}{2} & \frac{1}{2} & \\ & & & & & \frac{1}{2} & -\frac{3}{2} & 1 \\ & & & & & & 1 & -\frac{3}{2} \end{pmatrix}_{m\times m}$.

Then, $\det(C_m) = \begin{cases} \left(\frac{1}{2}\right)^{\frac{m}{2}}\left(\frac{3m}{2}+1\right), & \text{when } m \text{ is even;} \\ -\left(\frac{1}{2}\right)^{\frac{m-1}{2}}\left(\frac{3m+1}{2}\right), & \text{when } m \text{ is odd.} \end{cases}$

Proof. Let e_j represent the m-vector $(0,\ldots,0,1,0,\ldots,0)$, with 1 at the jth position. Then, we have $C_m = A_m - \frac{1}{2}e_1e_1^T$.
So, $\det(C_m) = \det(A_m) - \frac{1}{2}e_1^T adj(A_m)e_1 = \det(A_m) - \frac{1}{2}cof[A_m(1,1)]$. (Here, we denote by $cof[N(j,k)]$ the cofactor of the entry located at position (j,k) of a square matrix N).

Now, $\det(C_1) = -2$, $\det(C_2) = 2$, $\det(C_3) = -\frac{5}{2}$, and $\det(C_4) = \frac{7}{4}$. Hence, the lemma is proved for $m = 1,2,3,4$. In the other cases, when $5 \leq m \leq 2n$, we obtain

$$
\begin{aligned}
\det(C_m) &= \begin{cases} \det(A_m) - \frac{1}{2}\det(A_{m-1}), & \text{when } m \text{ is even;} \\ \det(A_m) - \frac{1}{2}\det(D_{m-1}), & \text{when } m \text{ is odd.} \end{cases} \\
&= \begin{cases} \left(\frac{1}{2}\right)^{\frac{m}{2}}\left(\frac{3m}{2}+1\right), & \text{when } m \text{ is even;} \\ -\left(\frac{1}{2}\right)^{\frac{m-1}{2}}\left(\frac{3m+1}{2}\right), & \text{when } m \text{ is odd.} \end{cases}
\end{aligned}
$$

And the result follows for any $m = 1,2,\ldots,2n$. □

Proof of Lemma 4. Let $\mathfrak{B}(\{j\}|\{k\})$ represent the sub-matrix of $\mathfrak{B}$ created by deleting its jth row and kth column of $\mathfrak{B}$. To find b_{3n-1} we proceed to examine the subsequent cases.
Case A1. Let us consider $1 \leq j \leq n$, then

$$
\det(-L_R(\{j\}|\{j\})) = \begin{vmatrix} -4I_{n-1} & -\sqrt{2}L_{V_{01}}(\{j\}|\{\}) \\ -\sqrt{2}L_{V_{01}}(\{j\}|\{\})^T & \chi \end{vmatrix} = \begin{vmatrix} -4I_{n-1} & 0 \\ 0 & \Re \end{vmatrix},
$$

where $\Re = \chi + \frac{1}{2}L_{V_{01}}(\{j\}|\{\})^T L_{V_{01}}(\{j\}|\{\})$ and $\chi = -L_{V_{11}}$.
By Lemma 2, we have $\det(-L_R(\{j\}|\{j\})) = \det(-4I_{n-1})\det(\Re)$, for $j = 1,2,\ldots,n$.
To estimate the $\det(\Re)$, we have to examine the sub-cases listed below.
Subcase 1(a): When $j = 1$, let $R_{2n} = \chi + \frac{1}{2}L_{V_{01}}(\{1\}|\{\})^T L_{V_{01}}(\{1\}|\{\})$. Then,

$$
R_{2n} = \begin{pmatrix} -2 & 1 & & & & & \\ 1 & -\frac{3}{2} & \frac{1}{2} & & & & \\ & \frac{1}{2} & -\frac{3}{2} & 1 & & & \\ & & & \ddots & & & \\ & & & & -\frac{3}{2} & \frac{1}{2} & \\ & & & & \frac{1}{2} & -\frac{3}{2} & 1 \\ & & & & & 1 & -2 \end{pmatrix}_{2n\times 2n} = C_{2n} + \frac{1}{2}e_{2n}e_{2n}^T.
$$

So,

$$
\begin{aligned}
\det(\Re_{2n}) &= \det(C_{2n}) + \frac{1}{2}e_{2n}^T adj(C_{2n})e_{2n} \text{ (see Lemma A3)} \\
&= \det(C_{2n}) + \frac{1}{2}cof[C_{2n}(2n,2n)] \\
&= \left(\frac{1}{2}\right)^n(3n+1) + \frac{1}{2}\left(\frac{1}{2}\right)^{n-1}(3n-1) \\
&= \left(\frac{1}{2}\right)^n 6n.
\end{aligned}
$$

Subcase 1(b): When $1 \leq j \leq n$,

$$
\begin{aligned}
&\chi + \frac{1}{2}L_{V_{01}}(\{j\}|\{\})^T L_{V_{01}}(\{j\}|\{\}) \\
&= \begin{pmatrix}
-\frac{3}{2} & 1 & 0 & 0 & \cdots & 0 & 0 & 0 & 0 & \cdots & \frac{1}{2} \\
1 & -\frac{3}{2} & \frac{1}{2} & 0 & \cdots & 0 & 0 & 0 & 0 & \cdots & 0 \\
0 & \frac{1}{2} & -\frac{3}{2} & 1 & \cdots & 0 & 0 & 0 & 0 & \cdots & 0 \\
\vdots & \vdots & \vdots & \vdots & \ddots & \vdots & \vdots & \vdots & \vdots & \ddots & \vdots \\
0 & 0 & 0 & 0 & \cdots & -2 & 0 & 0 & 0 & \cdots & 0 \\
0 & 0 & 0 & 0 & \cdots & 0 & -2 & 1 & 0 & \cdots & 0 \\
0 & 0 & 0 & 0 & \cdots & 0 & 0 & -\frac{3}{2} & \frac{1}{2} & \cdots & 0 \\
0 & 0 & 0 & 0 & \cdots & 0 & 0 & \frac{1}{2} & -\frac{3}{2} & \cdots & 0 \\
\vdots & \vdots & \vdots & \vdots & \ddots & \vdots & \vdots & \vdots & \vdots & \ddots & \vdots \\
\frac{1}{2} & 0 & 0 & 0 & \cdots & 0 & 0 & 0 & 0 & \cdots & -\frac{3}{2}
\end{pmatrix}_{2n\times 2n}
\end{aligned}
$$

$$
= \begin{pmatrix}
-\frac{3}{2} & 1 & 0 & 0 & \cdots & 0 & 0 & 0 & 0 & \cdots & 0 \\
1 & -\frac{3}{2} & \frac{1}{2} & 0 & \cdots & 0 & 0 & 0 & 0 & \cdots & 0 \\
0 & \frac{1}{2} & -\frac{3}{2} & 1 & \cdots & 0 & 0 & 0 & 0 & \cdots & 0 \\
\vdots & \vdots & \vdots & \vdots & \ddots & \vdots & \vdots & \vdots & \vdots & \ddots & \vdots \\
0 & 0 & 0 & 0 & \cdots & -2 & 0 & 0 & 0 & \cdots & 0 \\
0 & 0 & 0 & 0 & \cdots & 0 & -2 & 1 & 0 & \cdots & 0 \\
0 & 0 & 0 & 0 & \cdots & 0 & 0 & -\frac{3}{2} & \frac{1}{2} & \cdots & 0 \\
0 & 0 & 0 & 0 & \cdots & 0 & 0 & \frac{1}{2} & -\frac{3}{2} & \cdots & 0 \\
\vdots & \vdots & \vdots & \vdots & \ddots & \vdots & \vdots & \vdots & \vdots & \ddots & \vdots \\
0 & 0 & 0 & 0 & \cdots & 0 & 0 & 0 & 0 & \cdots & -\frac{3}{2}
\end{pmatrix} + \frac{1}{2}e_1 e_{2n}^T + \frac{1}{2}e_{2n}e_1^T
$$

$$
= \begin{pmatrix} C_{2j-2} & 0 \\ 0 & C_{2n-2j+2} \end{pmatrix} + \frac{1}{2}e_1 e_{2n}^T + \frac{1}{2}e_{2n}e_1^T \text{ (see Lemma A3).}
$$

Since, $\det\left(\begin{pmatrix} C_{2j-2} & 0 \\ 0 & C_{2n-2j+2} \end{pmatrix} + \frac{1}{2}e_1 e_{2n}^T\right) = \det\begin{pmatrix} C_{2j-2} & 0 \\ 0 & C_{2n-2j+2} \end{pmatrix}$,

$$
\begin{aligned}
\det\left(\chi + \frac{1}{2}L_{V_{01}}(\{j\}|\{\})^T L_{V_{01}}(\{j\}|\{\})\right) &= \det(C_{2j-2}) \cdot \det(C_{2n-2j+2}) \\
&\quad + (-1)^{2n+1}\frac{1}{2} \cdot \frac{1}{2}\det(C_{2j-3}) \cdot \det(C_{2n-2j+1}) \\
&= \left(\frac{1}{2}\right)^n 6n.
\end{aligned}
$$

Therefore, $\det\left(\chi + \frac{1}{2}L_{V_{01}}(\{j\}|\{\})^T L_{V_{01}}(\{j\}|\{\})\right) = \left(\frac{1}{2}\right)^n 6n$, for $1 \le j \le n$.

Case A2. Take the case when $n+1 \le j \le 3n$, let $r = j - n$, we have

$$
\det(-L_R(\{r\}|\{r\})) = \begin{vmatrix} -4I_n & -\sqrt{2}L_{V_{01}}(\{\}|\{r\}) \\ -\sqrt{2}L_{V_{01}}(\{\}|\{r\})^T & \chi(\{r\}|\{r\}) \end{vmatrix} = \begin{vmatrix} -4I_n & 0 \\ 0 & \Re_1 \end{vmatrix},
$$

where $\Re_1 = \chi(\{r\}|\{r\}) + \frac{1}{2}L_{V_{01}}(\{\}|\{r\})^T L_{V_{01}}(\{\}|\{r\})$ and $\chi = -L_{V_{11}}$.

Apply Lemma 2, $-4I_n$ in the preceding determinant, we have $\det(-L_R(\{r\}|\{r\})) = \det(-4I_n) \cdot \det(\Re_1)$, for $r = 1, 2, \ldots, 2n$. To estimate $\det(\Re_1)$, the following subcases need our attention:

Subcase 2(a): If $1 \le r \le 2n$,

$$
\begin{aligned}
\Re_1 &= \chi(\{r\}|\{r\}) + \frac{1}{2}L_{V_{01}}(\{\}|\{r\})^T L_{V_{01}}(\{\}|\{r\}) \\
&= \begin{pmatrix}
-\frac{3}{2} & 1 & 0 & 0 & \cdots & 0 & 0 & 0 & 0 & \cdots & \frac{1}{2} \\
1 & -\frac{3}{2} & \frac{1}{2} & 0 & \cdots & 0 & 0 & 0 & 0 & \cdots & 0 \\
0 & \frac{1}{2} & -\frac{3}{2} & 1 & \cdots & 0 & 0 & 0 & 0 & \cdots & 0 \\
\vdots & \vdots & \vdots & \vdots & \ddots & \vdots & \vdots & \vdots & \vdots & \ddots & \vdots \\
0 & 0 & 0 & 0 & \cdots & -\frac{3}{2} & 0 & 0 & 0 & \cdots & 0 \\
0 & 0 & 0 & 0 & \cdots & 0 & -\frac{3}{2} & \cdots & 0 & 0 & 0 \\
\vdots & \vdots & \vdots & \vdots & \ddots & \vdots & \vdots & \ddots & \vdots & \ddots & \vdots \\
0 & 0 & 0 & 0 & \cdots & 0 & 0 & \cdots & -\frac{3}{2} & \frac{1}{2} & 0 \\
0 & 0 & 0 & 0 & \cdots & 0 & 0 & \cdots & \frac{1}{2} & -\frac{3}{2} & 1 \\
\frac{1}{2} & 0 & 0 & 0 & \cdots & 0 & 0 & \cdots & 0 & 1 & -\frac{3}{2}
\end{pmatrix}_{2n-1\times 2n-1}
\end{aligned}
$$

$$
= \begin{pmatrix}
-\frac{3}{2} & 1 & 0 & 0 & \cdots & 0 & 0 & 0 & 0 & \cdots & 0 \\
1 & -\frac{3}{2} & \frac{1}{2} & 0 & \cdots & 0 & 0 & 0 & 0 & \cdots & 0 \\
0 & \frac{1}{2} & -\frac{3}{2} & 1 & \cdots & 0 & 0 & 0 & 0 & \cdots & 0 \\
\vdots & \vdots & \vdots & \vdots & \ddots & \vdots & \vdots & \vdots & \vdots & \ddots & \vdots \\
0 & 0 & 0 & 0 & \cdots & -\frac{3}{2} & 0 & 0 & 0 & \cdots & 0 \\
0 & 0 & 0 & 0 & \cdots & 0 & -\frac{3}{2} & \cdots & 0 & 0 & 0 \\
\vdots & \vdots & \vdots & \vdots & \ddots & \vdots & \vdots & \ddots & \vdots & \ddots & \vdots \\
0 & 0 & 0 & 0 & \cdots & 0 & 0 & \cdots & -\frac{3}{2} & \frac{1}{2} & 0 \\
0 & 0 & 0 & 0 & \cdots & 0 & 0 & \cdots & \frac{1}{2} & -\frac{3}{2} & 1 \\
0 & 0 & 0 & 0 & \cdots & 0 & 0 & \cdots & 0 & 1 & -\frac{3}{2}
\end{pmatrix} + \frac{1}{2}e_1 e_{2n-1}^T + \frac{1}{2}e_{2n-1}e_1^T
$$

$$= \begin{pmatrix} A_{r-1} & 0 \\ 0 & A_{2n-r} \end{pmatrix} + \frac{1}{2}e_1e_{2n-1}^T + \frac{1}{2}e_{2n-1}e_1^T \text{ (see Lemma A1)}$$
$$= \chi_1 + \frac{1}{2}e_{2n-1}e_1^T, \; where \; \chi_1 = \begin{pmatrix} A_{r-1} & 0 \\ 0 & A_{2n-r} \end{pmatrix}.$$

Since $\det\left(\chi_1 + \frac{1}{2}e_1e_{2n-1}^T\right) = \det(\chi_1) = \det(A_{r-1}) \cdot \det(A_{2n-r})$, then we have that

$$\det\left(\chi_1 + \frac{1}{2}e_1e_{2n-1}^T + \frac{1}{2}e_{2n-1}e_1^T)\right) =$$
$$\det\left(\chi_1 + \frac{1}{2}e_1e_{2n-1}^T\right) + \frac{1}{2}e_1^T \cdot adj\left(\chi_1 + \frac{1}{2}e_1e_{2n-1}^T\right) \cdot e_{2n-1} =$$
$$\begin{cases} det(\chi_1) + (-1)^{2n-1}\frac{det(A_{r-2})\cdot det(D_{2n-r-1})}{4}, & \text{if } r = \text{odd}; \\ det(\chi_1) + (-1)^{2n-1}\frac{det(A_{2n-r-1})\cdot det(D_{r-2})}{4}, & \text{if } r = \text{even}. \end{cases}$$
$$= -\left(\frac{1}{2}\right)^n 3n.$$

Subcase 2(b): If $r = 2n$, then:

$$\det\left(\chi(\{r\}|\{r\}) + \frac{1}{2}L_{V_{01}}(\{r\}|\{\})^T L_{V_{01}}(\{\}|\{r\})\right) = \det(A_{2n-1})$$
$$= -\left(\frac{1}{2}\right)^n 3n.$$

Therefore, for $1 \le r \le 2n$, i.e., for $n+1 \le j \le 3n$, one has

$$\det\left(\chi(\{r\}|\{r\}) + \frac{1}{2}L_{V_{01}}(\{\}|\{r\})^T L_{V_{01}}(\{\}|\{r\})\right) = -\left(\frac{1}{2}\right)^n 3n.$$

So,

$$\alpha_{3n-1} = \sum_{j=1}^{3n} \det(-L_R(\{j\}|\{j\}))$$
$$= \sum_{j=1}^{n} \det\left(-L_R(\{j\}|\{j\})\right) + \sum_{j=n+1}^{3n} \det\left(-L_R(\{j\}|\{j\})\right)$$
$$= \sum_{j=1}^{n}(-4)^{n-1} \cdot \left(\frac{1}{2}\right)^n 6n + \sum_{j=n+1}^{3n}(-4)^n \cdot (-1)\left(\frac{1}{2}\right)^n 3n$$
$$= (-1)^{n-1}2^{n-1} \cdot 15n^2. \quad \square$$

Proof of Lemma 5. Denote by $\mathfrak{B}(\{j,k\}|\{j,k\})$ the sub-matrix of the matrix $\mathfrak{B}$ after deleting the jth and kth rows and their corresponding columns. Thus,

$$\alpha_{3n-2} = \sum_{1 \le j < k \le 3n} \det(-L_R(\{j,k\}|\{j,k\}))$$
$$= \left(\sum_{1 \le j < k \le n} + \sum_{n+1 \le j < k \le 3n} + \sum_{\substack{1 \le j \le n \\ n+1 \le k \le 3n}}\right) \det(-L_R(\{j,k\}|\{j,k\})).$$

Therefore, we evaluate the subsequent cases.

Case A3. Take the case if $1 \leq j \leq n$,
$\det(-L_R(\{j,k\}|\{j,k\}) = \begin{vmatrix} -4I_{n-2} & -\sqrt{2}L_{V_{01}}(\{j,k\}|\{\}) \\ -\sqrt{2}L_{V_{01}}(\{j,k\}|\{\})^T & \chi \end{vmatrix}$, where $\chi = -L_{V_{11}}$.
Now, we have the subcases listed below.
Subcase 3.1: If $j = 1$ and $2 \leq k \leq n$, apply the Schur complement, we have

$$\begin{aligned} \det\left(\chi + \frac{1}{2}L_{V_{01}}(\{j,k\}|\{j,k\})^T L_{V_{V01}}(\{j,k\}|\{j,k\})\right) &= \begin{vmatrix} R_{2k-2} & 0 \\ 0 & R_{2n-2k+2} \end{vmatrix} \\ &= \det(R_{2k-2}) \cdot \det(R_{2n-2k+2}) \\ &= \left(\frac{1}{2}\right)^n 36(k-j)(n-k+1). \end{aligned}$$

Subcase 3.2: If $1 < j < k \leq n$, $R' = \chi + \frac{1}{2}L_{V_{01}}(\{j,k\}|\{j,k\})^T L_{V_{V01}}(\{j,k\}|\{j,k\})$

$$\begin{aligned} &= \begin{pmatrix} -\frac{3}{2} & 1 & 0 & 0 & \cdots & 0 & 0 & 0 & 0 & \cdots \\ 0 & 0 & 0 & 0 & 0 & \cdots & 0 & \frac{1}{2} \\ 1 & -\frac{3}{2} & \frac{1}{2} & 0 & \cdots & 0 & 0 & 0 & 0 & \cdots \\ 0 & 0 & 0 & 0 & 0 & \cdots & 0 & 0 \\ 0 & \frac{1}{2} & -\frac{3}{2} & 1 & \cdots & 0 & 0 & 0 & 0 & \cdots \\ 0 & 0 & 0 & 0 & 0 & \cdots & 0 & 0 \\ \vdots & \vdots & \vdots & \vdots & \ddots & \vdots & \vdots & \vdots & \vdots & \ddots \\ \vdots & \vdots & \vdots & \vdots & \vdots & \ddots & \vdots & \vdots \\ 0 & 0 & 0 & 0 & \cdots & -2 & 0 & 0 & 0 & \cdots \\ 0 & 0 & 0 & 0 & 0 & \cdots & 0 & 0 \\ 0 & 0 & 0 & 0 & \cdots & 0 & -2 & 1 & 0 & \cdots \\ 0 & 0 & 0 & 0 & 0 & \cdots & 0 & 0 \\ 0 & 0 & 0 & 0 & \cdots & 0 & 1 & -\frac{3}{2} & \frac{1}{2} & \cdots \\ 0 & 0 & 0 & 0 & 0 & \cdots & 0 & 0 \\ 0 & 0 & 0 & 0 & \cdots & 0 & 0 & \frac{1}{2} & -\frac{3}{2} & \cdots \\ 0 & 0 & 0 & 0 & 0 & \cdots & 0 & 0 \\ \vdots & \vdots & \vdots & \vdots & \ddots & \vdots & \vdots & \vdots & \vdots & \ddots \\ \vdots & \vdots & \vdots & \vdots & \vdots & \ddots & \vdots & \vdots \\ 0 & 0 & 0 & 0 & \cdots & 0 & 0 & 0 & 0 & \cdots \\ -\frac{3}{2} & 1 & 0 & 0 & 0 & \cdots & 0 & 0 \\ 0 & 0 & 0 & 0 & \cdots & 0 & 0 & 0 & 0 & \cdots \\ 1 & -2 & 0 & 0 & 0 & \cdots & 0 & 0 \\ 0 & 0 & 0 & 0 & \cdots & 0 & 0 & 0 & 0 & \cdots \\ 0 & 0 & -2 & 1 & 0 & \cdots & 0 & 0 \\ 0 & 0 & 0 & 0 & \cdots & 0 & 0 & 0 & 0 & \cdots \\ 0 & 0 & 1 & -\frac{3}{2} & \frac{1}{2} & \cdots & 0 & 0 \\ 0 & 0 & 0 & 0 & \cdots & 0 & 0 & 0 & 0 & \cdots \\ 0 & 0 & 0 & \frac{1}{2} & -\frac{3}{2} & \cdots & 0 & 0 \\ \vdots & \vdots & \vdots & \vdots & \ddots & \vdots & \vdots & \vdots & \vdots & \ddots \\ \vdots & \vdots & \vdots & \vdots & \vdots & \ddots & \vdots & \vdots \\ 0 & 0 & 0 & 0 & \cdots & 0 & 0 & 0 & 0 & \cdots \\ 0 & 0 & 0 & 0 & 0 & \cdots & -\frac{3}{2} & 1 \\ \frac{1}{2} & 0 & 0 & 0 & \cdots & 0 & 0 & 0 & 0 & \cdots \\ 0 & 0 & 0 & 0 & 0 & \cdots & 1 & -\frac{3}{2} \end{pmatrix} \\ &= \begin{pmatrix} C_{2j-2} & 0 & 0 \\ 0 & R_{2k-2j} & 0 \\ 0 & 0 & C_{2n-2k+2} \end{pmatrix} + \frac{1}{2}e_1 e_{2n}^T + \frac{1}{2}e_{2n}e_1^T. \end{aligned}$$

Now, $\det\left[\begin{pmatrix} C_{2j-2} & 0 & 0 \\ 0 & R_{2k-2j} & 0 \\ 0 & 0 & C_{2n-2k+2} \end{pmatrix} + \frac{1}{2}e_1 e_{2n}^T\right] = \det(C_{2j-2})\det(R_{2k-2j})\det(C_{2n-2k+2})$. Then,

$$\begin{aligned}\det(R') &= \det(C_{2j-2})\det(R_{2k-2j})\det(C_{2n-2k+2}) \\ &\quad + (-1)^{2n+1}\frac{1}{4}\det(C_{2j-3})\cdot\det(C_{2n-2k+1}) \\ &= \left(\frac{1}{2}\right)^n 36(k-j)(n-k+1).\end{aligned}$$

So, if $1 \le j < k \le n$,

$$\begin{aligned}\sum_{1\le j<k\le n} \det(-L_R(\{j,k\}|\{j,k\})) &= (-4)^{n-2}\sum_{1\le j<k\le n}\left(\frac{1}{2}\right)^n 36(k-j)(n-k+1) \\ &= (-4)^{n-2}\left(\frac{1}{2}\right)^n 3n^2(n-1)(n+1).\end{aligned}$$

Case A4. Consider the case when $n+1 \le j < k \le 3n$,

$$\det(-L_R(\{j,k\}|\{j,k\}) = \begin{vmatrix} -4I_n & -\sqrt{2}L_{V_{01}}(\{\}|\{j,k\}) \\ -\sqrt{2}L_{V_{01}}(\{\}|\{j,k\})^T & \chi(\{j,k\}|\{j,k\}) \end{vmatrix} = \begin{vmatrix} -4I_n & 0 \\ 0 & \Re_4 \end{vmatrix},$$

where $\Re_4 = \chi(\{j,k\}|\{j,k\}) + \frac{1}{2}L_{V_{01}}(\{\}|\{j,k\})^T L_{V_{V01}}(\{\}|\{j,k\})$ and $\chi = -L_{V_{11}}$.
$\det(-L_R(\{j,k\}|\{j,k\}) = \det(-4I_n)\det(\Re_4)$.
Let $r = j-n$ and $t = k-n$. We must examine the next subcases.
Subcase 4.1: $1 < r < t < 2n$, r-even and t-odd or r and t are both odd or both even, we have

$$\Re_4 = \begin{pmatrix} A_{r-1} & 0 & \frac{1}{2}e_1e_{2n}^T \\ 0 & A_{t-r-1} & 0 \\ \frac{1}{2}e_{2n}e_1^T & 0 & A_{2n-t} \end{pmatrix}.$$

Subcase 4.2: $1 < r < t < 2n$, r-odd and t-even, so

$$\Re_4 = \begin{pmatrix} A_{r-1} & 0 & \frac{1}{2}e_1e_{2n}^T \\ 0 & D_{t-r-1} & 0 \\ \frac{1}{2}e_{2n}e_1^T & 0 & A_{2n-t} \end{pmatrix}.$$

Subcase 4.3: $r = 1$, $1 < t < 2n$, and t even, we have

$$\Re_4 = \begin{pmatrix} D_{t-2} & 0 \\ 0 & A_{2n-t} \end{pmatrix}.$$

Subcase 4.4: $r = 1$, $1 < t < 2n$, and t-odd, we have

$$\Re_4 = \begin{pmatrix} A_{t-2} & 0 \\ 0 & A_{2n-t} \end{pmatrix}.$$

Subcase 4.5: $1 < r < 2n$, $r = 2n$, and r-even, we have

$$\Re_4 = \begin{pmatrix} A_{r-1} & 0 \\ 0 & A_{2n-r-1} \end{pmatrix}.$$

Subcase 4.6: $1 < r < 2n$, $r = 2n$, and r-odd, we have

$$\Re_4 = \begin{pmatrix} A_{r-1} & 0 \\ 0 & D_{2n-r-1} \end{pmatrix}.$$

As previously, we can proceed as follows:
$\chi(\{j,k\}|\{j,k\}) + \frac{1}{2}L_{V_{01}}(\{\}|\{j,k\})^T L_{V_{V01}}(\{\}|\{j,k\}) =$

$$\begin{cases} 9\left(\frac{1}{2}\right)^{n+2}(t-r)(2n-t+r), & \text{if } \{r,t\} \text{ are both even or both odd;} \\ \left(\frac{1}{2}\right)^{n+2}(3t-3r-1)(6n-3t+3r+1), & \text{if } r = \text{odd}, t = \text{even;} \\ \left(\frac{1}{2}\right)^{n+2}(3t-3r+1)(6n-3t+3r-1), & \text{if } r = \text{even}, t = \text{odd.} \end{cases}$$

So,

$$\sum_{n+1\le j<k\le 3n} \det(-L_R(\{j,k\}|\{j,k\})) = (-4)^n\left(\frac{1}{2}\right)^{n+2}\Bigg\{ \sum_{\substack{1\le r<t\le 2n\\ \{r,t\}=\{\text{even or odd}\}}} 9(t-r)(2n-t+r)$$
$$+ \sum_{\substack{1\le r<t\le 2n\\ r-\text{odd}, t-\text{even}}} (3t-3r-1)(6n-3t+3r+1)$$
$$+ \sum_{\substack{1\le r<t\le 2n\\ r-\text{even}, t-\text{odd}}} (3t-3r+1)(6n-3t+3r-1)\Bigg\}$$
$$= (-4)^n\left(\frac{1}{2}\right)^{n+2}\{6n(n^2-1)+(n-1)(3n^2+n+2)+(n+1)(3n^2-n+2)\}$$
$$= (-4)^n\left(\frac{1}{2}\right)^{n} n^2(3n^2-1).$$

Case A5. Suppose that $1 \le j \le n$ and $n+1 \le k \le 3n$. In such a case, we have that $\sum_{\substack{1\le j<n\\ n+1\le k\le 3n}} \det(-L_R(\{j,k\}|\{j,k\})) = \begin{vmatrix} -4I_{n-1} & V \\ V^T & \chi(\{k\}|\{k\}) \end{vmatrix}$, where V is a submatrix of $-\sqrt{2}L_{01}$ created by removing the jth row and kth column of $-\sqrt{2}L_{01}$. Taking $t = k-n$, we can compute $\det(\chi(\{t\}|\{t\}) + \frac{1}{2}V^TV)$:

$$\begin{cases}
\frac{(-1)^{n-1}(36(-j^2+iq+in)-9(t^2+2qn)+8(6j-3t-3n-2))}{2^{n+1}}, & \text{if } j>1, t<2j-2 \text{ and even;}\\
\frac{(-1)^{n-1}(36(-j^2+iq+in)-9(t^2+2qn)+30(2j-t-n-1)+5)}{2^{n+1}}, & \text{if } j>1, 1<t<2j-2 \text{ and odd;}\\
\frac{(-1)^{n-1}(36(-j^2+iq-in)-9(t^2+2qn)+8(6j-3qn-3n-2))}{2^{n+1}}, & \text{if } j>1, 2n>t>2j-2 \text{ and even;}\\
\frac{(-1)^{n-1}(36(-j^2+iq-in)-9(t^2+2qn)+30(2j-qn-n-1)+5)}{2^{n+1}}, & \text{if } j>1, t>2j-1 \text{ and odd;}\\
\frac{(-1)^{n-1}(9(2nq-t^2)+6(t-n)-1)}{2^{n+1}}, & \text{if } j=1, t=\text{odd;}\\
\frac{(-1)^{n-1}(9(2nq-t^2)+12(t-n)-4)}{2^{n+1}}, & \text{if } j=1, t=\text{even;}\\
\frac{(-1)^{n-1}(3n-1)}{2^{n-1}}, & \text{if } j>1, t=2j-1 \text{ or } 2j-2;\\
\frac{(-1)^{n-1}(9(ni-j^2)+4(6j-3n-4))}{2^{n-1}}, & \text{if } j>1, t=1;\\
\frac{(-1)^{n-1}(9(ni-j^2)+6(2j-n)-4)}{2^{n-1}}, & \text{if } j>1, t=2n.
\end{cases}$$

We have

$$\sum_{\substack{1\le j<n\\ n+1\le k\le 3n}} \det(-L_R(\{j,k\}|\{j,k\})) = -(-4)^{n-1}\left(\frac{1}{2}\right)^{n-1} n^2(3n^2+1).$$

Thus,

$$\alpha_{3n-2} = \sum_{1\le j<k\le 3n} \det(-L_R(\{j,k\}|\{j,k\})) = \sum_{1\le j<k\le n} \det(-L_R(\{j,k\}|\{j,k\}))$$
$$+ \sum_{n+1\le j<k\le 3n} \det(-L_R(\{j,k\}|\{j,k\})) + \sum_{\substack{1\le j<n\\ n+1\le k\le 3n}} \det(-L_R(\{j,k\}|\{j,k\}))$$
$$= (-4)^{n-2}\left(\frac{1}{2}\right)^{n} 3n^2(n^2-1) + (-4)^n\left(\frac{1}{2}\right)^{n}(3n^4-n^2)$$
$$+ (-4)^{n-1}\left(\frac{1}{2}\right)^{n-1} n^2(3n^2+1)$$
$$= -2^n n^2\frac{15(75n^2-11)}{16}. \quad \square$$

References

1. Spitzer, F. *Principles of Random Walk*; Springer Science and Business Media: Berlin/Heidelberg, Germany, 2013.
2. Perozzi, B.; Al-Rfou, R.; Skiena, S. Deepwalk: Online learning of social representations. In Proceedings of the 20th ACM SIGKDD International Conference on Knowledge Discovery and Data Mining (ACM), New York, NY, USA, 24–27 August 2014; pp. 701–710.
3. Yang, X.S.; Deb, S. Multi-objective cuckoo search for design optimization. *Comput. Oper. Res.* **2013**, *40*, 1616–1624. [CrossRef]
4. Adhikari, R.; Agrawal, R.K. A combination of artificial neural network and random walk models for financial time series forecasting. *Neural Comput. Appl.* **2014**, *24*, 1441–1449. [CrossRef]
5. Verstraete, F.; Wolf, M.M.; Cirac, J.I. Quantum computation and quantum-state engineering driven by dissipation. *Nat. Phys.* **2009**, *5*, 633–636. [CrossRef]
6. Codling, E.A.; Plank, M.J.; Benhamou, S. Random walk models in biology. *J. R. Soc. Interface* **2008**, *5*, 813–834. [CrossRef] [PubMed]
7. Mei, Q.; Zhou, D.; Church, K. Query suggestion using hitting time. In Proceedings of the 17th ACM Conference on Information and Knowledge Management (ACM), NapaValley, CA, USA, 26–30 October 2008; pp. 469–478.
8. Boccaletti, S.; Latora, V.; Moreno, Y.; Chavez, M.; Hwang, D.U. Complex networks: Structure and dynamics. *Phys. Rep. Rev. Sect. Phys. Lett.* **2006**, *424*, 175–308. [CrossRef]
9. Redner, S. *A Guide to First-Passage Processes*; Cambridge University Press: Cambridge, UK, 2001.
10. Polizzi, N.F.; Therien, M.J.; Beratan, D.N. Mean first-passage times in biology. *Isr. J. Chem.* **2016**, *56*, 816. [CrossRef] [PubMed]
11. Metzler, R.; Oshanin, G.; Redner, S. *First-Passage Phenomena and Their Applications*; World Scientific: Singapore, 2014.
12. Xie, Y.Y.; Chang, S.H.; Zhang, Z.P.; Zhang, M.; Yang, L. Efficient sampling of complex network with modified random walk strategies. *Phys. A Stat. Mech. Appl.* **2018**, *492*, 57–64. [CrossRef]
13. Kemeny, G.; Snell, J.L. *Finite Markov Chains*; Van Nostrand: Princeton, NJ, USA, 1960.
14. Van Mieghem, P. *Graph Spectra for Complex Networks*; Cambridge University Press: Cambridge, UK, 2011.
15. Zhu, H.Y.; Klein, D.J.; Lukovits, I. Extensions of the Wiener number. *J. Chem. Inf. Comput. Sci.* **1996**, *36*, 420–428. [CrossRef]
16. Gutman, I.; Mohar, B. The quasi-Wiener and the Kirchhoff indices coincide. *J. Chem. Inform. Comput. Sci.* **1996**, *36*, 982–985. [CrossRef]
17. Chandra, A.K.; Raghavan, P.; Ruzzo, W.L.; Smolensky, R. The electrical resistance of a graph captures its commute and cover times. In Proceedings of the Twenty-First Annual ACM Symposium on Theory of Computing, Edmonton, AB, Canada, 14–16 August 1989; pp. 574–586.
18. Levene, M.; Loizou, G. Kemeny's constant and the random surfer. *Am. Math.* **2002**, *109*, 741–745. [CrossRef]
19. Xiao, W.; Gutman, I. Resistance distance and Laplacian spectrum. *Theor. Chem. Acc.* **2003**, *110*, 284–289. [CrossRef]
20. Zhang, Z.; Wu, B.; Zhang, H.; Zhou, S.; Guan, J.; Wang, Z. Determining global mean-first-passage time of random walks on Vicsek fractals using eigenvalues of Laplacian matrices. *Phys. Rev. E* **2010**, *81*, 031118. [CrossRef] [PubMed]
21. Zaman, S.; Ullah, A. Kemeny's constant and global mean first passage time of random walks on octagonal cell network. *Math. Methods Appl. Sci* **2023**, *46*, 91779186. [CrossRef]
22. Ali, U.; Ahmad, Y.; Xu, S.A.; Pan, X.F. Resistance distance-based indices and spanning trees of linear pentagonal-quadrilateral networks. *Polycycl. Aromat. Compd.* **2021**, 42, 6352–6371. [CrossRef]
23. Ali, U.; Raza, H.; Ahmed, Y. On normalized Laplacians, degree-Kirchhoff index and spanning tree of generalized phenylene. *Symmetry* **2021**, *13*, 1374. [CrossRef]
24. Zhang, X.; Awais, H.M.; Javaid, M.; Siddiqui, M.K. Multiplicative Zagreb indices of molecular graphs. *J. Chem.* **2019**, *2019*, 5294198. [CrossRef]
25. Ullah, A.; Zeb, A.; Zaman, S. A new perspective on the modeling and topological characterization of H-Naphtalenic nanosheets with applications. *J. Mol. Model.* **2022**, *28*, 211. [CrossRef]
26. Kosar, Z.; Zaman, S.; Siddiqui, M.K. Structural characterization and spectral properties of hexagonal phenylene chain network. *Eur. Phys. J. Plus* **2023**, *138*, 415. [CrossRef]
27. Zaman, S. Spectral analysis of three invariants associated to random walks on rounded networks with $2n$-pentagons. *Int. J. Comp. Math.* **2022**, *99*, 465–485. [CrossRef]
28. Ali, U.; Li, J.; Ahmad, Y.; Raza, Z. Computing the Laplacian spectrum and Wiener index of pentagonal-derivation cylinder/Möbius network. *Heliyon* **2024**, *10*, e24182. [CrossRef]
29. Došlic, T.; Måloy, F. Chain hexagonal cacti: Matchings and independent sets. *Discrete Math.* **2010**, *310*, 1676–1690. [CrossRef]
30. Chen, X.; Zhao, B.; Zhao, P. Six-membered ring spiro chains with extremal Merrifield-Simmons index and Hosoya index. *Match Commun. Math. Comput. Chem.* **2009**, *62*, 657–665.
31. Huang, J.; Li, S.C.; Li, X.C. The normalized Laplacian degree-Kirchhoff index and spanning trees of the linear polyomino chains. *Appl. Math. Comput.* **2016**, *289*, 324–334. [CrossRef]
32. Zhang, F. (Ed.) *The Schur Complement and Its Applications*; Springer: New York, NY, USA, 2005.

mathematics MDPI

Article

Dupin Cyclides Passing through a Fixed Circle

Jean Michel Menjanahary [1,†] and Raimundas Vidunas [2,*,†]

[1] Institute of Computer Science, Vilnius University, 08303 Vilnius, Lithuania; jean.menjanahary@mif.vu.lt
[2] Institute of Applied Mathematics, Vilnius University, 03225 Vilnius, Lithuania
[*] Correspondence: raimundas.vidunas@mif.vu.lt
[†] These authors contributed equally to this work.

Abstract: Dupin cyclides are classical algebraic surfaces of low degree. Recently, they have gained popularity in computer-aided geometric design (CAGD) and architecture owing to the fact that they contain many circles. We derive algebraic conditions that fully characterize the Dupin cyclides passing through a fixed circle. The results are applied to the basic problem in CAGD of the blending of Dupin cyclides along circles.

Keywords: Dupin cyclide; cyclide blending; CAGD

MSC: 65D17; 14Q30

Citation: Menjanahary, J.M.; Vidunas, R. Dupin Cyclides Passing through a Fixed Circle. *Mathematics* **2024**, *12*, 1505. https://doi.org/10.3390/math12101505

Academic Editor: Martin Schlichenmaier

Received: 14 March 2024
Revised: 12 April 2024
Accepted: 4 May 2024
Published: 11 May 2024

1. Introduction

Dupin and Darboux cyclides are remarkable algebraic surfaces of degree four or three that contain many circles. They were discovered, respectively, by Charles Dupin [1] and Gaston Darboux [2] in the 19th century. Over the past few decades, they have gained popularity in computer-aided geometric design (CAGD) and architecture, making them interesting and important subjects for investigation. Dupin cyclides are used predominantly for blending surfaces along circles to model elaborate CAGD surfaces [3–10] or smoothly blending Dupin cyclides with natural quadrics and canal surfaces along the circles [11–16].

The prototypical example of a Dupin cyclide is a torus of revolution with major radius R and minor radius r. A canonical implicit equation of a torus is

$$\left(x^2+y^2+z^2+R^2-r^2\right)^2-4R^2(x^2+y^2)=0. \tag{1}$$

We must have $r<R$ for a smooth torus surface. A torus contains two orthogonal circles through each point. These circles are curvature lines of the torus and are called *principal circles*. A smooth torus has two additional circles through each point on a bitangent plane to the torus; see Figure 1a. They are called *Villarceau circles* [17].

A Dupin cyclide is the image of a torus under a Möbius transformation: for example, an inversion with respect to a sphere. These transformations preserve the angles and the set of circles and lines on the surfaces [18,19]. Accordingly, smooth Dupin cyclides inherit the property of having two principal circles and two Villarceau circles through each point; see Figure 1b. Some of these circles may degenerate to straight lines.

The implicit equation for a Dupin cyclide is of degree four or three and can be written in the form

$$\begin{aligned} a_0\left(x^2+y^2+z^2\right)^2 &+ 2(b_1x+b_2y+b_3z)\left(x^2+y^2+z^2\right)\\ &+c_1x^2+c_2y^2+c_3z^2+2d_1yz+2d_2xz+2d_3xy\\ &+2e_1x+2e_2y+2e_3z+f_0=0, \end{aligned} \tag{2}$$

with some $a_0, b_1, \ldots, f_0 \in \mathbb{R}$. For general values of the coefficients, this implicit equation defines a more general surface called a *Darboux cyclide* [20]. These cyclides typically have six circles through each point, and they are more challenging to use in geometric modeling [21]. The practical problem of distinguishing Dupin cyclides among Darboux cyclides is considered in [18].

The basic problem considered in this paper is the smooth blending of two Dupin cyclides along a fixed circle. Our approach is to match implicit equations (2) for the two Dupin cyclides we blend. To solve the basic problem algebraically, we first consider the general linear family of Darboux cyclides passing through a fixed circle. Then, we use the results in [18] to characterize the smaller family of Dupin cyclides in terms of the algebraic relations for the free coefficients of the general family of Darboux cyclides. This is considered in Section 3 together with the formulation of the main results of the paper. We prove them separately for quartic and cubic equations in Sections 4 and 5. The smooth blending between two implicit equations of Dupin cyclides along a fixed circle is investigated in Section 6. In the last section, we express the Möbius invariant from [18] of Dupin cyclides as applied to our particular families of Dupin cyclides.

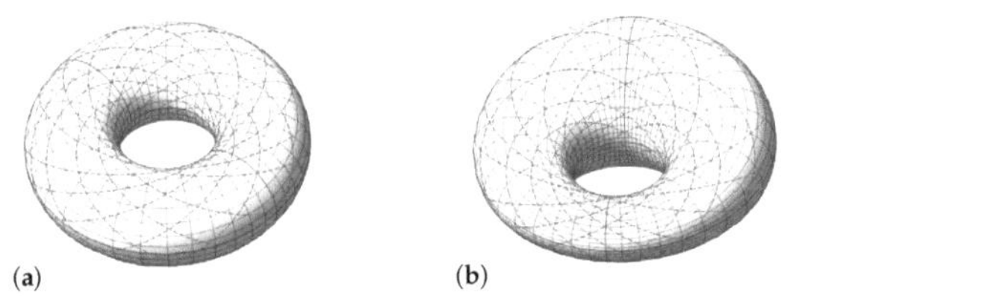

Figure 1. A smooth torus (**a**) and a smooth Dupin cyclide (**b**). The solid circles are principal circles, and the dashed circles are Villarceau circles.

2. Preliminaries

First off, let us recall the salient results in [18] on distinguishing Dupin cyclides among Darboux cyclides. They are formulated using the following abbreviations of algebraic expressions in the coefficients in (2):

$$\begin{aligned}
B_0 &= b_1^2 + b_2^2 + b_3^2, \\
C_0 &= c_1 + c_2 + c_3, \\
E_0 &= e_1^2 + e_2^2 + e_3^2, \\
W_1 &= c_1c_2 + c_1c_3 + c_2c_3 - d_1^2 - d_2^2 - d_3^2, \\
W_2 &= c_1c_2c_3 + 2d_1d_2d_3 - c_1d_1^2 - c_2d_2^2 - c_3d_3^2, \\
W_3 &= b_1^2c_1 + b_2^2c_2 + b_3^2c_3 + 2b_2b_3d_1 + 2b_1b_3d_2 + 2b_1b_2d_3, \\
W_4 &= c_1e_1^2 + c_2e_2^2 + c_3e_3^2 + 2d_1e_2e_3 + 2d_2e_1e_3 + 2d_3e_1e_2.
\end{aligned}$$

Let σ_{12}, σ_{13} denote the permutations of the variables $b_1, b_2, b_3; c_1, c_2, c_3; d_1, d_2, d_3;$ and e_1, e_2, e_3 that permute the indices $1, 2$ or $1, 3$, respectively.

To recognize quartic Dupin cyclides among the form (2), we can assume $a_0 = 1$ by dividing all coefficients by a_0. Then, we apply the shift

$$(x, y, z) \mapsto (x, y, z) - \tfrac{1}{2}(b_1, b_2, b_3) \tag{3}$$

to remove the cubic terms and reduce the equation to an intermediate Darboux form:

$$\begin{aligned}
(x^2 + y^2 + z^2)^2 + c_1x^2 + c_2y^2 + c_3z^2 + 2d_1yz + 2d_2xz + 2d_3xy \\
+ 2e_1x + 2e_2y + 2e_3z + f_0 = 0.
\end{aligned} \tag{4}$$

Theorem 1. *The surface in $\mathbb{R}^3$ defined by (4) is a Dupin cyclide only if the 12 equations*

$$K_1 = 0,\ \sigma_{12}K_1 = 0,\ \sigma_{13}K_1 = 0, \qquad L_1 = 0,\ \sigma_{12}L_1 = 0,\ \sigma_{13}L_1 = 0,$$
$$M_1 = 0,\ \sigma_{12}M_1 = 0,\ \sigma_{13}M_1 = 0, \qquad N_1 = 0, \quad N_2 = 0, \quad N_3 = 0,$$

are satisfied, where

$$\begin{aligned}
K_1 &= (c_3 - c_2)e_2e_3 + d_1(e_2^2 - e_3^2) + (d_2e_2 - d_3e_3)e_1, \\
L_1 &= (W_1 + 4f_0 - (c_2 + c_3)^2 - d_2^2 - d_3^2)e_1 \\
&\quad + (C_0d_3 + c_3d_3 - d_1d_2)e_2 + (C_0d_2 + c_2d_2 - d_1d_3)e_3, \\
M_1 &= 2(c_1e_1 + d_3e_2 + d_2e_3)(W_1 + 4f_0) + e_1(W_2 - C_0W_1 - 4E_0), \\
N_1 &= (4W_1 + 12f_0 - 3C_0^2)(W_1 + 4f_0) - 2C_0(W_2 - C_0W_1 - 6E_0) - 4W_4, \\
N_2 &= 4(W_2 - C_0W_1 - 2E_0)(W_1 + 4f_0) + (C_0^2 - 4f_0)(W_2 + C_0W_1 + 8C_0f_0 - 4E_0), \\
N_3 &= (W_2 + C_0W_1 + 8C_0f_0 - 4E_0)^2 - 4(W_1 + 4f_0)^3.
\end{aligned}$$

Proof. This result is covered by [18] (Proposition 3.6). We consider and use only the formulated necessity in the proof of the main new Theorem 3. □

Theorem 2. *The surface in $\mathbb{R}^3$ defined by (2) is a cubic Dupin cyclide only if the following equations are satisfied:*

$$a_0 = 0, \qquad e_1 = \tfrac{1}{4}E_1, \qquad e_2 = \tfrac{1}{4}\sigma_{12}E_1, \qquad e_3 = \tfrac{1}{4}\sigma_{13}E_1, \tag{5}$$

$$f_0 = \frac{W_3}{4B_0^2}\left(\frac{W_3}{B_0} - C_0\right)^2 + \frac{W_3W_1}{4B_0^2} + \frac{W_2 - C_0W_1}{4B_0}, \tag{6}$$

where

$$\begin{aligned}
E_1 = &-\frac{b_1}{B_0}\left(\frac{W_3}{B_0} - c_2 - c_3\right)^2 + \frac{2b_1^2}{B_0^2}(b_3c_3d_2 + b_2c_2d_3) - \frac{4b_1}{B_0^2}(b_3d_2 + b_2d_3)^2 \\
&+ \frac{2(b_3d_2 + b_2d_3)}{B_0^2}(b_2^2c_1 + b_3^2c_1 - 2b_2b_3d_1) - \frac{2b_2b_3}{B_0^2}(c_2 - c_3)(b_2d_2 - b_3d_3) \\
&+ \frac{b_1}{B_0}\left((c_1 - c_2)(c_1 - c_3) - d_1^2 + d_2^2 + d_3^2\right) + \frac{2d_1}{B_0}(b_2d_2 + b_3d_3).
\end{aligned}$$

Proof. This is covered by [18] (Theorem 2.4). □

3. Main Results

Without loss of generality, we assume that a fixed circle $\Gamma \subset \mathbb{R}^3$ with radius $r > 0$ is given by the equations

$$x = 0, \qquad y^2 + z^2 = r^2. \tag{7}$$

The Darboux cyclides passing through the circle Γ form a linear subspace of the space of coefficients in (2), as we formulate in Lemma 1. Computing the variety of Dupin cyclides passing through the circle Γ is less trivial. The defining equations are obtained by restricting the coefficients of (2) to cyclides passing through Γ and by considering the effects on the equations in Theorems 1 and 2.

Lemma 1. *A Darboux cyclide passing through the circle Γ has an implicit equation of the form*

$$\begin{aligned}
u_0(x^2 + y^2 + z^2 - r^2)^2 + 2(x^2 + y^2 + z^2 - r^2)(u_1x + u_2y + u_3z + u_4)& \\
+ 2x(v_1x + v_2y + v_3z + v_4) = 0,&
\end{aligned} \tag{8}$$

where $u_0, u_1, u_2, u_3, u_4, v_1, v_2, v_3, v_4$ are real coefficients.

Proof. The equation of a Darboux cyclide passing through the circle Γ will be in the ideal generated by x and $y^2+z^2-r^2$ of the polynomial ring $\mathbb{R}(r)[x,y,z]$ over the field $\mathbb{R}(r)$. The terms of degree four and three should match the Darboux form (2). Therefore, we expand the generator $y^2+z^2-r^2$ to $x^2+y^2+z^2-r^2$ so that the quartic and cubic terms

$$u_0(x^2+y^2+z^2-r^2)^2+2(x^2+y^2+z^2-r^2)(u_1x+u_2y+u_3z),$$

are contained in the ideal of the circle Γ. The remaining terms of degree $\leqslant 2$ should be in the same ideal; hence, they have the shape

$$2u_4(x^2+y^2+z^2-r^2)+2x\left(v_1x+v_2y+v_3z+v_4\right).$$

□

Following this lemma, the ambient-space of Darboux cyclides passing through the circle Γ are identified as $\mathbb{P}^8$, with the coordinates $(u_0:\ldots:u_4:v_1:\ldots:v_4)$. The Dupin cyclides defined over $\mathbb{R}$ are represented by real points on an algebraic variety $\mathcal{D}_\Gamma$ in this projective space. If we consider the radius r as a variable, the variety $\mathcal{D}_\Gamma$ should be invariant under the scaling of $(x,y,z)\in\mathbb{R}^3$. Accordingly, the obtained equations can be checked to also be weighted-homogeneous, with weight 1 for r and the respective weights $0,1,1,1,2,2,2,2,3$ of the coordinates of $\mathbb{P}^8$. We assume r to be a parameter $r\neq 0$ in our proofs and computations.

We define the variety $\mathcal{D}_\Gamma$ of Dupin cyclides as a specialized image of the variety $\mathcal{D}_0$ in [18] (Figure 1) that represents the whole variety of Dupin cyclides within the projective family (2) of Darboux cyclides. The specialization is identified by the projective subfamily (8). The variety $\mathcal{D}_\Gamma$ turns out to be reducible and to have several components with a maximum dimension of four. Section 4 provides a brief description distinguishing those components. We are interested in the components that generically correspond to irreducible cyclide surfaces defined over $\mathbb{R}$. There are two components fulfilling this interest, which reflects the fact that the circle Γ could be either a principal or a Villarceau circle on a Dupin cyclide; see Section 4. Accordingly, we split the main result into two Theorems as follows.

Theorem 3. *The surface in $\mathbb{R}^3$ defined by (8) is an irreducible Dupin cyclide containing Γ as a Villarceau circle if and only if the equations*

$$v_4-2r^2u_1=0, \qquad v_1+2u_4-2r^2u_0=0, \tag{9}$$

$$u_2v_2+u_3v_3-2u_1u_4=0, \qquad 4r^2(u_1^2+u_2^2+u_3^2)-4u_4^2-v_2^2-v_3^2=0, \tag{10}$$

and the inequality

$$u_4^2<r^2(u_2^2+u_3^2) \tag{11}$$

are satisfied.

Theorem 4. *The surface in $\mathbb{R}^3$ defined by (8) is an irreducible Dupin cyclide containing Γ as a principal circle only if the ranks of the following two matrices are equal to 1:*

$$\mathcal{N} = \begin{pmatrix} u_2 & v_2 \\ u_3 & v_3 \\ u_4 & v_4 \end{pmatrix}, \tag{12}$$

$$\mathcal{M} = \begin{pmatrix} u_2 & v_2(v_4 - 2r^2u_1) \\ u_3 & v_3(v_4 - 2r^2u_1) \\ u_4 & v_4(v_4 - 2r^2u_1) \\ 2u_0 & v_2^2 + v_3^2 - 4r^2u_1^2 \\ u_1 & 4r^2u_0v_4 - 2r^2(u_2v_2 + u_3v_3) - 4r^2u_1(v_1 + u_4) \\ v_1 & 4r^4(u_2^2 + u_3^2 + 2u_0v_1) - 4r^2(v_1 + u_4)^2 - (v_4 - 2r^2u_1)^2 \\ v_2 & -8r^4u_1u_2 - 4r^2v_2(v_1 + u_4 - 2r^2u_0) \\ v_3 & -8r^4u_1u_3 - 4r^2v_3(v_1 + u_4 - 2r^2u_0) \\ v_4 & -8r^4u_1u_4 - 4r^2v_4(v_1 + u_4 - 2r^2u_0) \end{pmatrix}. \tag{13}$$

Remark 1. *The rank conditions mean vanishing of the* 2×2 *minors of the matrices* $\mathcal{N}$ *and* $\mathcal{M}$*. The* 2×2 *minors from the first three rows of* $\mathcal{M}$ *differ from the minors of* $\mathcal{N}$ *by the common factor* $v_4 - 2r^2u_1$*. Incidentally, this factor appears as an equation for the Villarceau case. Localizing with* $(v_4 - 2r^2u_1)^{-1}$ *leads to the ideal for the principal circle case. But the Villarceau case equations of Theorem 3 do not imply a lesser rank of* $\mathcal{M}$*, as the second column does not necessarily vanish fully, particularly in the fourth row. Rather similarly, the* 2×2 *minors from the last three rows of* $\mathcal{M}$ *differ from the minors of* $\mathcal{N}$ *by the common factor* $-8r^4u_1$*, as the terms* $-4r^2v_i(v_1 + u_4 - 2r^2u_0)$ *are proportional to the first column. Therefore, the* 2×2 *minors formed only by the first three rows or only by the last three rows of* $\mathcal{M}$ *can be ignored.*

Remark 2. *The Hilbert series of the two algebraic varieties described by Theorems 3 and 4 can be computed using computer algebra systems Maple or Singular. The principal circle component of* $\mathcal{D}_\Gamma$ *has the Hilbert series* $H_p(t)/(1-t)^4$*, where*

$$H_p(t) = 1 + 4t + 7t^2 - 10t^3 + 10t^4 - 5t^5 + t^6. \tag{14}$$

Hence, the dimension of the variety equals 4, and the degree equals $H_p(1) = 8$*. The Zariski closure of the Villarceau circle component is a complete intersection. The Hilbert series of this component is* $(1 + 2t + t^2)/(1-t)^4$*. Hence, the dimension of this variety equals 4, and the degree equals 4.*

4. Distinguishing Principal and Villarceau Circles

As we will analyze in Section 5, the specialized variety $\mathcal{D}_\Gamma$ of Dupin cyclides turns out to be reducible. We discard some of the components because they:

- Either represent only reducible cyclide surfaces: namely, a pair of touching spheres (where one of the spheres could be a plane or degenerates to a point); see Remark 4;
- Or generically represent cyclide surfaces with complex (rather than real) coefficients in (8); real surfaces appear only in lower-dimensional intersections with the two main families described in Theorems 3 and 4.

We claim that the two main families are distinguished by the homotopy class of Γ as either a principal circle or a Villarceau circle. These two homotopical types can be discerned by inspecting the type of Γ on representative surfaces under Möbius transformations (which are finite compositions of inversions). Indeed, principal circles are preserved [19] (Theorem 3.14) by Möbius transformations. The components of $\mathcal{D}_\Gamma$ are invariant under the continuous action of Möbius transformations that fix the circle Γ. As mentioned in the introduction, any Dupin cyclide can be obtained from a torus by a Möbius transformation. Further, the torus can be chosen to pass through the circle Γ (by Euclidean similarity), and that circle can be considered as fixed. Therefore, it is enough to check the homotopy types for the toruses on both main components. Furthermore, the "vertical" principal circles (around the tube) and the "horizontal" principal circles (around the hole) can be interchanged by a Möbius transformation centered inside the torus tube; see [18] (§6.1). Hence, we consider only a fixed "vertical" principal circle in a moment.

Under Euclidean similarities, we can move the torus (1) so that the circle Γ is a principal circle (with radius r) or a Villarceau circle (with radius R). The principal circles on the vertical plane $x = 0$ are given by $(y \pm R)^2 + z^2 = r^2$. Identifying one of those circles with Γ by the shift $y \mapsto y + R$, we obtain an equation of the form (8) with

$$(u_0 : u_1 : u_2 : u_3 : u_4 : v_1 : v_2 : v_3 : v_4) = (1 : 0 : -2R : 0 : 2R^2 : -2R^2 : 0 : 0 : 0) \tag{15}$$

for the representative (under the Möbius transformations) tori with Γ as a principal circle. It is straightforward to check that the second columns of $\mathcal{N}$ and $\mathcal{M}$ consist of zeroes for the representative tori (15), while the second and fourth equations of Theorem 3 are not satisfied generically. Hence, Theorem 4 covers the cases where Γ is a principal circle.

Now consider a Villarceau circle of the torus (1) on the plane $z = \alpha x + \beta y$, where $\alpha = r/\varrho, \beta = 0, \varrho = \sqrt{R^2 - r^2}$. It is moved onto Γ by the Euclidean transformation

$$(x, y, z) \mapsto \left(\frac{rx + \varrho z}{R}, r - y, \frac{rz - \varrho x}{R} \right). \tag{16}$$

Then the torus equation becomes

$$\left(x^2 + y^2 + z^2 - 2ry + R^2\right)^2 - 4\left((rx + \varrho z)^2 + R^2(y - r)^2\right) = 0. \tag{17}$$

This identifies (8) with

$$(u_0 : u_1 : u_2 : u_3 : u_4 : v_1 : v_2 : v_3 : v_4) = (1 : 0 : -2r : 0 : 2r^2 : 2R^2 - 4r^2 : 0 : -4r\varrho : 0) \tag{18}$$

as an implicit equation for the representative tori with Γ as a Villarceau circle. The representative tori (18) satisfy the equations of Theorem 3, while the rows with u_2 and u_0 in the first column form a lower-triangular matrix with non-zero determinant generically. Hence, Theorem 3 describes the cases with Γ as a Villarceau circle.

Remark 3. *We must have $u_4^2 \leqslant r^2(u_2^2 + u_3^2)$ for real points on the Villarceau circle component. Indeed, eliminating v_3 in (10) gives a quadratic equation for v_2 with the discriminant*

$$16u_3^2(u_1^2 + u_2^2 + u_3^2)(r^2u_2^2 + r^2u_3^2 - u_4^2), \tag{19}$$

which has to be non-negative. The strict inequality (11) throws away horn cyclides; see the case $J_0 = 0$ in Section 7. Villarceau circles on horn cyclides coincide with "vertical" principal circles (that is, those around the tube). The Villarceau and principle circle components intersect exactly at the locus of horn Dupin cyclides on $\mathcal{D}_\Gamma$. In fact, Equations (9) and (10) together with rank $\mathcal{N} < 2$ imply the equation $r^2(u_2^2 + u_3^2) = u_4^2$ for horn cyclides already; then, the second column of $\mathcal{M}$ reduces to zero entries.

Remark 4. *The variety $\mathcal{D}_\Gamma$ contains a component of dimension 4 (and degree 10) that represents reducible surfaces (8) of two touching spheres (or a sphere and a tangent plane). This component is defined by the 2×2 minors of the matrix*

$$\mathcal{L} = \begin{pmatrix} u_2 & v_2 \\ u_3 & v_3 \\ u_4 & v_4 \\ u_0v_2 & 2(u_1v_2 - u_2v_1) \\ u_0v_3 & 2(u_1v_3 - u_3v_1) \\ u_0v_4 & 2(u_1v_4 - u_4v_1) \end{pmatrix}, \tag{20}$$

and the additional equation

$$4r^2(u_1^2 + u_2^2 + u_3^2) + v_2^2 + v_3^2 - 8v_1(r^2u_0 - u_4) - 4v_4u_1 - 4u_4^2 = 0. \tag{21}$$

The condition rank $\mathcal{L} \leqslant 1$ alone gives a reducible surface (8). Its spherical (or plane) components are defined by

$$x^2 + y^2 + z^2 + sx - r^2 = 0, \tag{22}$$

$$u_0(x^2 + y^2 + z^2) + (2u_1 - su_0)x + 2u_2y + 2u_3z + 2u_4 - r^2u_0 = 0, \tag{23}$$

where $s = v_i/u_i$ for some or (usually) all $i \in \{1,2,3\}$. Equation (21) is the touching condition. The touching point is

$$(x, y, z) = -\frac{(s(u_2^2 + u_3^2 - 2u_0u_4) + 2u_1u_4, u_2(su_1 - 2v_1 + 2u_4), u_3(su_1 - 2v_1 + 2u_4))}{2(u_1^2 + u_2^2 + u_3^2 - 2u_0v_1)}.$$

Further, we have surface degeneration to the circle Γ when $\text{rank}(\mathcal{L}) = 0$ and $u_1 = 0$, $v_1 = 2r^2u_0$. If we restrict the principal circle component to $\text{rank}(\mathcal{L}) = 0$, we have degeneration to a double sphere. The intersection of this degenerate component with the principal circle component represents the cases when the touching point is on Γ. The intersection with the Villarceau component represents a sphere through Γ and a point on Γ; this intersection has a lower dimension of two and is contained in the principal circle component as well.

5. Proving Theorems 3 and 4

Let us define the ring

$$\mathcal{R}_\Gamma = \mathbb{R}(r)[u_1, u_2, u_3, u_4, v_1, v_2, v_3, v_4], \tag{24}$$

and let us denote the 2×2 minors $\mathcal{N}$ as

$$T_2 = u_3v_4 - u_4v_3, \tag{25}$$

$$T_3 = u_2v_4 - u_4v_2, \tag{26}$$

$$T_4 = u_2v_3 - u_3v_2. \tag{27}$$

Let us also denote

$$U_0 = u_1^2 + u_2^2 + u_3^2. \tag{28}$$

We define the variety $\mathcal{D}_\Gamma$ in Section 3 as the specialized image of the variety $\mathcal{D}_0$ in [18] (Figure 1). The variety $\mathcal{D}_0$, including the cubic part of Theorem 2, can be obtained from the 12 equations of Theorem 1 by applying the shift (3) backwards and homogenizing with a_0, as explained in [18] (§5). By straightforward Euclidean equivalence of cyclide surfaces, it is enough to consider (8) separately as a quartic equation that can be simplified by translating to (4) or as a cubic equation. Accordingly, we split the proofs into two cases and use Theorems 1 and 2 in a parallel way. We arrive at parallel options to simplify the reducible variety $\mathcal{D}_\Gamma$ from the full consideration of equations in those Theorems. Most of the particular equations or factors considered by us appear naturally in examined Gröbner bases. Even if an equation like (31) appears as an arbitrary choice, a formal proof does not have to justify the consideration.

5.1. Proof for Quartic Cyclides

Without loss of generality, we may assume $u_0 = 1$ while considering quartic cyclides. To apply Theorem 1, it is necessary to apply the shift (3) with $(b_1, b_2, b_3) = (u_1, u_2, u_3)$ so as to bring the cyclide equation (8) to the form (4). The obtained expression is

$$
\begin{aligned}
&\left(x^2+y^2+z^2\right)^2+\left(2(u_4+v_1-r^2)-u_1^2-\frac{U_0}{2}\right)x^2 \\
&+\left(2(u_4-r^2)-u_2^2-\frac{U_0}{2}\right)y^2+\left(2(u_4-r^2)-u_3^2-\frac{U_0}{2}\right)z^2 \\
&-2u_2u_3yz+2(v_3-u_1u_3)xz+2(v_2-u_1u_2)xy \\
&-(2u_1v_1+u_2v_2+u_3v_3-2v_4-u_1(U_0-2u_4))x \\
&-(u_1v_2-u_2(U_0-2u_4))y-(u_1v_3-u_3(U_0-2u_4))z \\
&-\frac{3U_0^2}{16}+\frac{U_0(u_4+r^2)+u_1(u_1v_1+u_2v_2+u_3v_3-2v_4)}{2}-2r^2u_4+r^4=0.
\end{aligned}
\tag{29}
$$

Identification with the coefficients $c_1, c_2, \ldots, f_0$ in (4) defines the ring homomorphism

$$\rho : \mathbb{R}[c_1, c_2, c_3, d_1, d_2, d_3, e_1, e_2, e_3, f_0] \to \mathcal{R}_\Gamma.$$

Let $\mathcal{I}_\Gamma \subset \mathcal{R}_\Gamma$ denote the ideal generated by the ρ-images of the 12 polynomials in Theorem 1. The polynomials in this ideal have to vanish when (8) is a Dupin cyclide. The polynomial $\rho(K_1)$ factors in $\mathcal{R}_\Gamma$: namely, $\rho(K_1) = -\frac{1}{4}T_4V_0$, where

$$V_0 = u_1^2(2u_1u_4-u_2v_2-u_3v_3)+(u_2^2+u_3^2-2u_4)(2u_1u_4+2u_1v_1+u_2v_2+u_3v_3-2v_4).$$

This shows that the variety defined by $\mathcal{I}_\Gamma$ is reducible. To investigate real points of the variety, we consider three possible options: $T_4 \neq 0$, $V_0 \neq 0$, and $T_4 = V_0 = 0$.

First, assume that $T_4 \neq 0$. Elimination of v_2, v_3, v_4 gives the product $V_1V_2 \in \mathcal{I}_\Gamma$ in the remaining variables, where

$$V_1 = v_1 + 2u_4 - 2r^2, \qquad V_2 = (u_1^2+u_2^2+u_3^2-2u_4)^2 + 4r^2u_1^2. \tag{30}$$

If $V_2 = 0$, then $U_0 - 2u_4 = 0$, $u_1 = 0$ as we look only for real components. The augmented ideal contains this sum of squares: $v_4^2 + r^2V_1^2 = 0$. Therefore, $V_1 = 0$ is inevitable for the real components with $T_4 \neq 0$. The ideal $\mathcal{I}_\Gamma + (V_1)$ in $\mathcal{R}_\Gamma[T_4^{-1}]$ contains several multiples of the polynomial $V_3 = v_4 - 2r^2u_1$. Localizing $V_3 \neq 0$ gives the trivial ideal of $\mathcal{R}_\Gamma[T_4^{-1}, V_3^{-1}]$, which is, hence, an empty variety. With $V_3 = 0$, we obtain the equations of Theorem 3 in the homogenized form with u_0. The points on the corresponding variety describe cases when Γ is a Villarceau circle, as analyzed in Section 4.

Secondly, assume that $V_0 \neq 0$. Localization of $\mathcal{I}_\Gamma$ in the ring $\mathcal{R}_\Gamma[V_0^{-1}]$ gives an ideal generated by the 2×2 minors of the matrix $\mathcal{L}$ in (20) and the additional equation (21) with $u_0 = 1$. Here, we obtain the reducible Dupin cyclides of Remark 4.

The last option is $T_4 = V_0 = 0$. We notice polynomial multiples of $T_2^2 + T_3^2$ in the Gröbner basis of $(\mathcal{I}_\Gamma, T_4, V_0)$. Localization at $T_2^2 + T_3^2 \neq 0$ gives an ideal that contains the four polynomials of Theorem 3. Hence, it describes some points in the Villarceau circle component (of the option $T_4 \neq 0$). We assume further that $T_2 = T_3 = 0$. Consideration of the following polynomial allows further progress:

$$
\begin{aligned}
V_4 = {} & (2r^2u_1+v_4)(U_0-2u_4-2v_1)-u_1(4r^2u_4+v_2^2+v_3^2) \\
& +(v_1-4r^2)(u_2v_2+u_3v_3)+8r^2v_4.
\end{aligned}
\tag{31}
$$

The localization $V_4 \neq 0$ leads to a subcase (describing touching spheres) of the option $V_0 \neq 0$. Hence, we assume that $V_4 = 0$. Elimination of v_2, v_3, v_4 in the ideal $(\mathcal{I}_\Gamma, T_2, T_3, T_4, V_0, V_4)$ leads to some generators that factor with

$$V_5 = u_1^2(u_2^2+u_3^2) + (u_2^2+u_3^2-2u_4)^2. \tag{32}$$

The further localization $V_5 \neq 0$ leads to the principal circle component in Theorem 4. The remaining case $V_5 = 0$ splits into these two subcases, as we are interested in the real points only:

(i) $u_1 \neq 0$, so that $u_2 = u_3 = 0$, and eventually $u_4 = 0$. The obtained ideal is reducible, with the prominent factor $V_6 = u_1^2(v_2^2 + v_3^2) + 4v_4^2$ after elimination of v_1. The localization $V_7 \neq 0$ belongs to the principal circle component. The case $V_6 = 0$ simplifies to $v_2 = v_3 = v_4 = 2v_1 - u_1^2 = 0$, and the cyclide degenerates to a double-sphere case.

(ii) $u_1 = 0$, $u_2^2 + u_3^2 - 2u_4 = 0$. Elimination of the variables u_1, u_2, u_3, u_4 gives us a principal ideal, and the generator factors with

$$V_7 = (v_2^2 + v_3^2)^3 + (v_1 v_2^2 + v_1 v_3^2 + 2v_4^2)^2. \tag{33}$$

The localization $V_7 \neq 0$ belongs to the principal circle component. With $V_7 = 0$ we get $v_2 = v_3 = v_4 = 0$, and the resulting ideal contains the product $(u_2^2 + u_3^2 + 2v_1)^2(u_2^2 + u_3^2 + 2v_1 - 4r^2)$. Either of the factors leads to points on the principal circle component.

5.2. *Proof for Cubic Cyclides*

We use Theorem 2 to recognize cubic Dupin cyclides in the form (8) with $u_0 = 0$. The equation is first transformed to the form (2)

$$\begin{aligned} &2(u_1x + u_2y + u_3z)(x^2 + y^2 + z^2) + 2(u_4 + v_1)x^2 + 2u_4y^2 + 2u_4z^2 \\ &\quad + 2v_2xy + 2v_3xz + 2(v_4 - r^2u_1)x - 2r^2u_2y - 2r^2u_3z - 2r^2u_4 = 0. \end{aligned} \tag{34}$$

Let

$$\rho_0 : \mathbb{R}[b_1, b_2, b_3, c_1, c_2, c_3, d_1, d_2, d_3, e_1, e_2, e_3, f_0] \to \mathcal{R}_\Gamma.$$

be the ring homomorphism defined by the coefficient identification. Since $\rho_0(B_0) = U_0$, all remaining computations are considered over the localized ring $\mathcal{R}_\Gamma[U_0^{-1}]$. Let us denote by $\mathcal{I}_\Gamma^*$ the ideal generated by the numerators of the ρ_0-images of the four equations in Theorem 2. This ideal contains the product $T_4V_0^*$, where

$$V_0^* = 2u_1u_4U_0 + 2u_1v_1(u_2^2 + u_3^2) + (u_2v_2 + u_3v_3)(u_2^2 + u_3^2 - u_1^2). \tag{35}$$

Like in the quartic case, we consider the three options: $T_4 \neq 0$, $V_0^* \neq 0$, and $T_4 = V_0^* = 0$.

The localization $T_4 \neq 0$ gives us directly the $u_0 = 0$ part of the Villarceau circle component in Theorem 3.

Localizing $V_0^* \neq 0$ gives an ideal containing the 2×2 minors of the matrix $\mathcal{L}$ and Equation (21). This case describes only reducible cyclides of Remark 4.

With $T_4 = V_0^* = 0$, the ideal $(\mathcal{I}_\Gamma^*, T_4, V_0^*)$ contains the sum of squares $T_2^2 + T_3^2$. Hence, $T_2 = T_3 = 0$ since we are looking only for real points of the variety $\mathcal{D}_\Gamma$. The further candidate for localization to consider is

$$V_1^* = 4r^2u_1^2 + v_2^2 + v_3^2 - 4u_1v_4. \tag{36}$$

By comparing Gröebner bases, the localization of $(\mathcal{I}_\Gamma^*, T_2, T_3, T_4, V_0^*)$ at $V_1^* \neq 0$ indeed coincides with the ideal of the principal circle defined by the 2×2 minors of $\mathcal{N}$ and $\mathcal{M}$. The remaining case $V_1^* = 0$ can be localized further at $V_2^* = u_2^2 + u_3^2 + u_4^2$. The localization $V_2^* \neq 0$ defines points on the principal circle component. The case $V_2^* = 0$ simplifies to $u_2 = u_3 = u_4 = 0$, and the cyclide equation degenerates to a subcase of a touching sphere + plane case.

6. Smooth Blending of Cyclides

Here, we apply the main results to the practical problem of blending smoothly two Dupin cyclides along a common circle. Smooth blending in this context means that the cyclides share tangent planes along their common circle.

Lemma 2. *Consider two cyclide equations of the form* (8) *with possibly different coefficients* $u_0, \ldots, u_4, v_1, \ldots, v_4$. *Then they are joined smoothly along the circle* Γ *if and only if the rational function*

$$\mathcal{F}(y,z) = \frac{v_2y + v_3z + v_4}{u_2y + u_3z + u_4} \tag{37}$$

is the same function on the circle Γ *for both cyclides.*

Proof. The normal vector of cyclides (8) along the circle Γ is defined by the gradient of the defining polynomial. The gradient is computed as

$$\big(v_2y + v_3z + v_4, 2y(u_2y + u_3z + u_4), 2z(u_2y + u_3z + u_4)\big).$$

On the two given cyclides, the paired gradient vectors should be proportional along the circle in order to obtain smooth blending. After the division by $u_2y + u_3z + u_4$, the gradient vectors are rescaled to $(\mathcal{F}(y,z), 2y, 2z)$ for direct comparison. □

A special case is when the rational function (37) is a constant on Γ. This is equivalent to $\mathrm{rank}(\mathcal{N}) = 1$. Therefore, the rational function $\mathcal{F}$ is constant when Γ is a principal circle case of a Dupin cyclide. As the following Lemma implies, the envelope surface of tangent planes of any cyclide equation satisfying $\mathrm{rank}(\mathcal{N}) = 1$ along Γ is a circular cone or cylinder. It is known [7] that the envelope appearing as a cone or cylinder occurs in the case of Dupin cyclides if the circle is principal. This is due to the representation of Dupin cyclides as canal surfaces, where they are considered as conics in the four-dimensional Minkowski space, and the tangent lines to those conics represent circular cones or cylinders; see [7] for details.

Lemma 3. *If the function* $\mathcal{F}(y,z) \equiv \lambda$ *on the circle* Γ *for some constant* λ*, then the envelope surface of tangent planes of the cyclide* (8) *along* Γ *is given by the equation*

$$y^2 + z^2 = \left(r - \frac{\lambda x}{2r}\right)^2. \tag{38}$$

It is a circular cone if $\lambda \neq 0$ *or a cylinder if* $\lambda = 0$.

Proof. We parametrize the circle by $(0, r\cos\varphi, r\sin\varphi)$. The envelope line passing through such a point is orthogonal to the rescaled gradient vector $(\lambda, 2r\cos\phi, 2r\sin\phi)$ and to the tangent vector $(0, -\sin\phi, \cos\phi)$ to the circle. The line therefore follows the direction of the cross-product vector $(2r, -\lambda\cos\phi, -\lambda\sin\phi)$. The envelope of tangent planes is parametrized therefore as

$$(x,y,z) = (0, r\cos\varphi, r\sin\varphi) + t\,(2r, -\lambda\cos\varphi, -\lambda\sin\varphi). \tag{39}$$

Hence, $x = 2rt$, $y^2 + z^2 = (r - \lambda t)^2$. Elimination of t gives (38). □

Remark 5. *The envelope of tangent planes degenerates to the plane* $x = 0$ *of the circle* Γ *when* $\lambda = \infty$. *If the circle is a Villarceau circle, then the envelope of tangent planes is a more complicated surface of degree four. As mentioned in Remark 3, the condition* $\mathrm{rank}(\mathcal{N}) = 1$ *combined with the equations of the Villarceau component leads to singular horn cyclides. On the other hand, the cone envelope occurs also in the degenerate case of Remark* 4.

6.1. Smooth Blending along Principal Circles

In this section, we focus on smooth blending between Dupin cyclides having Γ as a principal circle. The main case to investigate is by fixing a tangent cone along the circle Γ and finding Dupin cyclides that fit the blending conditions along the circle; see Figure 2a.

Proposition 1. *Let us fix the parameter* $\lambda \neq 0$ *and the cone* (38) *containing the circle* Γ*. The Dupin cyclides that join the fixed cone smoothly along* Γ *as a principle circle are fully characterized by the five equations*

$$v_2 = \lambda u_2, \qquad v_3 = \lambda u_3, \qquad v_4 = \lambda u_4, \tag{40}$$
$$4r^2 u_1(\lambda u_0 - u_1) + \lambda^2(u_2^2 + u_3^2) - 2\lambda u_0 u_4 = 0, \tag{41}$$
$$16r^4(\lambda u_0 - u_1)^2 + 4\lambda^2 r^2 u_1^2 - \lambda^2(\lambda^2 + 4r^2)(u_2^2 + u_3^2) - 8\lambda^2 r^2 u_0 v_1 = 0. \tag{42}$$

Proof. From Lemmas 2 and 3, the tangency conditions along the circle are given by $v_i = \lambda u_i$ for $i \in \{2,3,4\}$. We specialize u_0, v_2, v_3, v_4 in the ideal generated by the 2×2 minors of $\mathcal{N}$ and $\mathcal{M}$ and obtain an ideal $\mathcal{I}_\lambda$ in $\mathcal{R}_\lambda = \mathbb{R}(r)[u_1, u_2, u_3, u_4, v_1, \lambda, \lambda^{-1}]$. We notice many multiples of u_2, u_3, u_4 in a Gröbner basis of $\mathcal{I}_\lambda$. If $u_2u_3u_4 \neq 0$, we obtain an ideal $\mathcal{I}_\lambda^* \subset \mathcal{R}_\lambda[(u_2u_3u_4)^{-1}]$ generated by the five equations of the proposition. The points with $u_2u_3u_4 = 0$ satisfy the equations of $\mathcal{I}_\lambda^* \cup \mathcal{R}_\lambda$ by checking the cases $u_2 = u_3 = u_4 = 0$, $u_i = 0, u_ju_k \neq 0$ or $u_i = u_j = 0, u_k \neq 0$ with $i,j,k \in \{2,3,4\}$ being pairwise distinct. Each of the resulting ideals $\mathcal{R}_\Gamma[\lambda, \lambda^{-1}]$ contains $\mathcal{I}_\lambda^* \cup \mathcal{R}_\lambda$. □

Remark 6. *The five equations of Proposition 1 are linear in the five variables u_4, v_1, v_2, v_3, v_4. Hence, we can easily solve the equations for those variables and obtain a parametrization of the family of Dupin cyclides touching the cone along the circle Γ. Apart from the first three equations, the variables u_2, u_3 appear only within the expression $u_2^2 + u_3^2$, representing a rotational degree of freedom: rotating the two Dupin cyclide patches independently around the x-axis preserves the smooth blending along the circle Γ.*

The limit cases $\lambda = 0$ and $\lambda = \infty$ contain interesting families of Dupin cyclides as well. The family with $\lambda = 0$ allows us to blend two toruses or a torus with a Dupin cyclide; see Figure 2b–d. The family in the case $\lambda = \infty$ allows us to blend a Dupin cyclide with a plane; see Figure 2e.

Proposition 2. *Let us fix the cylinder defined by the parameter $\lambda = 0$ in (38). The only Dupin cyclides that join this cylinder smoothly along Γ are characterized by the equations*

$$u_1 = v_2 = v_3 = v_4 = 0, \tag{43}$$
$$2r^2 u_0 v_1 + r^2(u_2^2 + u_3^2) - (v_1 + u_4)^2 = 0. \tag{44}$$

Those Dupin cyclides are symmetric with respect to plane $x = 0$ of the circle Γ.

Proof. The equations $v_2 = v_3 = v_4 = 0$ follow from the condition $\lambda = 0$ and the tangent conditions in Lemma 2. With those constraints, the ideal of the principal circle component reduces to the other two equations $u_1 = 0$ and (44). The symmetry property with the plane $x = 0$ follows from Equation (43). □

Proposition 3. *Let us fix the plane $x = 0$ (of the circle Γ) defined by the parameter $\lambda = \infty$ in (38). The only Dupin cyclides that join this plane smoothly along the circle Γ are characterized by the equations*

$$u_2 = u_3 = u_4 = 0, \qquad v_4 = 2r^2 u_1, \tag{45}$$
$$16r^4 u_0^2 + 4r^2 u_1^2 - (v_2^2 + v_3^2) - 8r^2 u_0 v_1 = 0. \tag{46}$$

This family of Dupin cyclides is preserved by the reflection with respect to the plane of the circle.

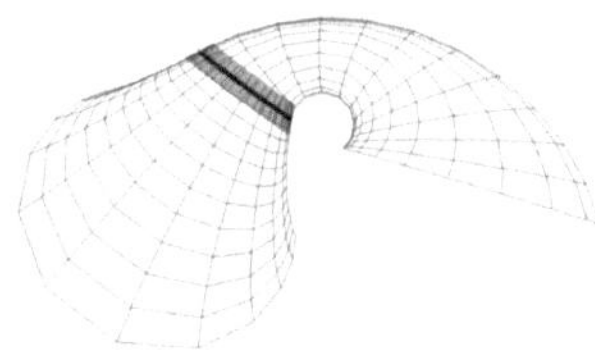

(a) $(1:-\frac{49}{30}:0:\frac{76}{15}:\frac{323}{30}:-\frac{1669}{120}:0:-\frac{76}{15}:-\frac{323}{30})$
$(1:-2:-5:0:\frac{17}{2}:-\frac{93}{8}:5:0:-\frac{17}{2})$

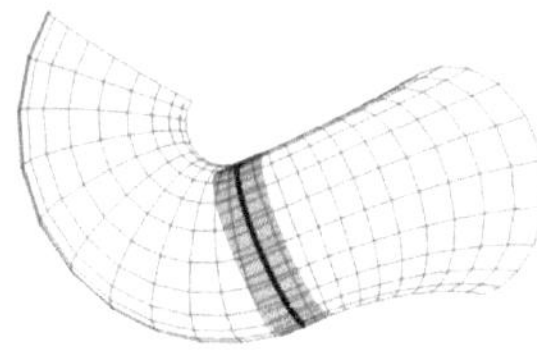

(b) $(1:0:-3:0:\frac{9}{2}:-\frac{9}{2}:0:0:0)$
$(1:0:0:\frac{76}{15}:\frac{323}{30}:-\frac{361}{30}:0:0:0)$

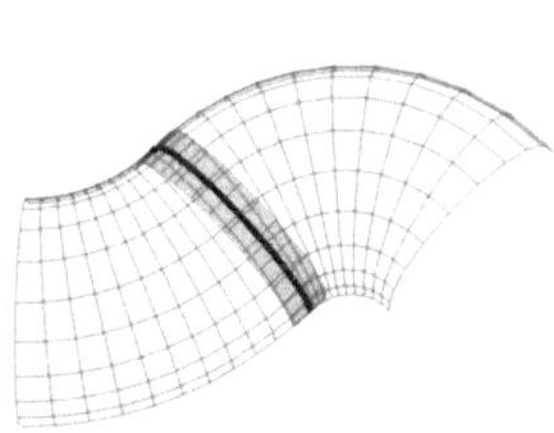

(c) $(1:0:5:0:\frac{25}{2}:-\frac{25}{2}:0:0:0)$
$(1:0:-3:0:\frac{9}{2}:-\frac{9}{2}:0:0:0)$

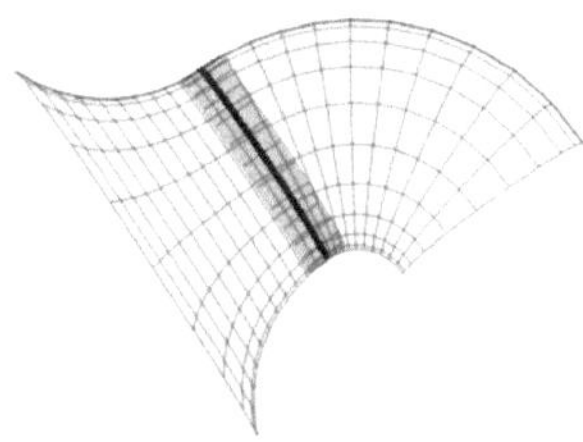

(d) $(1:0:0:0:-4:8:0:0:0)$
$(1:0:-3:0:\frac{9}{2}:-\frac{9}{2}:0:0:0)$

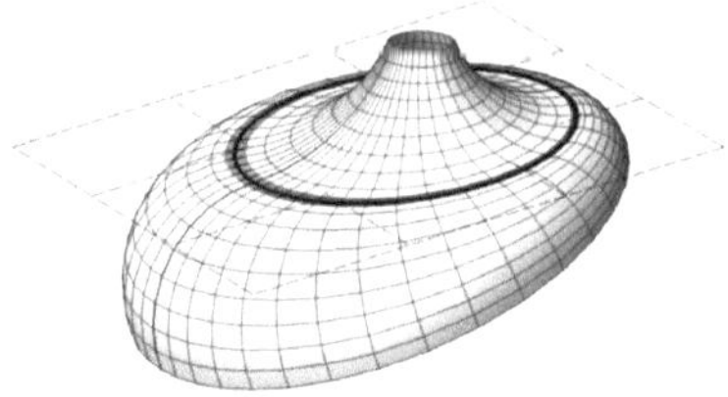

(e) $(1:a:0:0:0:\frac{1}{2}a^2+\frac{15}{8}:1:0:2a)$

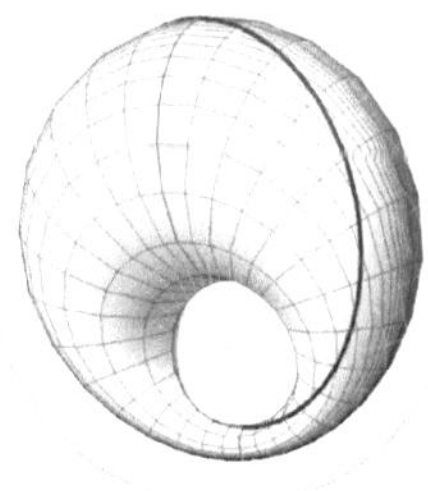

(f) $(1+t:0:1:0:\frac{12}{13}:\frac{2}{13}+2t:0:-\frac{10}{13}:0)$

Figure 2. Two Dupin cyclide equations with different coefficient values $(u_0:\ldots:u_4:v_1:\ldots:v_4)$ are smoothly blended along the circle Γ with $r=1$. The two cyclides on *(e)* are obtained from the parameter values $a=1$ and $a=1.8$. The two cyclides on *(f)* are obtained from the parameter values $t=0$ and $t=0.4$.

Proof. Similar to the proof of Proposition 2. The equations $u_2=u_3=u_4=0$ follow from the tangent condition $\lambda=\infty$, and the ideal of the principal circle component reduces to the other two equations of the proposition. The reflection $(x,y,z)\mapsto(-x,y,z)$ with respect to the plane $x=0$ preserves the coefficients u_0,u_2,u_3,u_4,v_1 and symmetries u_1,v_2,v_3,v_4 to $-u_1,-v_2,-v_3,-v_4$ in (8). This transformation preserves Equations (45) and (46). □

Remark 7. *The cubic cyclides with $u_0 = 0$ in the family of Proposition 3 degenerate to reducible surfaces: namely, the cases of touching sphere + plane.*

It is interesting to distinguish torus surfaces in the principal circle component. We get two cases depending on the position of the circle Γ (wrapping around the torus hole or around the torus tube). Figure 2c,d illustrate two different configurations of torus blending using those two kinds of principal circles. The circle wraps around the torus tube of both toruses in Figure 2c. The circle wraps around the torus tube for one torus and around the torus hole for the other torus in Figure 2d. The examples satisfy the pertinent algebraic conditions exactly; this article does not consider the issue of numerical stability.

Proposition 4. *Equation (8) defines a torus having Γ as the principal circle if and only if one of the following applies:*

(i) $u_0 = 1, \quad u_2^2 + u_3^2 = 2u_0u_4, \quad v_1 = -u_4, \quad v_2 = v_3 = v_4 = 0;$

(ii) $u_0 = 1, \quad u_2 = u_3 = v_2 = v_3 = 0, \quad u_4 = \dfrac{2r^2u_1(\lambda - u_1)}{\lambda^2},$

$$v_1 = \frac{\lambda^2u_1^2 + 4r^2(\lambda - u_1)^2}{2\lambda^2}, \quad v_4 = \lambda u_4 = \frac{2r^2u_1(\lambda - u_1)}{\lambda}.$$

Proof. Assume that the circle Γ is wrapping around the torus tube. Then we have a tangent cylinder along the circle, defined by $v_2 = v_3 = v_4 = 0$ as in Proposition 2. The cross section of (8) with the plane $x = 0$ is a pair of circles with the same radius (Γ, Γ'):

$$\Gamma' : x = \left(y + \frac{u_2}{u_0}\right)^2 + \left(z + \frac{u_3}{u_0}\right)^2 - \frac{r^2u_0^2 - 2u_0u_4 + u_2^2 + u_3^2}{u_0^2} = 0.$$

We need $u_2^2 + u_3^2 = 2u_0u_4$ for the equality of radii. Equation (44) then factors into $(v_1 + u_4)(v_1 + u_4 - 2r^2u_0)$. Due to the rotations in the yz-plane that preserve the circle Γ, we can assume that the revolution axis of the torus is parallel to the z-axis. Then $u_3 = 0$, and we say $u_2 = \sqrt{2u_0u_4}$. Note that $u_0u_4 > 0$ by the derived equation $u_2^2 + u_3^2 = 2u_0u_4$. The rotated cyclide equation must be

$$u_0\left(x^2 + \left(y - \sqrt{\frac{u_4}{2u_0}}\right)^2 + z^2 - r^2 + \frac{u_4}{2u_0}\right)^2 - 2u_4\left(y - \sqrt{\frac{u_4}{2u_0}}\right)^2 + 2v_1x^2 = 0. \tag{47}$$

Comparing with (1), we recognize a torus equation (with shifted y) when $v_1 = -u_4$. The other option $v_1 = 2r^2u_0 - u_4$ gives a surface that is not symmetric around the revolution axis; hence, that is not a torus. This shows possibility *(i)*.

Assume now that the circle Γ is wrapping around the torus hole. Then we have a tangent cone along the circle, i.e., $v_2 = \lambda u_2$, $v_3 = \lambda u_3$, $v_4 = \lambda u_4$ as in Proposition 1. The section with $x = 0$ should be a pair of concentric circles. Hence, $u_2 = u_3 = 0$. Again, with $u_0 = 1$ and the parametrization in Proposition 1, the cyclide equation reduces to

$$\left(\left(x + \frac{u_1}{2}\right)^2 + y^2 + z^2 + \frac{r^2(\lambda - u_1)^2}{\lambda^2} - \frac{u_1^2(\lambda^2 + 4r^2)}{4\lambda^2}\right)^2 - \frac{4r^2(\lambda - u_1)^2}{\lambda^2}(y^2 + z^2) = 0.$$

This is a torus equation, comparable to (1). □

6.2. Smooth Blending along Villarceau Circles

By Remarks 3 and 5, it is not possible to smoothly blend a Dupin cyclide that has Γ as a principle circle with a Dupin cyclide that has Γ as a Villarceau circle. It is left to investigate blending between cyclides in the Villarceau circle component. The following result is illustrated in Figure 2f.

Proposition 5. *Let D denote a Dupin cyclide (8) that has Γ as a Villarceau circle. The only Dupin cyclides that join D smoothly along Γ are obtained by perturbing the equation of D by*

$$(x^2 + y^2 + z^2 - r^2)^2 + 4r^2x^2.$$

Those cyclides have Γ as a Villarceau circle.

Proof. Let $D' = (u_0 : u_1' : \ldots : u_4' : v_1' : \ldots : v_4')$ be a Dupin cyclide that has Γ as a Villarceau circle and assume that D' and D are smoothly blending along the circle Γ. We obtain the matrix equation:

$$\begin{pmatrix} 0 & 0 & 0 & 2 & 1 & 0 & 0 & 0 \\ -2r^2 & 0 & 0 & 0 & 0 & 0 & 0 & 1 \\ 0 & r^2v_2 & 0 & v_4 & 0 & -r^2u_2 & 0 & -u_4 \\ 0 & 0 & r^2v_3 & v_4 & 0 & 0 & -r^2u_3 & -u_4 \\ 0 & v_3 & v_2 & 0 & 0 & -u_3 & -u_2 & 0 \\ 0 & v_4 & 0 & v_2 & 0 & -u_4 & 0 & -u_2 \\ 0 & 0 & v_4 & v_3 & 0 & 0 & -u_4 & -u_3 \end{pmatrix} \begin{pmatrix} u_1' \\ u_2' \\ u_3' \\ u_4' \\ v_1' \\ v_2' \\ v_3' \\ v_4' \end{pmatrix} = \begin{pmatrix} 2r^2u_0 \\ 0 \\ 0 \\ 0 \\ 0 \\ 0 \\ 0 \\ 0 \end{pmatrix}.$$

The first two rows of the matrix are linear equations obtained from D' being in the Villarceau circle component. The last five rows are the tangency conditions for the given Dupin cyclide D from Lemma 2. Note that the 7×8 matrix has the full rank seven symbolically. We must have $v_i \neq 0$ for some $i \in \{2,3,4\}$ to avoid rank $\mathcal{N} < 2$ and degeneracy to a horn cyclide. Then, by setting $s = u_i'/v_i$, we can solve

$$u_j' = su_j, \qquad v_j' = sv_j, \qquad \text{for } j \in \{2,3,4\}, \tag{48}$$

$$u_1' = s\frac{v_4}{2r^2} = su_1, \qquad v_1' = 2r^2u_0 - 2su_4. \tag{49}$$

After dividing the equation of D' by s, all coefficients are fixed except $v_1' = 2r^2u_0/s - 2u_4$, and u_0 becomes u_0/s. Hence, with $t = u_0/s - u_0$, u_0 and v_1' become $u_0 + t$ and $2r^2u_0 - 2u_4 + 2r^2t = v_1 + 2r^2t$, respectively. This is exactly a perturbation by amount t. □

7. The Möbius Invariant J_0

In this section, we compute a Möbius invariant denoted by J_0 [18] (Section 6) for Dupin cyclides in the Villarceau and principal circle components described by Theorems 3 and 4, respectively. This invariant extends the Möbius invariant

$$J_0 = \frac{r^2}{R^2}\left(1 - \frac{r^2}{R^2}\right) \tag{50}$$

for toruses to the Dupin cyclides. The smooth Dupin cyclides are characterized by $0 < J_0 \leqslant 1/4$, and the singular Dupin cyclides are characterized by $J_0 \leqslant 0$. A singular Dupin cyclide can be obtained from a spindle or a horn torus (see Figure 3) by Möbius transformations.

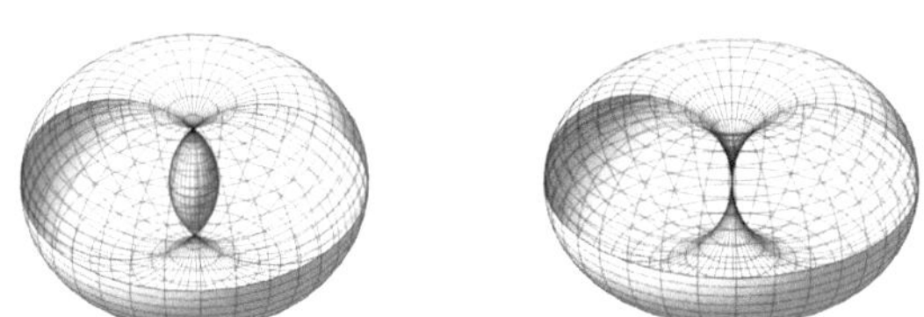

(a) (b)

Figure 3. A cutaway view of singular toruses: (**a**) a spindle torus ($J_0 < 0, r > R$); (**b**) a horn torus ($J_0 = 0, r = R$).

We use [18] ((6.15) and (6.17)) to compute J_0 for, respectively, the quartic equation (8) with $u_0 \neq 0$ and the cubic equation (8) with $u_0 = 0$. The obtained expression gives the Möbius invariant when the equation defines a Dupin cyclide. It is convenient to subtract $1/4$ from J_0 and obtain a perfect square expression frequently. Let us denote by $\widehat{J}_0$ the remainder $1/4 - J_0$. The goal is to have a compact equivalent formula for J_0 in each of the two components.

Obtaining a J_0-expression for quartic Dupin cyclides in the principal circle case is not straightforward. Consider the ideal $\mathcal{I}_\lambda$ generated by the five equations of Proposition 1. By incorporating separately the numerator and the denominator of $\widehat{J}_0$ in the ideal $\mathcal{I}_\lambda$ and by eliminating the linear variables $u_4, v_1, \ldots, v_4$, we obtain a representative numerator and a representative denominator with a common factor. This gives a new expression of $\widehat{J}_0$ up to a constant multiplier. It is easy to find this constant by solving it from the difference of the two expressions of $\widehat{J}_0$ modulo $\mathcal{I}_\lambda$. The resulting J_0 expression is

$$J_0 = \frac{1}{4} - \frac{\left(8r^4(\lambda u_0 - u_1)^2 - 4r^2(\lambda^2 + 4r^2)u_1^2 + \lambda^2(\lambda^2 + 2r^2)(u_2^2 + u_3^2)\right)^2}{16r^4\left(4r^2(\lambda u_0 - u_1)^2 - \lambda^2(u_2^2 + u_3^2)\right)^2}. \tag{51}$$

By further elimination of $u_2^2 + u_3^2$ using (41)–(42), we obtain the more compact form

$$J_0 = \frac{1}{4} - \frac{\left(4r^4\lambda u_0 - 2r^2(\lambda^2 + 6r^2)u_1 + \lambda(\lambda^2 + 2r^2)u_4\right)^2}{16r^4\left(2r^2\lambda u_0 - 2r^2 u_1 - \lambda u_4\right)^2}. \tag{52}$$

It is interesting that this compact form (52) also covers the J_0 expression of the family of cubic Dupin cyclides $u_0 = 0$ in Proposition 1.

Since the majority of Dupin cyclides in the principal circle component belong to the family of Dupin cyclides in Proposition 1, three equivalent expressions for J_0 in the principal circle component are obtained by substituting $\lambda = v_i/u_i$ into (52) for each $i = 2, 3, 4$. The equality of two different J_0 expressions can be checked by reducing the numerator of the difference between them modulo the ideal of the principal circle component.

In the two limiting cases of Propositions 2 and 3 of the principal circle component, we use the same method and obtain the expression

$$J_0 = \frac{1}{4} - \frac{(4r^2u_0 - 4u_4 - 3v_1)^2}{4v_1^2} \tag{53}$$

for the family $\lambda = 0$ of Proposition 2, and

$$J_0 = \frac{1}{4} - \frac{(3r^2u_0 - v_1)^2}{4r^4u_0^2} \tag{54}$$

for the family $\lambda = \infty$ of Proposition 3. Note that the latter formula is always well-defined because the family of Proposition 3 does not contain irreducible cubic Dupin cyclides by Remark 7.

In the Villarceau circle case, the simplification of J_0 in [18] (6.15) modulo the equations (9) and (10) is straightforward. Elimination of v_2, v_3, and v_4 gives a common factor of the numerator and the denominator and leads to the expression

$$J_0 = \frac{r^2u_2^2 + r^2u_3^2 - u_4^2}{16(r^2u_2^2 + r^2u_3^2 - u_4^2) + 4v_1^2}. \tag{55}$$

Alternative eliminations give

$$J_0 = \frac{1}{4} - \frac{r^2 v_1^2}{4\left(r^2(v_1^2 + v_2^2 + v_3^2) - v_4^2\right)}, \tag{56}$$

$$= \frac{1}{4} - \frac{v_1^2}{16r^2\left(u_2^2 + u_3^2 + u_0 v_1 - r^2 u_0^2\right)}. \tag{57}$$

These expressions are applicable to cubic Dupin cyclides as well. The invariant values should be positive because singular cyclides have no real Villarceau circles. Indeed, the numerator in (55) is positive by the inequality $u_4^2 < r^2 u_2^2 + r^2 u_3^2$ in (11). The denominator is positive as well from the same condition. The limiting case $u_4^2 = r^2 u_2^2 + r^2 u_3^2$ of Theorem 3 represents horn cyclides since $J_0 = 0$ from (55), as mentioned in Remark 3.

8. Conclusions

This paper derives the algebraic conditions that fully characterize the general family of Dupin cyclides passing through the fixed circle (7). The algebraic conditions restrict the coefficients of the general family (8) of Darboux cyclides passing through the circle. The main results are divided to Theorems 3 and 4, which reflect the position of the circle as either a Villarceau circle or a principal circle of the Dupin cyclides. The two obtained general families are four-dimensional; see Remark 2. The main results can be applied to check whether a particular surface (8) is a Dupin cyclide or to generate parametric families of Dupin cyclides (by considering subvarieties of $\mathcal{D}_\Gamma$).

The found algebraic conditions are used in Section 6 to characterize and exemplify pairs of Dupin cyclides that blend smoothly along circles. The construction of smooth blending constitutes the basic application of Dupin cyclides in CAGD. The focal case of smooth blending requires fixing a tangent cone along the circle (7), which reduces the dimension of general families of smoothly matching Dupin cyclides to three; see Proposition 1. Even if we would like to join two Dupin cyclides continuously along a circle at a constant angle [9], the straightforward way of modeling is to fix the tangent cones meeting at the desired angle. This leads to choosing within two distinct families of Dupin cyclides in the context of Section 6. The J_0-invariant of Section 7 determines (up to Möbius transformations) the proportions of a whole Dupin cyclide.

Using implicit equations like (8) rather than parametrizations amounts to an alternative technique of blending cyclides. Like in [18], the algebraic conditions on implicit equations for Dupin cyclides are quite non-linear. Their derivation and concise presentation required particular earnestness and attention. The derivation in Section 5 was facilitated by the computer algebra systems Maple 2018 and Singular 4.2.1, employment of a Gröbner basis, elimination and localization techniques, and syzygy computations [22].

Future work may establish blending routines of using implicit equations for Dupin cyclides and compare their practicability, efficiency, and accuracy to existing parametrization techniques [3–8]. The results could be applied to uniformize investigation of blending Dupin cyclides at two fixed circles or on fixed spheres, cones, or cylinders [11–16].

Author Contributions: Conceptualization, R.V.; methodology, J.M.M. and R.V.; software, J.M.M. and R.V.; investigation, J.M.M. and R.V.; writing—original draft preparation, J.M.M.; writing—review and editing, J.M.M. and R.V.; visualization, J.M.M.; supervision, R.V.; project administration, R.V.; funding acquisition, R.V. All authors have read and agreed to the published version of the manuscript.

Funding: This work is part of a project that has received funding from the European Union's Horizon 2020 Research and Innovation Programme under Marie Skłodowska–Curie grant agreement No. 860843.

Data Availability Statement: Data are contained within the article.

Conflicts of Interest: The authors declare no conflicts of interest.

References

1. Dupin, C. *Applications de Géométrie et de Méchanique: à la Marine aux Ponts et Chaussées, etc., pour Faire Suite aux Développements de Géométrie;* Bachelier: Paris, France, 1822.
2. Darboux, G. *Principes de Géométrie Analytique;* Gauthier-Villars: Paris, France, 1917.

3. Martin, R.R. *Principal Patches—A New Class of Surface Patch Based on Differential Geometry*; Elsevier: Amsterdam, The Netherlands, 1983.
4. Pratt, M.J. Cyclides in computer aided geometric design. *Comput. Aided Geom. Des.* **1990**, *7*, 221–242. [CrossRef]
5. Pratt, M.J. Cyclides in computer aided geometric design II. *Comput. Aided Geom. Des.* **1995**, *12*, 131–152. [CrossRef]
6. Zube, S.; Krasauskas, R. Representation of Dupin cyclides using quaternions. *Graph. Model.* **2015**, *82*, 110–122. [CrossRef]
7. Krasauskas, R.; Mäurer, C. Studying cyclides with Laguerre geometry. *Comput. Aided Geom. Des.* **2000**, *17*, 101–126. [CrossRef]
8. Garnier, L.; Barki, H.; Foufou, S.; Puech, L. Computation of Yvon-Villarceau circles on Dupin cyclides and construction of circular edge right triangles on tori and Dupin cyclides. *Comput. Math. Appl.* **2014**, *68*, 1689–1709. [CrossRef]
9. Mesnil, R.; Douthe, C.; Baverel, O.; Léger, B. Generalised cyclidic nets for shape modelling in architecture. *Int. J. Archit. Comput.* **2017**, *15*, 148–168. [CrossRef]
10. Salkov, N. Application of the Dupin cyclide in temple architecture. *J. Phys. Conf. Ser.* **2020**, *1546*, 012042. [CrossRef]
11. Boehm, W. On cyclides in geometric modeling. *Comput. Aided Geom. Des.* **1990**, *7*, 243–255. [CrossRef]
12. Pottmann, H.; Peternell, M. Applications of Laguerre geometry in CAGD. *Comput. Aided Geom. Des.* **1998**, *15*, 165–186. [CrossRef]
13. Allen, S.; Dutta, D. Cyclides in pure blending I. *Comput. Aided Geom. Des.* **1997**, *14*, 51–75. [CrossRef]
14. Allen, S.; Dutta, D. Cyclides in pure blending II. *Comput. Aided Geom. Des.* **1997**, *14*, 77–102. [CrossRef]
15. Shene, C.K. Blending two cones with Dupin cyclides. *Comput. Aided Geom. Des.* **1998**, *15*, 643–673. [CrossRef]
16. Druoton, L.; Langevin, R.; Garnier, L. Blending canal surfaces along given circles using Dupin cyclides. *Int. J. Comput. Math.* **2014**, *91*, 641–660. [CrossRef]
17. Villarceau, A.Y. Extrait d'une note communiquée à M. Babinet par M. Yvon Villarceau. *Comptes Rendus Hebd. Des SÉAnces L'AcadÉMie Des Sci.* **1848**, *27*, 246.
18. Menjanahary, J.M.; Vidunas, R. Dupin Cyclides as a Subspace of Darboux Cyclides. *arXiv* **2022**, arXiv:2212.14015.
19. Ottens, L. Dupin Cyclides. Ph.D. Thesis, Faculty of Science and Engineering, University of Groningen, Groningen, The Netherlands, 2012.
20. Pottmann, H.; Shi, L.; Skopenkov, M. Darboux cyclides and webs from circles. *Comput. Aided Geom. Des.* **2012**, *29*, 77–97. [CrossRef]
21. Zhao, M.; Jia, X.; Tu, C.; Mourrain, B.; Wang, W. Enumerating the morphologies of non-degenerate Darboux cyclides. *Comput. Aided Geom. Des.* **2019**, *75*, 101776. [CrossRef]
22. Cox, D.; Little, J.; O'shea, D.; Sweedler, M. *Ideals, Varieties, and Algorithms*; Springer: Berlin/Heidelberg, Germany, 1997; Volume 3.

mathematics

Article

Maximizing Closeness in Bipartite Networks: A Graph-Theoretic Analysis

Fazal Hayat [1] and Daniele Ettore Otera [2,*]

[1] School of Mathematics and Statistics, Gansu Center for Applied Mathematics, Lanzhou University, Lanzhou 730000, China; fhayatmaths@gmail.com
[2] Institute of Data Science and Digital Technologies, Vilnius University, 08412 Vilnius, Lithuania
* Correspondence: daniele.otera@mif.vu.lt or daniele.otera@gmail.com

Abstract: A fundamental aspect of network analysis involves pinpointing nodes that hold significant positions within the network. Graph theory has emerged as a powerful mathematical tool for this purpose, and there exist numerous graph-theoretic parameters for analyzing the stability of the system. Within this framework, various graph-theoretic parameters contribute to network analysis. One such parameter used in network analysis is the so-called closeness, which serves as a structural measure to assess the efficiency of a node's ability to interact with other nodes in the network. Mathematically, it measures the reciprocal of the sum of the shortest distances from a node to all other nodes in the network. A bipartite network is a particular type of network in which the nodes can be divided into two disjoint sets such that no two nodes within the same set are adjacent. This paper mainly studies the problem of determining the network that maximize the closeness within bipartite networks. To be more specific, we identify those networks that maximize the closeness over bipartite networks with a fixed number of nodes and one of the fixed parameters: connectivity, dissociation number, cut edges, and diameter.

Keywords: closeness; bipartite graph; connectivity; dissociation number; diameter; cut edge

MSC: 05C12; 05C35; 68M15

Citation: Hayat, F.; Otera, D.E. Maximizing Closeness in Bipartite Networks: A Graph-Theoretic Analysis. *Mathematics* **2024**, *12*, 2039. https://doi.org/10.3390/math12132039

Academic Editor: Mario Gionfriddo

Received: 2 May 2024
Revised: 19 June 2024
Accepted: 26 June 2024
Published: 30 June 2024

1. Introduction

A network is typically depicted using an undirected simple graph, where nodes represent vertices and the connections between them are represented by edges. The central aspect of network analysis involves identifying which nodes hold significant positions within the network. Graph theory has become one of the most powerful mathematical tools in network analysis, offering numerous techniques and methodologies. One of the most important tasks of network analysis is to determine which nodes or links are more critical in a network. One such parameter, *closeness*, serves as a means of identifying nodes capable of efficiently disseminating information throughout the network. In simpler terms, a node with high closeness is one that can reach other nodes in the network quickly and efficiently. It signifies that the node is closely connected to the rest of the network and can potentially influence or be influenced by other nodes more rapidly than nodes with lower closeness values. Nodes with high closeness are crucial in various network applications, such as communication networks, social networks, and transportation networks, as they can facilitate rapid information flow, influence decision-making processes, and enhance overall network resilience. Thus, understanding the closeness of nodes provides valuable insights into the structural and functional characteristics of complex networks.

Closeness is measured on a scale from 0 to 1. A node with a value nearing 0 suggests it is relatively distant from other nodes within the network. Consequently, reaching other nodes from this point necessitates traversing numerous links. Conversely, a node with a value approaching 1 indicates it is in close proximity to other nodes. As a result, only a few connections are needed to reach neighbouring nodes from this node within the network.

Freeman first introduced the concept of closeness [1], but it turned out to be ineffective for disconnected graphs and exhibited weaknesses during graph operations. Addressing the first limitation, Latora and Marchiori introduced a novel measure of closeness for disconnected graphs [2], yet it still remains susceptible to the second weakness. Subsequently, Danglachev proposed an alternative definition [3], which effectively addresses the challenges posed by disconnected graphs and facilitates the creation of convenient formulas for graph operations. Following this definition of closeness, various vulnerability measures have been formulated to quantify the resilience of a network. Among these novel measures are the vertex (or edge) residual closeness parameters, which assess the closeness of a graph following the removal of vertices (or edges) [3]. Another measure is the additional closeness, which identifies the maximum potential of the closeness of a network, by means of the addition of a connection [4,5]. For further information on these new finer parameters, we recommend referring to [6–12].

The computation of closeness across various classes of graphs has gained significant attention in recent years [3,13–15]. For instance, Danglachev investigated the closeness of splitting graphs [16]. In [17], the same author determined the closeness of line graphs for certain fundamental graphs, as well as the closeness of line graphs connected by a bridge of two basic graphs. Closeness formulas for various graph classes were derived by Golpek [18]. Poklukar and Žerovnik [19] identified the graphs that minimize and maximize closeness among all connected graphs and trees with a fixed order, respectively. They also determined the graphs that uniquely maximize closeness among all cacti of fixed order and number of cycles, posing an open problem for the minimum case. The open problem posed by Poklukar and Žerovnik [19] was solved by Hayat and Xu [20], which obtained the unique graph that minimizes closeness across all cacti with fixed numbers of vertices and cycles. The notion of closeness in spectral graph theory was recently combined by Zheng and Zhou [21]. They also investigated the closeness matrix and established the connection between the closeness eigenvalues and the graph structure.

Basic Notations and Definitions

Let G be a simple connected graph with vertex set $V(G)$ and edge set $E(G)$. For a vertex $v \in V(G)$, $N_G(v)$ refers to the set of vertices adjacent to v in G. The *degree* of a vertex $v \in V(G)$, denoted by $d_G(v)$, is the number of vertices in $N_G(v)$. A *pendent vertex* in a graph is a vertex with degree one and an edge incident to a pendent vertex is called a *pendent edge*. For an edge $e \in E(G)$, $G - e$ denotes the subgraph of G obtained by removing e, and $G + xy$ represents a graph formed from G by adding an edge between x and y, where $x, y \in V(G)$. Deleting a vertex $v \in V(G)$ (along with its incident edges) from G is denoted by $G - v$. The union of two graphs H_1 and H_2, denoted by $H_1 \cup H_2$ is the graph with $V(H_1 \cup H_2) = V(H_1) \cup V(H_2)$ and $E(H_1 \cup H_2) = E(H_1) \cup E(H_2)$. The *join of two graphs H_1 and H_2*, denoted by $H_1 \vee H_2$ is a graph obtained from H_1 and H_2 by joining each vertex of H_1 to all vertices of H_2. For disjoint graphs $H_1, H_2, \ldots, H_t$ with $t \geq 3$, the *sequential join* $H_1 \vee H_2 \vee \cdots \vee H_t$ is the graph obtained from $H_1, H_2, \ldots, H_t$ by joining each vertex of H_1 to all vertices of H_2 and then joining each vertex of H_2 to all vertices of H_3, and continuing in this manner, finally connecting each vertex of H_{t-1} to all vertices of H_t. For simplicity, tG (and $[t]G$) is used to represent the union (and sequential join) of t disjoint copies of G. For example $tK_1 = \overline{K_t}$ which is the t isolated vertices and $[a]H_1 \vee H_2 \vee [b]H_3$ is the sequential join $\underbrace{H_1 \vee H_1 \vee \cdots \vee H_1}_{a} \vee H_2 \vee \underbrace{H_3 \vee H_3 \vee \cdots \vee H_3}_{b}$.

A *matching* in G is a set of edges that do not have a set of common vertices. A *perfect matching* in G is a matching that covers each vertex of G.

For vertices $u, v \in V(G)$, the *distance* between u and v in G is the length of the shortest path connecting them, and denoted by $d_G(u, v)$. Whereas, the *diameter* of G is the maximum distance between any pair of vertices in G.

By P_n and K_n we denote the path and complete graph on n vertices, respectively. In [3], for a vertex u of G, the *closeness of u in G* is defined as

$$C_G(u) = \sum_{v \in V(G) \setminus \{u\}} 2^{-d_G(u,v)}.$$

The closeness of G is defined as

$$C(G) = \sum_{u \in V(G)} C_G(u) = \sum_{u \in V(G)} \sum_{v \in V(G) \setminus \{u\}} 2^{-d_G(u,v)}.$$

A *bipartite graph* is a graph in which $V(G)$ can be divided into two disjoint subsets V_1 and V_2 such that no two vertices within the same set are adjacent. A bipartite graph in which every two vertices from different partition classes are adjacent is called complete, and it is denoted by $K_{a,b}$, where $a = |V_1|, b = |V_2|$. Bipartite graphs serve as powerful tools for modeling complex systems with two distinct sets of entities, enabling analyses of and solutions to a wide range of real-world problems across different domains [22,23].

The *(vertex) connectivity* of a graph G is the minimum number of vertices whose removal from G results in a disconnected graph or in the trivial graph, and it is denoted by $k(G)$. If G is trivial or disconnected, then $k(G) = 0$, obviously. An edge e of a connected graph G is a *cut edge* if $G - e$ is disconnected. A subset $M \subseteq V(G)$ is called a *dissociation set* if the induced subgraph $G[M]$ does not include P_3 as a subgraph. A maximum dissociation set of G is one with the greatest cardinality. Finally, the *dissociation number* of G is the cardinality of a maximum dissociation set within G.

In order to explore the connection between closeness and the structural characteristics of a graph, we will investigate extremal problems aimed at maximizing closeness within certain classes of bipartite graphs.

2. Main Results

In this section we will state our results. Specifically, we will determine those graphs which maximize closeness over the bipartite graphs of order n and one of the fixed parameters, such as dissociation number, connectivity, cut edges, and diameter.

The following Lemma will be helpful for the proofs of the main results.

Lemma 1 ([3,12]). *If u and v are vertices in a graph G where there is no edge between them, then adding the edge uv increases the closeness of G.*

Our first main result establishes an upper bound on the closeness of a bipartite graphs with a fixed order and dissociation number α, and identified the graph that attain the bound.

Theorem 1. *Let G be a bipartite graph of order n with dissociation number α. Then,*

$$C(G) \leq \frac{n(n-1)}{4} + \frac{\alpha(n-\alpha)}{2}$$

with equality if and only if $G \cong K_{\alpha,n-\alpha}$.

For $r \geq 1$, we define N_r as the graph comprising r isolated vertices. Let $B_r(m_1, m_2)$ be the graph obtained from N_r and $K_1 \cup K_{m_1,m_2}$ by adding the edges between the vertices in N_r and the vertices belonging to partitions of size m_1 in K_{m_1,m_2} and K_1, respectively (see Figure 1). It is evident that $K_{r,n-r} = B_r(n-r-1, 0)$.

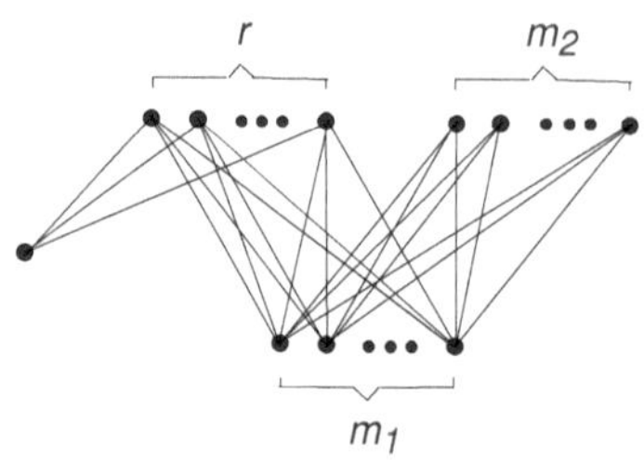

Figure 1. The graph $B_r(m_1, m_2)$.

Our second result identifies the graph that maximizes the closeness within bipartite graphs of order n and fixed connectivity r.

Theorem 2. *Let G be a bipartite graph of order n with connectivity r, where $1 \leq r \leq \lfloor \frac{n-1}{2} \rfloor$. Then,*

$$\begin{aligned} C(G) \quad \leq \quad & \frac{1}{4}\left(\left\lceil \frac{n-2r-1}{2} \right\rceil + 6r + 1\right)\left\lceil \frac{n-2r-1}{2} \right\rceil + \left\lceil \frac{n-2r-1}{2} \right\rceil \left\lfloor \frac{n-2r-1}{2} \right\rfloor \\ + \quad & \frac{1}{4}\left(\left\lfloor \frac{n-2r-1}{2} \right\rfloor + 6r\right)\left\lfloor \frac{n-2r-1}{2} \right\rfloor + \frac{r(3r+2)}{2} \end{aligned}$$

with equality if and only if $G \cong B_r\left(\left\lceil \frac{n-2r-1}{2} \right\rceil + r, \left\lfloor \frac{n-2r-1}{2} \right\rfloor\right)$.

For positive integers s, ℓ, and n, where $2 \leq s \leq \frac{n-\ell}{2}$, let $A_\ell(s, n-s-\ell)$ be the graph obtained by attaching ℓ pendent vertices to a vertex with degree $n-s-\ell$ in $K_{s,n-s-\ell}$ (see Figure 2).

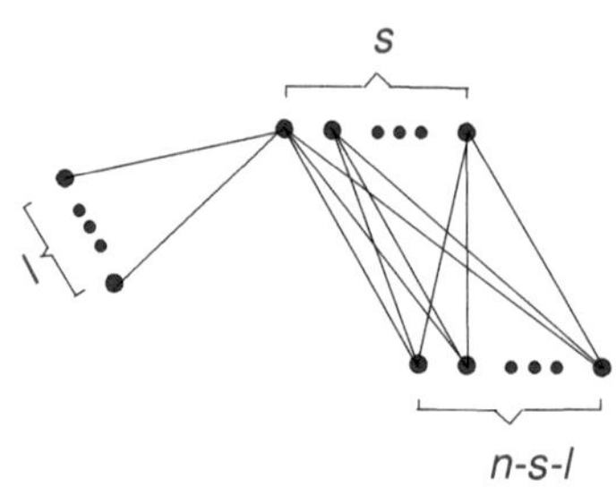

Figure 2. The graph $A_\ell(s, n-s-\ell)$.

The next result characterizes all bipartite graphs with n vertices and ℓ cut edges having the largest closeness.

Theorem 3. *Let G be a bipartite graph of order $n \geq 5$ with ℓ cut edges.*

(i) *If $\ell = n-1$, then $C(G) \leq \frac{(n-1)(n+2)}{4}$ with equality if and only if $G \cong K_{1,n-1}$;*

(ii) *If $\frac{3n}{4} - 3 \leq \ell \leq n-4$, then $C(G) \leq \frac{n^2+3n-3\ell-8}{4}$ with equality if and only if $G \cong A_\ell(2, n-2-\ell)$.*
In the following cases, $1 \leq \ell \leq \frac{3n}{4} - 3$.

(iii) *If $3n - 4\ell \equiv 0 (mod\ 6)$, then $C(G) \leq \frac{27n^2-18n+20\ell^2+54\ell-27n\ell}{72}$ with equality if and only if $G \cong A_\ell(\frac{n}{2} - \frac{2\ell}{3}, \frac{n}{2} - \frac{\ell}{3})$;*

(iv) *If* $3n - 4\ell \equiv 1 (mod\ 6)$, *then* $C(G) \leq \frac{27n^2-18n+20\ell^2+55\ell-27n\ell-1}{72}$ *with equality if and only if* $G \cong A_\ell(\frac{n}{2} - \frac{2\ell}{3} - \frac{1}{6}, \frac{n}{2} - \frac{\ell}{3} + \frac{1}{6})$;

(v) *If* $3n - 4\ell \equiv 2 (mod\ 6)$, *then* $C(G) \leq \frac{27n^2-18n+20\ell^2+56\ell-27n\ell-4}{72}$ *with equality if and only if* $G \cong A_\ell(\frac{n}{2} - \frac{2\ell}{3} - \frac{1}{3}, \frac{n}{2} - \frac{\ell}{3} + \frac{1}{3})$;

(vi) *If* $3n - 4\ell \equiv 3 (mod\ 6)$, *then* $C(G) \leq \frac{27n^2-18n+20\ell^2+57\ell-27n\ell-9}{72}$ *with equality if and only if* $G \cong A_\ell(\frac{n}{2} - \frac{2\ell}{3} - \frac{1}{2}, \frac{n}{2} - \frac{\ell}{3} + \frac{1}{2})$;

(vii) *If* $3n - 4\ell \equiv 4 (mod\ 6)$, *then* $C(G) \leq \frac{27n^2-18n+20\ell^2+52\ell-27n\ell-4}{72}$ *with equality if and only if* $G \cong A_\ell(\frac{n}{2} - \frac{2\ell}{3} + \frac{1}{3}, \frac{n}{2} - \frac{\ell}{3} - \frac{1}{3})$;

(viii) *If* $3n - 4\ell \equiv 5 (mod\ 6)$, *then* $C(G) \leq \frac{27n^2-18n+20\ell^2+53\ell-27n\ell-1}{72}$ *with equality if and only if* $G \cong A_\ell(\frac{n}{2} - \frac{2\ell}{3} + \frac{1}{6}, \frac{n}{2} - \frac{\ell}{3} - \frac{1}{6})$.

In a bipartite graph G with n vertices and diameter d, suppose $P = u_0u_1 \cdots u_d$ represents a diametrical path of G. We can then partition $V(G)$ as follows:

$$V(G) = X_0 \cup X_1 \cup \cdots \cup X_d, \tag{1}$$

where $X_0 = u_0$ and $X_i = v \in V(G) : d_G(v, u_0) = i$ for $i = 1, 2, \ldots, d$.

Let

$$F(n,d) = \lceil (d-1)/2 \rceil K_1 \vee \lfloor (n-d-1)/2 \rfloor K_1 \vee \lceil (n-d-1)/2 \rceil K_1 \vee \lceil (d-1)/2 \rceil K_1,$$

where d is odd. Let

$$\mathcal{H}(n,d) = \{H(n,d) = \lceil d/2 - 1 \rceil K_1 \vee aK_1 \vee \lfloor (n-d+2)/2 \rfloor K_1 \vee bK_1 \vee \lceil d/2 - 1 \rceil K_1\},$$

where d is even, and $a + b = \lceil (n-d+2)/2 \rceil$.

Clearly, $F(n,d)$ is a bipartite graph of order n with diameter d, and $\mathcal{H}(n,d)$ is a set of n-vertex bipartite graphs having diameter d.

Evidently, K_2 (resp. P_n) is the unique bipartite graph of diameter one (resp. $n-1$). In what follows, we consider $2 \leq d \leq n-2$.

Our last main result identifies the bipartite graphs with n vertices and diameter d that maximize the closeness

Theorem 4. *Let G be a bipartite graph of order n with diameter d having maximum closeness.*

(i) *If* $d = 2$, *then* $G \cong K_{\lfloor \frac{n}{2} \rfloor, \lceil \frac{n}{2} \rceil}$;

(ii) *If* $d \geq 3$, *then* $G \cong F(n,d)$ *for odd* d, *and* $G \in \mathcal{H}(n,d)$ *otherwise.*

3. Proof of Theorem 1

In this section, we give the proof of Theorem 1, which establishes an upper bound on the closeness of a bipartite graphs with a fixed order and dissociation number α, and we identify the graph that attains the bound.

Proof. Let G be a bipartite graph of order n and dissociation number α that maximizes $C(G)$. Denote the partition of $V(G)$ as (V_1, V_2), assuming without loss of generality that $|V_1| \geq |V_2|$. Let Q be the maximum dissociation set of G. Then $|V_1| \leq |Q| = \alpha$. If $|V_1| = \alpha$, then by Lemma 1, $G \cong K_{\alpha, n-\alpha}$.

Now, we consider the case where $|V_1| < \alpha$. Let $Q = Q_1 \cup Q_2$ with $Q_1 \subseteq V_1$, $Q_2 \subseteq V_2$, and $Q_1' = Q \setminus Q_1$, $Q_2' = Q \setminus Q_2$. It can be observed that $|Q_2'| < |Q_1|$ and $|Q_1'| < |Q_2|$. Since G is a bipartite graph with maximum closeness, by Lemma 1, each vertex in Q_1 (resp. Q_1') is adjacent to each vertex in Q_2 (resp. V_2).

If $|Q_1| \leq |Q_2|$, then there exists $S \subseteq Q_2$ with $|Q_2| = |S|$ such that $G[Q_1 \cup S]$ forms a perfect matching. Thus, we have:

$$\begin{aligned}C(G) =& \frac{1}{4}[2|Q_1||Q_1'| + 2|Q_2'||Q_2| + |Q_1|(|Q_1| - 1) + |Q_2|(|Q_2| - 1) + |Q_1'|(|Q_1'| - 1) \\ &+ |Q_2'|(|Q_2'| - 1)] + \frac{1}{2}[2|Q_1||Q_1'| + 2|Q_1'||Q_2'| + 2|Q_1'||Q_2| + 2|Q_1|] \\ &+ \frac{1}{8}[2|Q_1|(|Q_1| - 1) + 2|Q_1|(|Q_2| - |Q_1|)],\end{aligned}$$

and

$$\begin{aligned}C(K_{|Q_1|+|Q_2|,|Q_1'|+|Q_2'|}) =& \frac{1}{4}[(|Q_1| + |Q_2|)(|Q_1| + |Q_2| - 1) + (|Q_1'| + |Q_2'|)(|Q_1'| + |Q_2'| - 1))] \\ &+ \frac{1}{2}[2(|Q_1| + |Q_2|)(|Q_1'| + |Q_2'|)].\end{aligned}$$

We deduce,

$$C(G) - C(K_{|Q_1|+|Q_2|,|Q_1'|+|Q_2'|}) = \frac{1}{4}[|Q_1|(3 + 2|Q_1'| - 4|Q_2'| - |Q_2|)] + \frac{1}{2}[|Q_2'|(|Q_1'| - |Q_2|)].$$

Note that since G is connected, we have $max|Q_1'|, |Q_2'| \geq 1$. If $|Q_1'| = 0$, then $|Q_2'| \geq 1$, implying $2 \leq |Q_1| \leq |Q_2|$. If $|Q'1| \geq 1$, then $2 \leq |Q_2|$, and thus $C(G) < C(K|Q_1| + |Q_2|, |Q_1'| + |Q'2|)$, which contradicts $\alpha(G) = |Q| = |Q_1| + |Q_2| = \alpha(K|Q_1| + |Q_2|, |Q_1'| + |Q_2'|)$.

If $|Q_1| > |Q_2|$, then by a similar argument as above, we arrive at a contradiction to the choice of G. Therefore, $G \cong K_{\alpha,n-\alpha}$. By direct calculation, we obtain:

$$\begin{aligned}C(K_{\alpha,n-\alpha}) &= [\alpha(\alpha-1) + (n-\alpha)(n-\alpha-1)] \times 2^{-2} + [2\alpha(n-\alpha)] \times 2^{-1} \\ &= \frac{n(n-1)}{4} + \frac{\alpha(n-\alpha)}{2}. \quad \square\end{aligned}$$

4. Proof of Theorem 2

To establish the main result, we first require the following Lemma.

Lemma 2. *Let a, b and r be positive integers.*
(i) If $r + b > a$, then $C(B_r(a,b)) < C(B_r(a+1, b-1))$;
(ii) If $r + b + 1 < a$, then $C(B_r(a,b)) < C(B_r(a-1, b+1))$.

Proof. By the definition of closeness, we have

$$\begin{aligned}C(B_r(a,b)) =& [2a + 2rb + r(r-1) + a(a-1) + b(b-1)] \times 2^{-2} \\ &+ (2r + 2ra + 2ab) \times 2^{-1} + 2b \times 2^{-3},\end{aligned}$$

$$\begin{aligned}C(B_r(a+1, b-1)) =& [2(a+1) + 2r(b-1) + r(r-1) + a(a+1) + (b-1)(b-2)] \times 2^{-2} \\ &+ [2r + 2r(a+1) + 2(a+1)(b-1)] \times 2^{-1} + 2(b-1) \times 2^{-3},\end{aligned}$$

and

$$\begin{aligned}C(B_r(a-1, b+1)) =& [2(a-1) + 2r(b+1) + r(r-1) + (a-1)(a-2) + b(b+1)] \times 2^{-2} \\ &+ [2r + 2r(a-1) + 2(a-1)(b+1)] \times 2^{-1} + 2(b+1) \times 2^{-3}.\end{aligned}$$

(i) If $r+b>a$, we have

$$\begin{aligned}&C(B_r(a,b))-C(B_r(a+1,b-1))\\&=(2r-2a+2b-4)\times 2^{-2}+(-2r+2a-2b+2)\times 2^{-1}+2\times 2^{-3}\\&=[2a+1-2(b+r)]\times 2^{-2}<0.\end{aligned}$$

Thus, $C(B_r(a,b))<C(B_r(a+1,b-1))$.

(i) If $r+b+1<a$, we have

$$\begin{aligned}&C(B_r(a,b))-C(B_r(a-1,b+1))\\&=(-2r+2a-2b)\times 2^{-2}+(2r-2a+2b+2)\times 2^{-1}-2\times 2^{-3}\\&=[-2a+2(b+r+1)+1]\times 2^{-2}<0.\end{aligned}$$

Thus, $C(B_r(a,b))<C(B_r(a-1,b+1))$. □

By Lemma 3 (ii), we immediately get the following Corollary.

Corollary 1. *If $1\le r\le\lfloor\frac{n-1}{2}\rfloor$, then $C(K_{r,n-r})<C(B_r(n-r-2,1))$.*

Proof. By direct calculation, we have

$$\begin{aligned}&C\left(B_r\left(\left\lceil\frac{n-2r-1}{2}\right\rceil+r,\left\lfloor\frac{n-2r-1}{2}\right\rfloor\right)\right)\\
&=\frac{1}{2}\left[2r+2r\left(\left\lceil\frac{n-2r-1}{2}\right\rceil+r\right)+2\left(\left\lceil\frac{n-2r-1}{2}\right\rceil+r\right)\left\lfloor\frac{n-2r-1}{2}\right\rfloor\right]\\
&\quad+\frac{1}{4}\left[2\left(\left\lceil\frac{n-2r-1}{2}\right\rceil+r\right)+\left(\left\lceil\frac{n-2r-1}{2}\right\rceil+r\right)\left(\left\lceil\frac{n-2r-1}{2}\right\rceil+r-1\right)\right.\\
&\quad\left.+\left\lfloor\frac{n-2r-1}{2}\right\rfloor\left(\left\lfloor\frac{n-2r-1}{2}\right\rfloor-1\right)+2r\left\lfloor\frac{n-2r-1}{2}\right\rfloor+r(r-1)\right]+\frac{2}{8}\left\lfloor\frac{n-2r-1}{2}\right\rfloor\\
&=\frac{1}{4}\left(\left\lceil\frac{n-2r-1}{2}\right\rceil+6r+1\right)\left\lceil\frac{n-2r-1}{2}\right\rceil+\left\lceil\frac{n-2r-1}{2}\right\rceil\left\lfloor\frac{n-2r-1}{2}\right\rfloor\\
&\quad+\frac{1}{4}\left(\left\lfloor\frac{n-2r-1}{2}\right\rfloor+6r\right)\left\lfloor\frac{n-2r-1}{2}\right\rfloor+\frac{r(3r+2)}{2}.\end{aligned}$$

Let G be a bipartite graph of order n and connectivity r such that $C(G)$ is maximized. Let $W\subseteq G$ contain r vertices, and let $H_1,H_2,\dots,H_k$ be the components of $G-W$, where $k\ge 2$. If any component H_i of $G-W$ contains at least two vertices, then by Lemma 1, it must be a complete bipartite graph. If one of the components is a singleton set, denoted as $H_i=v$, then v is adjacent to all vertices in W; otherwise, if G's connectivity is less than r, $G[W]$ contains isolated vertices.

Case 1. *At least one component of $G-W$ comprises a minimum of two vertices.*

In this case, $G-W$ comprises exactly two components. Otherwise, by introducing some edges in G, we would obtain a complete bipartite graph G' among the vertices of $H_1\cup H_2\cup\dots\cup H_{k-1}$, with order n and connectivity r. According to Lemma 1, $C(G)<C(G')$, contradicting the maximality of G. Let H_1 and H_2 be the components of G. Then either $H_1=K_1$ or $H_2=K_1$. Otherwise, $G-U$ has the partitions (M_1,M_2) and (Q_1,Q_2), respectively. Let $W=W_1\cup W_2$ represent the bipartition of W. As G possesses

maximum closeness, by Lemma 1, there must exist edges between the vertices of M_1 and M_2, Q_1 and Q_2, W_1 and W_2. Considering the definition of closeness, we have:

$$\begin{aligned}C(G) =&\frac{1}{4}[2|M_1||W_1| + 2|M_1||Q_1| + 2|M_2||Q_2| + 2|M_2||W_2| + 2|W_1||Q_1| + 2|W_2||Q_2| \\ &+|M_1|(|M_1| - 1) + |M_2|(|M_2| - 1) + |Q_1|(|Q_1| - 1) + |Q_2|(|Q_2| - 1) \\ &+|W_1|(|W_1| - 1) + |W_2|(|W_2| - 1)] + \frac{1}{8}[2|M_1||Q_2| + 2|M_2||Q_1|] \\ &+ \frac{1}{2}[2|M_1|(|M_2| + |W_2|) + 2|W_1|(|M_2| + |W_2| + |Q_2|) + 2|Q_1|(|W_2| + |Q_2|)].\end{aligned}$$

Note that $|W_2| + |Q_2| \geq |W|$, and $|Q_2| \geq |W_1|$. Let $Q_2 = YUZ$, and $G' = G - \{q_1z : q_1 \in V(Q_1), z \in V(Z)\} + \{m_1q_2 : m_1 \in V(M_1), q_2 \in V(Q_2)\} + \{qm_2 : q \in V(Q_1) \setminus \{q_1\}, m_2 \in V(M_2)\}$. Clearly, G' is a bipartite graph of order n having vertex cut $W_2 \cup Y$ contain r vertices. We have

$$\begin{aligned}C(G') =&\frac{1}{4}[(|M_1| + |Q_1| + |W_1|)(|M_1| + |Q_1| + |W_1| - 1) \\ &+ (|M_2| + |Q_2| + |W_2|)(|M_2| + |Q_2| + |W_2| - 1)] + \frac{1}{8}[2|M_2| + 2|Q_2| - 2|W_1|] \\ &+ \frac{1}{2}[2(|M_1| + |Q_1| + |W_1| - 1)(|M_2| + |Q_2| + |W_2|) + 2(|W_1| + |W_2|)].\end{aligned}$$

So

$$C(G) - C(G') = -\frac{3}{4}[|M_2|(|Q_1| - 1) + |Q_2|(|M_1| - 1) + |W_1|] < 0$$

this leads to a contradiction. Without loss of generality, let us assume that $H_2 = K_1 = u$. Then, $H_1 = K_{a,b}$, and u is connected to all vertices of W, while each vertex of W is connected to every vertex of H_1 that is in the same partition as u. Thus, $G = B_r(a, b)$, where $r = |W|$, and $a \geq r$. Since G maximizes closeness, by Lemma 3, we have $r + b - 1 \leq a \leq r + b + 1$, which implies $G \cong B_r\left(\left\lceil \frac{n-2r-1}{2} \right\rceil + r, \left\lfloor \frac{n-2r-1}{2} \right\rfloor\right)$.

Case 2. *All components of $G - W$ consist of a single vertex.*

In this case $G = K_{n-r,r}$. By Corollary 1, $k \geq \lfloor \frac{n-1}{2} \rfloor$.
Hence, $G \cong B_r\left(\left\lceil \frac{n-2r-1}{2} \right\rceil + r, \left\lfloor \frac{n-2r-1}{2} \right\rfloor\right)$. □

5. Proof of Theorem 3

Lemma 3 ([19])**.** *Let G represent a connected graph containing a cut edge $e = uv$. Let G' denote the graph resulting from contracting edge e into a new vertex w, which becomes adjacent to every vertex in $N_G(u) \cup N_G(v)$ except for u and v, and then attaching a pendent edge at w. Then $C(G') > C(G)$.*

Lemma 4. *Let u, v be the two vertices on the same partition of a complete bipartite graph H, and G be a graph formed from H by attaching pendent vertices $x_1, x_2, \ldots, x_s$ (resp. $y_1, y_2, \ldots, y_t$) to u (resp. v). Let $G' = G - \{ux_i : i = 1, 2, \ldots, s\} + \{vx_i : i = 1, 2, \ldots, s\}$. Then, $C(G') > C(G)$.*

Proof. By the definition of closeness, we have

$$\begin{aligned}
& C(G') - C(G) \\
= \;& 2\sum_{i=1}^{s}\left(2^{-d_{G'}(x_i,u)} - 2^{-d_G(x_i,u)}\right) + 2\sum_{i=1}^{s}\left(2^{-d_{G'}(x_i,v)} - 2^{-d_G(x_i,v)}\right) \\
+ \;& 2\sum_{i=1}^{s}\sum_{j=1}^{t}\left(2^{-d_{G'}(x_i,y_j)} - 2^{-d_G(x_i,y_j)}\right) \\
= \;& 2\sum_{i=1}^{s}\left(2^{-[d_G(x_i,u)+2]} - 2^{-d_G(x_i,u)}\right) + 2\sum_{i=1}^{s}\left(2^{-[d_G(x_i,v)-2]} - 2^{-d_G(x_i,v)}\right) \\
+ \;& 2\sum_{i=1}^{s}\sum_{j=1}^{t}\left(2^{-[d_G(x_i,y_j)-2]} - 2^{-d_G(x_i,y_j)}\right) \\
= \;& 2\sum_{i=1}^{s}2^{-d_G(x_i,u)}[2^{-2}-1] + 2\sum_{i=1}^{s}2^{-d_G(x_i,u)}[2^{-2}-1] \\
+ \;& 2\sum_{i=1}^{s}\sum_{j=1}^{t}2^{-d_G(x_i,y_j)}[2^{-2}-1] \\
= \;& \frac{6a+3ab}{8} > 0.
\end{aligned}$$

Hence, $C(G') > C(G)$. □

Lemma 5. *Let $K_{p,q}$ be a graph with vertex partition $V_p = \{x_1, \ldots, x_p\}$ and $V_q = \{y_1, \ldots, y_q\}$, and G be a graph obtained from $K_{p,q}$ by attaching pendent vertices $a_1, a_2, \ldots, a_s$ (resp. $b_1, b_2, \ldots, b_t$) to x_2 (resp. y_2) . Let $G' = G - \{x_2a_i : i = 1, 2, \ldots, s\} + \{y_2a_i : i = 1, 2, \ldots, s\}$. Then, $C(G') > C(G)$.*

Proof. By the definition of closeness, we have

$$\begin{aligned}
& C(G') - C(G) \\
= \;& 2\sum_{i=1}^{s}\sum_{j=1}^{t}\left(2^{-d_{G'}(a_i,b_j)} - 2^{-d_G(a_i,b_j)}\right) + 2\sum_{i=1}^{s}\sum_{j=1}^{p}\left(2^{-d_{G'}(a_i,x_j)} - 2^{-d_G(a_i,x_j)}\right) \\
+ \;& 2\sum_{i=1}^{s}\sum_{j=1}^{q}\left(2^{-d_{G'}(a_i,y_j)} - 2^{-d_G(a_i,y_j)}\right) \\
= \;& 2\sum_{i=1}^{s}\sum_{j=1}^{t}\left(2^{-[d_G(a_i,b_j)-1]} - 2^{-d_G(a_i,b_j)}\right) + 2\sum_{i=1}^{s}\sum_{j=1}^{p}\left(2^{-[d_G(a_i,x_j)+1]} - 2^{-d_G(a_i,x_j)}\right) \\
+ \;& 2\sum_{i=1}^{s}\sum_{j=1}^{q}\left(2^{-[d_G(a_i,y_j)-1]} - 2^{-d_G(a_i,y_j)}\right) \\
= \;& 2\sum_{i=1}^{s}\sum_{j=1}^{t}2^{-d_G(a_i,b_j)}[2-1] + 2\sum_{i=1}^{s}\sum_{j=1}^{p}2^{-d_G(a_i,x_j)}[2^{-1}-1] \\
+ \;& 2\sum_{i=1}^{s}\sum_{j=1}^{q}2^{-d_G(a_i,y_j)}[2-1] \\
= \;& \frac{ab}{4} > 0.
\end{aligned}$$

Hence, $C(G') > C(G)$. □

Proof. For $\ell = n-1$, $K_{1,n-1}$ stands as the unique bipartite graph, with its closeness calculated directly as $C(K_{1,n-1}) = \frac{(n-1)(n+2)}{4}$.

Consider a bipartite graph G of order n containing ℓ cut edges, maximizing $C(G)$. Note that for any bipartite graph with ℓ cut edges, $\ell \neq n-2$ and $\ell \neq n-3$. Hereafter, we consider the case $1 \leq \ell \leq n-4$. Let $e_1, e_2, \ldots, e_\ell$ denote the ℓ cut edges of G. Our claim is that each component of $G \setminus \{e_1, e_2, \ldots, e_\ell\}$ forms either a single vertex or a complete bipartite graph.

Suppose there exists a component H of $G \setminus \{e_1, e_2, \ldots, e_\ell\}$ that is not a complete bipartite graph. Let G' be the graph formed by adding an edge between two vertices from different partitions in H. Then, according to Lemma 1, $C(G') > C(G)$, contradicting the selection of G. Thus, each component of $G \setminus \{e_1, e_2, \ldots, e_\ell\}$ is either a single vertex or a complete bipartite graph. By Lemma 3, $e_1, e_2, \ldots, e_\ell$ must be pendent edges in G. Since G is a complete bipartite graph, these edges must be incident to a single vertex, denoted as s. Therefore, $G \cong A_\ell(s, n-s-\ell)$ by Lemmas 4 and 5.

By direct calculation, we have

$$C(A_\ell(s, n-s-\ell)) = g(s) = \frac{-2s^2 + (2n-3\ell)s + n^2 - n + 3\ell}{4}.$$

For $\frac{3n}{4} - 3 \leq \ell \leq n-4$, we get $C(G) \leq g(2) = \frac{n^2+3n-3\ell-8}{4}$ with equality if and only if $G \cong A_\ell(2, n-2-\ell)$.

For $1 \leq \ell \leq \frac{3n}{4} - 3$, we obtain

$$max \quad g(s) = \begin{cases} g(\frac{n}{2} - \frac{2\ell}{3}), & \text{if } 3n - 4\ell \equiv 0 (\text{mod } 6); \\ g(\frac{n}{2} - \frac{2\ell}{3} - \frac{1}{6}), & \text{if } 3n - 4\ell \equiv 1 (\text{mod } 6); \\ g(\frac{n}{2} - \frac{2\ell}{3} - \frac{1}{3}), & \text{if } 3n - 4\ell \equiv 2 (\text{mod } 6); \\ g(\frac{n}{2} - \frac{2\ell}{3} - \frac{1}{2}), & \text{if } 3n - 4\ell \equiv 3 (\text{mod } 6); \\ g(\frac{n}{2} - \frac{2\ell}{3} + \frac{1}{3}), & \text{if } 3n - 4\ell \equiv 4 (\text{mod } 6); \\ g(\frac{n}{2} - \frac{2\ell}{3} + \frac{1}{6}), & \text{if } 3n - 4\ell \equiv 5 (\text{mod } 6). \end{cases}$$

Therefore, we get

$$C(S) \leq \begin{cases} \frac{27n^2-18n+20\ell^2+54\ell-27n\ell}{72}, & \text{with equality iff } G \cong A_\ell(\frac{n}{2} - \frac{2\ell}{3}, \frac{n}{2} - \frac{\ell}{3}); \\ \frac{27n^2-18n+20\ell^2+55\ell-27n\ell-1}{72}, & \text{with equality iff } G \cong A_\ell(\frac{n}{2} - \frac{2\ell}{3} - \frac{1}{6}, \frac{n}{2} - \frac{\ell}{3} + \frac{1}{6}); \\ \frac{27n^2-18n+20\ell^2+56\ell-27n\ell-4}{72}, & \text{with equality iff } G \cong A_\ell(\frac{n}{2} - \frac{2\ell}{3} - \frac{1}{3}, \frac{n}{2} - \frac{\ell}{3} + \frac{1}{3}); \\ \frac{27n^2-18n+20\ell^2+57\ell-27n\ell-9}{72}, & \text{with equality iff } G \cong A_\ell(\frac{n}{2} - \frac{2\ell}{3} - \frac{1}{2}, \frac{n}{2} - \frac{\ell}{3} + \frac{1}{2}); \\ \frac{27n^2-18n+20\ell^2+52\ell-27n\ell-4}{72}, & \text{with equality iff } G \cong A_\ell(\frac{n}{2} - \frac{2\ell}{3} + \frac{1}{3}, \frac{n}{2} - \frac{\ell}{3} - \frac{1}{3}); \\ \frac{27n^2-18n+20\ell^2+53\ell-27n\ell-1}{72}, & \text{with equality iff } G \cong A_\ell(\frac{n}{2} - \frac{2\ell}{3} + \frac{1}{6}, \frac{n}{2} - \frac{\ell}{3} - \frac{1}{6}). \end{cases}$$

This completes the proof. □

6. Proof of Theorem 4

Proof. Let G be a bipartite graph of order n and diameter d with maximum closeness. Let (V_1, V_2) be the partition of $V(G)$.

(i) If $d = 2$, then by Lemma 1, $G \cong K_{t,n-t}$ where $t, n-t \geq 2$. By direct calculation, we get

$$\begin{aligned} C(K_{t,n-t}) &= \frac{n(n-1)}{4} + \frac{t(n-t)}{2} \\ &\leq \frac{n(n-1)}{4} + \frac{1}{2}\left\lfloor \frac{n}{2} \right\rfloor \left\lceil \frac{n}{2} \right\rceil \end{aligned}$$

with equality if and only if $t = \lfloor \frac{n}{2} \rfloor, n - t = \lceil \frac{n}{2} \rceil$, i.e., $G \cong K_{\lfloor \frac{n}{2} \rfloor, \lceil \frac{n}{2} \rceil}$.

(ii) Let $P = u_0 u_1 \cdots u_d$ represent a diametrical path of G. Then G maintains the same vertex partition as that described in Equation (1). We proceed with the following claims.

Claim 1. *For $i = 1, 2, \ldots, d$, all the vertices in $G[X_i]$ are isolated and $|X_d| = 1$.*

Proof. Let us assume there are two vertices, x_1 and x_2, in some X_i such that there is an edge between them, $x_1x_2 \in E(G[X_i])$. This implies the existence of two paths, P_1 and P_2, between x_0 and x_1 (or between x_0 and x_2). The combination of P_1, P_2, and the edge x_1x_2 forms an odd cycle in G. Specifically, if P_1 and P_2 do not share any internal vertex, then their union with x_1x_2 creates an odd cycle. Otherwise, if u is the last common internal vertex of P_1 and P_2, then combining $P_1(u, x_1)$ with $P_2(u, x_2)$ and x_1x_2 forms an odd cycle. This contradicts the assumption of G being bipartite.

In case $|X_d| \geq 2$, we can select $w \in X_d \setminus u_d$ and augment G by adding edges $wx_3 : x_3 \in X_{d-3}$. This augmentation results in a bipartite graph G' of order n and diameter d, featuring a vertex partition $X_0 \cup X_1 \cup \cdots \cup (X_{d-2} \cup w) \cup X_{d-1} \cup (X_d \setminus w)$. According to Lemma 1, $C(G') > C(G)$, leading to a contradiction. Hence, $|X_d| = 1$. □

Claim 2. *$G[X_{i-1} \cup X_i]$ is a complete bipartite graph for each $i = 1, 2, \ldots, d$.*

Proof. Let us assume that for some i, $G[X_{i-1} \cup X_i]$ is not a complete bipartite graph. According to claim 1, all vertices in $G[X_i]$ are isolated, and $|X_d| = 1$. Now, consider $v_1 \in X_{i-1}$ and $v_2 \in X_i$. We create a new graph, $G' = G + v_1v_2$. It is evident that G' is a bipartite graph of order n with diameter d. Using Lemma 1, we deduce that $C(G') > C(G)$, which contradicts our earlier assumption. Hence, we conclude that $G[X_{i-1} \cup X_i]$ is a complete bipartite graph for each $i = 1, 2, \ldots, d$. □

Claim 3. *(i) If $d \geq 3$ is odd, then*

$$|X_0| = |X_1| = |X_2| = \cdots = |X_{\frac{d-3}{2}}| = |X_{\frac{d+3}{2}}| = \cdots = |X_{d-1}| = |X_d| = 1,$$

and $\left||X_{\frac{d-1}{2}}| - |X_{\frac{d+1}{2}}|\right| \leq 1.$

(ii) If $d \geq 3$ is even, then

$$|X_0| = |X_1| = |X_2| = \cdots = |X_{\frac{d-4}{2}}| = |X_{\frac{d+4}{2}}| = \cdots = |X_{d-1}| = |X_d| = 1,$$

and $\left||X_{\frac{d-2}{2}}| + |X_{\frac{d+2}{2}}| - |X_{\frac{d}{2}}|\right| \leq 1.$

Proof. (*i*) When $d = 3$, the result is straightforward. We now focus on the case where $d \geq 5$. Given that $|X_0| = |X_d| = 1$, we aim to demonstrate that $|X_1| = |X_2| = \cdots = |X_{\frac{d-3}{2}}| = |X_{\frac{d+3}{2}}| = \cdots = |X_{d-1}| = 1$.

Let us assume $|X_1| \geq 2$. Consider $G' = G - u_0x_1 + x_1x_4$, where $x_1 \in X_1$ and $x_4 \in X_4$. From the construction of G', it is evident that $C_G(x_1) = C_{G'}(x_1) + \frac{3}{8} - \sum_{i=4}^{d} \frac{3|X_i|}{2^{i-1}}$, $C_G(v) = C_{G'}(v) + \frac{3}{8}$ for each $v \in X_0$, $C_G(v) = C_{G'}(v)$ for each $v \in (X_1 \setminus \{x_1\}) \cup X_2 \cup X_3$, $C_G(v) = C_{G'}(v) - \frac{3}{2^{i-1}}$ for each $v \in X_4 \cup X_5 \cup \cdots \cup X_d$. We get

$$\begin{aligned}
C(G) - C(G') &= \sum_{u \in V(G)} C_G(u) - \sum_{u \in V(G')} C_{G'}(u) \\
&= \sum_{u \in X_0} [C_G(u) - C_{G'}(u)] + \sum_{i=4}^{d} \sum_{u \in X_i} [C_G(u) - C_{G'}(u)] + C_G(x_1) - C_{G'}(x_1) \\
&= \frac{3}{8} - \sum_{i=4}^{d} \frac{3}{2^{i-1}} + \frac{3}{8} - \sum_{i=4}^{d} \frac{3|X_i|}{2^{i-1}} \\
&= \frac{3}{4} - 3\sum_{i=4}^{d} \frac{1 + |X_i|}{2^{i-1}} < 0,
\end{aligned}$$

implying $C(G) < C(G')$, a contradiction to the choice of G. Thus, $|X_1| = 1$. Similarly, we can show that $|X_2| = \cdots = |X_{\frac{d-3}{2}}| = |X_{\frac{d+3}{2}}| = \cdots = |X_{d-1}| = 1$.

Next we show that if $d \geq 3$ is odd, then $\left||X_{\frac{d-1}{2}}| - |X_{\frac{d+1}{2}}|\right| \leq 1$. Without loss of generality, we assume that $|X_{\frac{d-1}{2}}| \geq |X_{\frac{d+1}{2}}|$. Then, it suffices to show that $|X_{\frac{d-1}{2}}| - |X_{\frac{d+1}{2}}| \leq 1$. Suppose that $|X_{\frac{d-1}{2}}| - |X_{\frac{d+1}{2}}| \geq 2$. Choose $z \in X_{\frac{d-1}{2}}$, and let $G' = G - zu + zv$, where $u \in X_{\frac{d+1}{2}}, v \in X_{\frac{d+3}{2}}$. Then, the vertex partition of G' is $X_0 \cup X_1 \cup \cdots \cup X_{\frac{d+3}{2}} \cup (X_{\frac{d-1}{2}} \setminus \{z\}) \cup (X_{\frac{d+1}{2}} \cup \{z\}) \cup X_{\frac{d+3}{2}} \cup \cdots \cup X_d$. By direct calculation, we have

$$\begin{aligned} C(G) - C(G') &= \left[\frac{1}{4}|X_{\frac{d-1}{2}}| + (|X_{\frac{d+1}{2}}| - 1)\right] - \left[(|X_{\frac{d-1}{2}}| - 1) + \frac{1}{4}|X_{\frac{d+1}{2}}|\right] \\ &= -\frac{3}{4}\left(|X_{\frac{d-1}{2}}| - |X_{\frac{d+1}{2}}|\right) < 0, \end{aligned}$$

i.e., $C(G) < C(G')$ a contradiction. Thus, $\left||X_{\frac{d-1}{2}}| - |X_{\frac{d+1}{2}}|\right| \leq 1$.

(ii) By the same arguments as above, we can show that $|X_0| = |X_1| = |X_2| = \cdots = |X_{\frac{d-4}{2}}| = |X_{\frac{d+4}{2}}| = \cdots = |X_{d-1}| = |X_d| = 1$. To complete the proof it suffices to show that $\left||X_{\frac{d-2}{2}}| + |X_{\frac{d+2}{2}}| - |X_{\frac{d}{2}}|\right| \leq 1$. Without loss of generality, we assume that $|X_{\frac{d-2}{2}}| + |X_{\frac{d+2}{2}}| > |X_{\frac{d}{2}}|$. Suppose that $\left||X_{\frac{d-2}{2}}| + |X_{\frac{d+2}{2}}| - |X_{\frac{d}{2}}|\right| \geq 2$. Since one of $X_{\frac{d-2}{2}}$ and $X_{\frac{d+2}{2}}$ contains at least two vertices. Assume that $|X_{\frac{d-2}{2}}| \geq 2$. Choose $w \in X_{\frac{d-2}{2}}$, and let $G'' = G - wu + wv$, where $u \in X_{\frac{d}{2}}, v \in X_{\frac{d+2}{2}}$. Then, the vertex partition of G'' is $X_0 \cup X_1 \cup \cdots \cup (X_{\frac{d-2}{2}} \setminus \{z\}) \cup (X_{\frac{d}{2}} \cup \{z\}) \cup X_{\frac{d+2}{2}} \cup \cdots \cup X_d$. We have

$$\begin{aligned} C(G) - C(G') &= \left[\frac{1}{4}(|X_{\frac{d-2}{2}}| + |X_{\frac{d+2}{2}}|) + (|X_{\frac{d}{2}}| - 1)\right] - \left[(|X_{\frac{d-2}{2}}| + |X_{\frac{d+2}{2}}| - 1) + \frac{1}{4}|X_{\frac{d}{2}}|\right] \\ &= -\frac{3}{4}\left(|X_{\frac{d-2}{2}}| + |X_{\frac{d+2}{2}}| - |X_{\frac{d}{2}}|\right) < 0, \end{aligned}$$

i.e., $C(G) < C(G')$ a contradiction. This completes the proof of Claim 3.

Observing that $|X_{\frac{d-1}{2}}| - |X_{\frac{d+1}{2}}| = n - d + 1$ for odd d, and $|X_{\frac{d-2}{2}}| + |X_{\frac{d+2}{2}}| - |X_{\frac{d}{2}}| = n - d + 2$, we conclude the following:

For odd d, G is isomorphic to $F(n,d)$. For even d, G belongs to $\mathcal{H}(n,d)$. □

□

7. Concluding Remarks

In this study, we have identified the networks that maximize the closeness over the bipartite networks with a given number of nodes and one of the fixed parameters like dissociation number, connectivity, cut edges, and diameter. However, the characterization of networks which minimize closeness within this same category remains an open problem. Actually, this represents an interesting and consecutive research problem, i.e., to identify the networks that minimize closeness over the bipartite networks with fixed number of nodes and one of the fixed parameters such as dissociation number, connectivity, cut edges, and diameter.

Author Contributions: Conceptualization, F.H.; Methodology, F.H.; Validation, D.E.O.; Investigation, F.H. and D.E.O. All authors have read and agreed to the published version of the manuscript.

Funding: This research received no external funding.

Data Availability Statement: No data were used to support this study.

Acknowledgments: We thank the anonymous referees for their careful reading of the manuscript and suggestions which have immensely helped us in getting the article to its present form.

Conflicts of Interest: The authors declare no conflicts of interest.

References

1. Freeman, L. Centrality in social networks conceptual clarification. *Soc. Netw.* **1978**, *1*, 215–239. [CrossRef]
2. Latora, V.; Marchiori, M. Efficient behavior of small-world networks. *Phys. Rev. Lett.* **2001**, *87*, 198701. [CrossRef] [PubMed]
3. Dangalchev, C. Residual closeness in networks. *Phys. A Stat. Mech. Its Appl.* **2006**, *365*, 556–564. [CrossRef]
4. Dangalchev, C. Additional closeness and networks growth. *Fundam. Inform.* **2020**, *176*, 1–15. [CrossRef]
5. Dangalchev, C. Additional closeness of cycle graphs. *Int. J. Found. Comput. Sci.* **2022**, *33*, 1–21. [CrossRef]
6. Aytaç, A.; Berberler, Z.N.O. Robustness of regular caterpillars. *Int. J. Found. Comput. Sci.* **2017**, *28*, 835–841. [CrossRef]
7. Aytac, A.; Odabas, Z.N. Residual closeness of wheels and related networks. *Int. J. Found. Comput. Sci.* **2011**, *22*, 1229–1240. [CrossRef]
8. Cheng, M.; Zhou, B. Residual closeness of graphs with given parameters. *J. Oper. Res. Soc. China* **2022**, *11*, 839–856. [CrossRef]
9. Dangalchev, C. Residual closeness and generalized closeness. *Int. J. Found. Comput. Sci.* **2011**, *22*, 1939–1948. [CrossRef]
10. Li, C.; Xu, L.; Zhou, B. On the residual closeness of graphs with cut vertices. *J. Comb. Optim.* **2023**, *45*, 115. [CrossRef]
11. Wang, Y.; Zhou, B. Residual closeness, matching number and chromatic number. *Comput. J.* **2022**, *66*, 1156–1166. [CrossRef]
12. Zhou, B.; Li, Z.; Guo, H. Extremal results on vertex and link residual closeness. *Int. J. Found. Comput. Sci.* **2021**, 32, 921–941. [CrossRef]
13. Aytac, A.; Turaci, T. Closeness centrality in some splitting networks. *Comput. Sci. J. Mold.* **2018**, *26*, 251–269.
14. Odabas, Z.N.; Aytac, A. Residual closeness in cycles and Related Networks. *Fundam. Inform.* **2013**, *124*, 297–307. [CrossRef]
15. Dangalchev, C. Residual closeness of generalized Thorn graphs. *Fundam. Inform.* **2018**, *126*, 1–15. [CrossRef]
16. Dangalchev, C. Closeness of splitting graphs. *Proc. Bulg. Acad. Sci.* **2020**, *73*, 461–463.
17. Dangalchev, C. Closeness of some line graphs. *arXiv* **2023**, arXiv:2308.14491v1.
18. Golpek, H.T. Closeness of some tree structures. *Soft Comput.* **2023**, *28*, 5751–5763. [CrossRef]
19. Rupnik Poklukar, D.; Žerovnik, J. Network with extremal closeness. *Fundam. Inform.* **2019**, *167*, 219–234. [CrossRef]
20. Hayat, F.; Xu, S.-J. Solution to an open problem on the closeness of graphs. *arXiv* **2023**, arXiv:2311.18671v1.
21. Zheng, L.; Zhou, B. The closeness eigenvalues of graphs. *J. Algebr. Comb.* **2023**, *58*, 741–760. [CrossRef]
22. Hopcroft, J.E.; Karp, R.M. An $n^{5/2}$ algorithm for maximum matchings in bipartite graphs. *SIAM J. Comput.* **1973**, 2, 225–231. [CrossRef]
23. Newman, M.E.J. The structure and function of complex networks. *SIAM Rev.* **2003**, *45*, 167–256. [CrossRef]

mathematics

MDPI

Article

Topological Interactions Between Homotopy and Dehn Twist Varieties

Susmit Bagchi

Department of Software Engineering (Earlier: Department of Aerospace and Software Engineering (Informatics)), IT Engineering College, Gyeongsang National University, Jinju 660-701, Republic of Korea; profsbagchi@gmail.com

Abstract: The topological Dehn twists have several applications in mathematical sciences as well as in physical sciences. The interplay between homotopy theory and Dehn twists exposes a rich set of properties. This paper generalizes the Dehn twists by proposing the notion of pre-twisted space, orientations of twists and the formation of pointed based space under a homeomorphic continuous function. It is shown that the Dehn twisted homotopy under non-retraction admits a left lifting property (LLP) through the local homeomorphism. The LLP extends the principles of Hurewicz fibration by avoiding pullback. Moreover, this paper illustrates that the Dehn twisted homotopy up to a base point in a based space can be formed by considering retraction. As a result, two disjoint continuous functions become point-wise continuous at the base point under retracted homotopy twists. Interestingly, the oriented Dehn twists of a pre-twisted space under homotopy retraction mutually commute in a contractible space.

Keywords: topology; Dehn twist; homotopy; retraction

MSC: 54E15; 55P05; 55P15

Citation: Bagchi, S. Topological Interactions Between Homotopy and Dehn Twist Varieties. *Mathematics* **2024**, *12*, 3282. https://doi.org/10.3390/math12203282

Academic Editor: Daniele Ettore Otera

Received: 8 September 2024
Revised: 17 October 2024
Accepted: 17 October 2024
Published: 19 October 2024

1. Introduction

In general, the mathematical concepts of twisting have applications in physical systems and in mathematics, which have interplays with topology as well as the topological dynamics of the respective systems [1–4]. Interestingly, algebraic operator-based twisting can be formulated by employing the homotopy theory of Donovan–Karoubi, and it leads to the notion of symmetric spectra of a topological space (E, X) under retraction as well as the twist $M(k) \times M(l) \xrightarrow{twist} M(l) \times M(k)$, where E is the total space, X is the retracted topological space and $M(k) \times M(l)$ represents a Cartesian product of monoids [5,6]. A Dehn twist is a special class of twisted structure, which can be formulated by employing the algebraic operators (named after mathematician Max Dehn). Interestingly, if we consider that the topological surface is a Klein bottle, then the Dehn twist and the corresponding $Y-$ homeomorphism are essentially the varieties of automorphisms [1]. Dehn twists have several applications in analyzing physical systems [1–3]. It is known that the topologically ordered state of matter is stable if it is in a topologically trivial state preventing degeneracy [2]. However, under degeneracy, Dehn twists can be applied to form braid structures, and corresponding nontrivial operations are obtained. Moreover, from the application point of view, it is shown that Dehn twists encode the topological spins of parity-symmetric anyons (i.e., the exchanges of such anyons) in a physical system [1,2]. In addition to applications in physical systems, a Dehn twist has interplays with homotopy and associated algebraic structures, exposing a rich set of interesting mathematical properties. First, we present the concept of a Dehn twist, in brief (Section 1.1). Next, we present the motivation and contributions made in this paper in Sections 1.2 and 1.3, respectively. In this paper, the unit interval in real values is denoted by I; the index set is denoted by Λ; and the sets of real numbers and integers are denoted by R, Z, respectively. If A and B are homeomorphic, then it is denoted as $Hom(A, B)$.

1.1. General Dehn Twist

Let us consider an oriented (arbitrary) surface of genus g, represented as (S, g), containing a simple closed curve $f : I \to S$. Suppose N_f is a regular neighborhood of the curve $f(.)$ and there exists an orientation-preserving homeomorphism given by $h : S^1 \times I \to N_f$. If the function $T_f : S^1 \times I \to S^1 \times I$ is a directed twist such that $T_f(\theta, t) = (\theta \pm 2\pi t, t)$, $t \in I$, then we can define a standard Dehn twist as follows [7,8]:

Definition 1. *If the continuous function $T_f : S \to S$ is a homeomorphism on (S, g), then it is a Dehn twist about $f : I \to S$ if it preserves the following properties:*

$$\begin{aligned} &[x \in N_f] \Rightarrow [T_f(x) = (h \circ T_f \circ h^{-1})(x)], \\ &[x \in S \backslash N_f] \Rightarrow [T_f(x) = x]. \end{aligned} \tag{1}$$

Remark 1. *Note that a Dehn twist can have directions, such as a right twist or left twist, as indicated by the corresponding signs. Moreover, if we consider two simple closed (disjoint) curves $f : I \to S$ and $v : I \to S$ in an isotopy class, then the Dehn twist admits the commutative algebraic property, which is given as $T_f T_v = T_v T_f$.*

The fundamental property of a Dehn twist is its uniqueness, as presented in the following Lemma [7]:

Lemma 1. *If we consider two Dehn twists $T_f : S \to S$ and $T_v : S \to S$ about the respective disjoint and simple closed curves, then we can conclude that $[T_f = T_v] \Rightarrow [f(I) = v(I)]$ and $[f(I) \neq v(I)] \Rightarrow [T_f \neq T_v]$.*

It is interesting to note that a Dehn twist can be formulated considering a fundamental group $\pi_1(S, p)$ on a surface (S, g) without requiring any additional modifications of the concept [8].

1.2. Motivation

Homotopy analysis methods have wide arrays of applications. For example, homotopy analysis methods are applied for solving integrodifferential equations by admitting the convergence criteria of the associated series [9]. Note that in such applications, the homotopy is employed as an operator. Interestingly, the metrizable topological space of Grothendieck manifold admits the coarse sheaf cohomology as well as cohomology groups [10]. In this case, the coarse cohomologies are homotopy invariant [10]. There are interplays between the homotopy of algebraic topology, Dehn twists and the lifting with a rich set of properties. For example, suppose $Tor^2 \subset R^2$ is a flat torus and there exists the area-preserving homeomorphism $f : Tor^2 \to Tor^2$, where $f(.)$ is homotopic to the identity of the respective flat torus. If $f_l : R^2 \to R^2$ is a lifting of $f(.)$, then there is a rotation set $\rho(f_l)$, which is a generalization of the rotational number of circle homeomorphisms preserving the orientations [11]. Moreover, let us consider a (area-preserving) homeomorphism $f : T_D(Tor^2) \to T_D(Tor^2)$, where $T_D(Tor^2)$ denotes a set of homotopic Dehn twists of the respective flat torus. If $f_{Tl} : T_D(Tor^2) \to S^1 \times R$ is lifting with a zero vertical rotational number, then all points have uniformly bounded motion under the corresponding lifting [12,13]. This has applications in dynamical systems and in fixed point theory [13]. Note that the aforesaid topological properties are restricted to the flat torus under Dehn twists while preserving the area.

It is known that homotopy and retraction are two inter-related concepts in algebraic topology, where Dehn twists play an interesting role. Thus, the relevant motivating question is as follows: *can we further generalize or extend a Dehn twist in relation to its application in homotopy and retraction*? More specifically, interesting questions are (1) *what are the topological properties of interactions between extended Dehn twists and non-contractible spaces under homotopy*; (2) *what are the interplays between the homotopic retraction of a topological space and Dehn twists*? Furthermore, the question is as follows: *is there any lifting of such twisted homotopy and what is its relationship with Hurewicz fibration*? This paper addresses these questions in relative detail from the viewpoint of algebraic topology.

1.3. Contributions

First, we note the following fundamental observation presented as Theorem 1 [14]. We present our proof (formulated by the author of this paper) of the corresponding theorem (Theorem 1).

Theorem 1. *If $f : I \to (S, g)$ is a simple closed curve on a compact oriented surface (S, g) of genus g, then the generalized Dehn twists about $f : I \to (S, g)$ generate automorphism of fundamental group $\pi(S, f(0))$. Moreover, it forms the corresponding homotopy class $[f]$ on (S, g) under the Dehn twists.*

Proof. Let (S, g) be a compact oriented surface of genus g. Suppose $A \subset S$ is a connected based subspace such that $f : I \to A$ is a simple closed curve with the base point $f(0) = f(1) = b$. Thus, it forms a fundamental group $\pi_1(A, b)$ on (S, g). If $T_D : A \to A$ is a base point preserving a Dehn twist about $f : I \to A$, then $T_D(f(I))$ admits the conditions given by (1) $Hom(T_D(f(I)), f(I))$, (2) $Hom(T_D(f(I)), S^1)$ and (3) $T_D^n(\{b\}) \cong \{b\}$, where $1 \leq n < +\infty$. Thus, it results in the formation of homotopy class $[f] = \{T_D^n(f(I)) : n \in [1, k], k < +\infty\}$, where $\forall h \in [f]$ and the fundamental group $\pi_1(A, b)$ admits automorphism under a finite number of Dehn twists. □

The important constraint on $T_D(f(I))$ is that it should result in a set of simple closed curves in the homotopy class $[f]$ within the based space.

Theorem 1 and our proof illustrate that a based topological space plays an interesting role in generating fundamental groups under Dehn twists. This paper introduces the notion of pre-twisted space and the formation of an $f - base$ space under homeomorphism, such that the $f - base$ space essentially becomes a based topological space. The formulation of a generalized as well as an extended Dehn twist of a pre-twisted space is presented in this paper, where a Dehn twist has a specific orientation and the Dehn twists with opposite orientations mutually commute. We show that a non-contractible space can be subjected to the extended Dehn twists under homotopy and the resulting twisted homotopy with non-retraction can be lifted (LLP) by employing the local homeomorphism. Thus, the proposed formulation extends the principles of Hurewicz fibration by avoiding pullback. Furthermore, the topological properties of twisted homotopy up to an $f - base$ point with retraction under a Dehn twist are presented in this paper. As a result, two disjoint continuous functions become continuous at the $f - base$ point under the Dehn-twisted homotopy with retraction. We show that the commutative relation between the homotopic retraction and Dehn twists is preserved.

The rest of the paper is organized as follows: Section 2 presents preliminary concepts. The definitions of pre-twisted space, extended Dehn twists and twisted homotopy are presented in Section 3. The topological properties of the varieties of twisted homotopies are presented in Section 4. Finally, Section 5 concludes the paper.

2. Preliminaries

We present the preliminary concepts in two parts. First, we present the results related to Dehn twists in Section 2.1. Next, we present the discussions about the Dehn twists, isotopy and fibration in Section 2.2.

2.1. Curves and Dehn Twists

Suppose we consider an oriented surface of genus g represented as (S, g) and let $f : I \to S$ be a simple closed curve. The curve is called trivial if $A \subset S : f(I) = \partial A$ and it maintains the condition given by $Hom(A^o, D_2)$, where $D_2 = D_2^o$ represents an open disk. Note that every trivial curve $f : I \to S$ admits a Dehn twist, which is equivalent to the corresponding diffeomorphism [15]. There is an inter-relationship between the closed curve, the Dehn twist about the curve and the respective automorphic homeomorphism of a closed surface, which is presented as follows [15,16]:

Lemma 2. *Let (S, g) denote a closed surface S of genus g and the two-sided closed curve on S be given as $f : I \to S$. Suppose T_f is a Dehn twist about $f(.)$ and $h : S \to S$ is an automorphic homeomorphism preserving $f : I \to S$. If the Dehn twist T_f reverses the orientations of neighborhoods of $f : I \to S$, then the following properties are preserved:*

$$\begin{aligned} &T_f = h(T_f)^{-1}h^{-1}, \\ &\forall n \in Z : (T_f)^{2n} = (T_f)^n (T_f)^n. \end{aligned} \tag{2}$$

The corresponding commutator under homeomorphism can be denoted as $[(T_f)^n, h]$. Note that in this case, the closed two-sided curve is not bounding any disk. The concept of a compression body and the associated Dehn twist on a manifold with a boundary are defined as follows [17]:

Definition 2. *A compression body is a connected three-manifold M^3 generated from a compact surface S with no components such that the $Hom(S, S^2)$ property is preserved, where $S \times \{1\}$ is the attached one-handle.*

It is important to note that a compression body is irreducible.

Definition 3. *Let M^3 be a three-manifold with a boundary and the continuous function $h : M^3 \to M^3$ be a homeomorphism. The function restricted to boundary $h|_{\partial M^3} : M^3 \to M^3$ is a Dehn twist if it is isotopic to the identity of the subspace and it is complement to a set of closed as well as simple curves $\{f_i : I \to \partial M^3 : i \in \Lambda\}$, such that $[i \neq k] \Rightarrow [f_i(I) \cap f_k(I) = \varphi]$.*

Remark 2. *Note that the Dehn twist on a closed surface about a closed two-sided curve does not bound any disk. However, in the case of manifold with a boundary, the Dehn twist (restricted to the boundary) about a set of disjoint closed and simple curves essentially bounds a set of disks generated by $\{f_i(I)\}$.*

This leads to the following theorem involving the Dehn twist of a compression body [17]:

Theorem 2. *Let S be a compression body and $h : S \to S$ be a homeomorphism. The Dehn twist about the function $h : S \to S$ is a composition of a set of Dehn twists about the simple, closed and disjoint curves $\{f_i : I \to \partial S : i \in \Lambda\}$, which are isotopic, and each of $f_i(I)$ bounds a disk such that the $Hom(f_i(I), S^1)$ condition is maintained.*

There are interplays between the Dehn twists and the intersection numbers of multiple simple closed curves generated by $f : I \to S$ and $g : I \to S$ on the surface (S, g) with genus g. Let us denote the intersection number as $\lambda = |f(I) \cap g(I)|$. This results in the commutative invariance theorem of Dehn twists of T_f, T_g if the $\lambda = 0$ condition is maintained on the surface [18].

Theorem 3. *If $f : I \to S$ and $g : I \to S$ are two-sided curves on the surface (S, g) such that $Hom(f(I), S^1)$ and $Hom(g(I), S^1)$ conditions are maintained, then $\exists j, k \in Z^+$ such that the following implication is admitted:* $[(T_f)^j (T_g)^k = (T_g)^k (T_f)^j] \Rightarrow [\lambda = 0]$.

The proof of the commutative invariance under multiple Dehn twists about the non-intersecting curves is detailed in [18]. A similar result can be extended to Lagrangian n-sphere S^n_L embedded within the symplectic m-manifold M^m for $m = n = 2$ admitting Milnor fibration, where the twist is a standard Dehn twist [19]. Moreover, in such a case, the standard Dehn twist commutes considering two disjoint Lagrangian S^n_L for $n = 2$. Interestingly, there may not be any inter-relationship between two Dehn twists, even if the intersection number is non-zero, which is presented in the Ishida theorem as follows [19]:

Theorem 4. *Let a surface of genus g and the puncture p be given as (S, g, p). Suppose two simple closed curves are $f : I \to (S, g, p)$ and $g : I \to (S, g, p)$ such that $\lambda \geq 2$. In this case, there is no inter-relationship between the Dehn twists T_f, T_g.*

Note that the value of λ is considered to be minimum in this case. A detailed discussion is given in [19,20].

2.2. Dehn Twists, Isotopy and Fibration

The topological properties of Dehn twists vary depending on the dimensions of the spaces. The Dehn twist around a non-trivial loop on a surface $(S, g > 1)$ with a non-zero genus generates a one-dimensional Teichmüller disk [21]. A Teichmüller disk is completely geodesic with respect to the Teichmüller metric. If we consider a two-manifold M^2 representing a surface, then there is an isotopy $\lambda : M^2 \times [0,1] \to M^2$ without fixing ∂M^2 such that it is homotopic up to a periodic and irreducible variety [22]. If $h : M^2 \to M^2$ is a homeomorphism fixing ∂M^2, then the fractional Dehn twist coefficient of $h(.)$ represents the winding number of the arc $\{b\} \times [0,1]$, where $b \in \partial M^2$ is a base point [22].

Interestingly, there is an inter-relationship between the fundamental group and Hurewicz arc system on a two-disk (represented as D_2). Let us consider a Lefschetz fibration $f : X \to D_2$, where X is a compact four-manifold. Let us choose a base point $b \in \partial D_2$ and a finite set of points $\{p_i\} \subset (D_2)^o$. If we consider a set of arcs $\{A_i\} \subset D_2$ such that $A_i \cap A_k = \{b\}$, then $\langle\{p_i\}, \{A_i\}\rangle$ is a Hurewicz arc system admitting a right-handed Dehn twist generating $\pi_1(D_2 \backslash \{p_i\}, b)$, which is called the Hurewicz generator system [23].

It is known that the Dehn twists of various four-manifolds may not always preserve the smooth isotopy with respect to the identity function along the twist. For example, Kronheimer and Mrowka have shown that if we consider a manifold $K3\#K3$, then the Dehn twist along the submanifold S^3 within the respective manifold does not admit smooth isotopy with respect to the identity function [24,25]. In order to avoid non-smooth isotopy, the sequences of stabilizations are often necessary. Interestingly, the Dehn twist along S^3 within $K3\#K3$ cannot be made smooth after a single stabilization [24].

3. Homotopy Under Dehn Twists: Definitions

Let a topological space be given as (X, τ_X) such that $\dim(X) = n$ and $n \in (1, +\infty)$. We denote a real plane of dimension $m \leq n$ as RP^m, and a planar convex open m-disk is denoted as $D_m = \{x \in RP^m : |x| < 1\}$. If we consider a topological subspace $F \subset X$, then the corresponding homotopy can be formulated through $H_n : F \times I \to Y$ by following the conventions of algebraic topology. Let us denote a homotopic subspace of $A = F \times \{a \in I\}$ as $A_{(F,a)} \subset F \times I$. Moreover, if $f : I \to F \times I$ is a continuous function such that $f(\{b\} \subset I) \cap A_{(F,a)} = \{x_{ab}\}$, then we represent the position of the point x_{ab} as $p(\theta_b, a)$, where θ_b is a clock-wise angular displacement with respect to a fixed reference point on $A_{(F,a)}$. Let us consider the low-dimensional topological space such that $n \leq 3$, for simplicity. First, we present the definition of *pre-twist* θ_{Dp} of a Dehn variety as follows:

Definition 4. *Let $X \subset R^2$ be a topological space and $F \subset X$ such that the $Hom(F, \overline{D_2})$ condition is preserved. If $f : I \to \partial F \times I$ and $g : I \to \partial F \times I$ are two disjoint continuous functions, where $g(.)$ maintains the $Hom(g(I), P_g \subset RP^1)$ property, then $\theta_{Dp} \geq 0$ is the pre-twist of a Dehn variety if the following conditions are maintained:*

$$\begin{aligned} \{x_{ac}\} &= g(I) \cap A_{(F,a)}, \\ \{x_{ab}\} &= f(I) \cap A_{(F,a)}, \\ \theta_{Dp} &= |p(\theta_c, a) - p(\theta_b, a)|. \end{aligned} \tag{3}$$

It is important to note that $\theta_{Dp} \geq 0$ is considered as extremely small, such that $\inf\theta_{Dp} = \lim_{k \to M} (2\pi/k)$ in general, where $M \in (1, +\infty]$ and $M >> 1$. It is important to note that in the remaining sections of this paper, we are algebraically denoting the position $p(\theta_b, a)$ and the corresponding point x_{ab} together as $p(\theta_b, a)$ to avoid representational complexities (i.e., $x_{ab} \equiv p(\theta_b, a)$ for simplicity).

Definition 5. *Let U be a simply connected topological space such that $U = \overline{U}$ and let $f : U \to Y$ be a continuous function. The ordered pair $(U, f)_Y$ is defined as an $f - base$ forming a fixed based space $(Y, y_*)_f$ if $f(U) = \{y_*\}$. The point y_* is called an $f - base$ point in Y.*

Note that the $f - base$ $(U, f)_Y$ admits homeomorphism such that if $h : Y \to V$ is a homeomorphism, then $(h \circ f)(U) = h(y_*)$.

Remark 3. *There exists an $H_{2*} : F \times I \to Y$, which is a null-homotopy up to an $f - base$ point $y_* \in Y$ in a fixed-based space $(Y, y_*)_f$ such that $H_{2*}(A_{(F,1)}) = \{y_*\}$. Note that in this case, F is also a simply connected space. Moreover, if $r : F \to F$ is a retraction and $h : F \to Y$ is continuous, then $\exists c \in F$ such that $(h \circ r)(F) = h(c) = \{y_*\}$. Furthermore, it can be observed that $H_{2*}(A_{(F,1)}) = (h \circ r)(F)$, indicating that in this case, $H_{2*} : F \times I \to Y$ is a null-homotopic retraction up to the $f - base$ point y_*.*

Definition 6. *Let a continuous function be given as $\Delta_{D(\pm m\varepsilon)} : F \times I \to F \times I$, where $\varepsilon \in R^1$ and $m \in Z^+$. The function $\Delta_{D(\pm m\varepsilon)}$ is an extended Dehn twist if $\forall p(\theta_{Dp}, t) \in F \times \{t\}$; the function induces twist as $\Delta_{D(\pm m\varepsilon)}(p(\theta_{Dp}, t)) = p((\theta_{Dp} \pm 2\pi m\varepsilon t), t)$, such that $\varepsilon \in (0, 1]$ and $t \in I$.*

The extended Dehn twist generalizes the standard Dehn twist by admitting a variable factor or weight ε of the twist, while covering a finite order $m \in [1, +\infty)$ of the twist. Note that the extended Dehn twist introduces the notion of the direction of a twist within a homotopy space.

Remark 4. *If we consider that $\varepsilon = 1$, then the extended twist $\Delta_{D(\pm m\varepsilon)}$ is transformed into a standard Dehn twist of order m. If we consider a positively (clock-wise) oriented twist $\Delta_{D(+m\varepsilon)}$, then the corresponding inverse is given by $\Delta_{D(-m\varepsilon)}$. It is important to note that, in general, the directed as well as extended Dehn twists are mutually commutative such that they admit the condition given as $(\Delta_{D(+m\varepsilon)} \circ \Delta_{D(-m\varepsilon)}) = (\Delta_{D(-m\varepsilon)} \circ \Delta_{D(+m\varepsilon)}) = id_{F \times I}$, where $id_{F \times I} : F \times I \to F \times I$ is an identity function.*

4. Topological Properties

In this section, we present the topological properties of extended Dehn twists on two varieties of homotopy spaces. First, we present the topological analysis of the application of an extended Dehn twist on a homotopy space, which is not contractible and not null-homotopic. Next, we consider a null-homotopic topological space and we apply the extended Dehn twist on the respective homotopy space.

4.1. Extended Dehn Twist in Non-Contractible Space

Let us consider a continuous function $g : I \rightarrow S^1 \times I$ such that the $Hom(g(I), P_g \subset RP^1)$ property is maintained. Suppose we consider that $p(\theta_{Dp}, 0) = g(0)$ and $p(\theta_{Dp}, 1) = g(1)$. Suppose a homotopy is given by $H : S^1 \times I \rightarrow E$ and a covering map is given by $q : E \rightarrow X$. We define a homotopy under the extended Dehn twist, which is given by $H_\Delta : S^1 \times I \rightarrow X$, such that the following algebraic properties are preserved:

$$\begin{aligned} &t \in [0,1] : H_\Delta(S^1 \times \{t\}) \cong (H \circ \Delta_{D(\pm m\varepsilon)})(S^1 \times \{t\}), \\ &t \in [0,1] : Hom(H_\Delta(S^1 \times \{t\}), S^1 \times \{t\}). \end{aligned} \tag{4}$$

Note that, in this particular case, we can consider that $\theta_{Dp} = 0$ with respect to $P_g \subset RP^1$ and the corresponding twisted homotopy can be formulated as $H_\Delta(S^1 \times \{t\}) = q_*(H \circ \Delta_{D(\pm m\varepsilon)})(S^1 \times \{t\})$. As a result, we obtain $\Delta_{D(\pm 11)}(p(0,t) \in S^1 \times \{t\}) = p(\pm 2\pi t, t)$, where $t \in [0,1]$. It results in the following commutative diagram as illustrated in Figure 1, where $(H \circ \Delta_{D(\pm m\varepsilon)}) : S^1 \times I \rightarrow E$ is a homotopy lifting under the extended Dehn twist and $h : E \rightarrow S^1 \times \{0\}$ is a local homeomorphism in E:

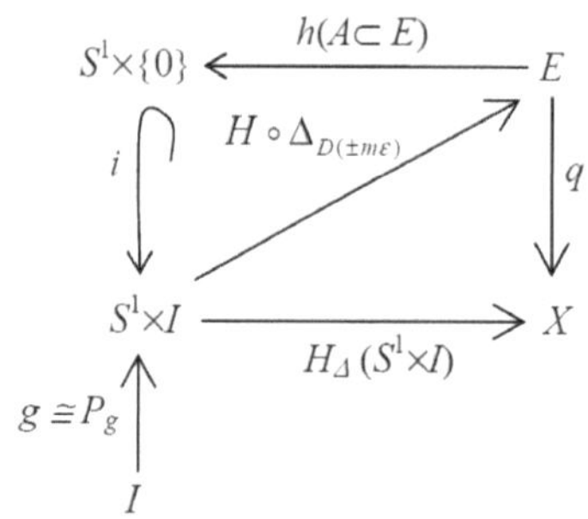

Figure 1. Twisted homotopy lifting and fibration with no retraction.

Interestingly, the homotopy lifting under the extended Dehn twist with no retraction have resemblances to the Hurewicz fibration with necessary modifications.

Remark 5. *It is important to note that the covering map of a homotopic extended Dehn twist $q : E \rightarrow X$ has a left lifting property (LLP) because it admits the condition given by $(q \circ (H \circ \Delta_{D(\pm m\varepsilon)}) \circ i \circ h) = (H_\Delta \circ i)$. Furthermore, the lifting $(H \circ \Delta_{D(\pm m\varepsilon)}) : S^1 \times I \rightarrow E$ is a twisted homotopy lifting because it preserves the $q_* H \circ \Delta_{D(\pm m\varepsilon)} = H_\Delta$ property.*

Theorem 5. *If $H_\Delta : S^1 \times I \rightarrow X$ is a twisted homotopy with $m\varepsilon = 1$, then it admits the following two properties: (a) $H_\Delta(S^1, 0) \cong H(S^1, 0)$ and (b) $H_\Delta(S^1, 1) \cong H(S^1, 1)$.*

Proof. Let us consider a twisted homotopy $H_\Delta : S^1 \times I \rightarrow X$. Note that in this case, $\Delta_{D(\pm 11)}(p(0,t) \in S^1 \times \{t\}) = p(\pm 2\pi t, t)$ for all $t \in [0,1]$. Let us consider an identity function given as $id : S^1 \times I \rightarrow S^1 \times I$. As a result, the extended Dehn twist results in the following properties:

$$\begin{aligned} &\Delta_{D(\pm 11)}(S^1 \times \{0\}) = id(S^1 \times \{0\}), \\ &and, \\ &\Delta_{D(\pm 11)}(S^1 \times \{1\}) = id(S^1 \times \{1\}). \end{aligned} \tag{5}$$

Hence, we can conclude that $H_\Delta(S^1, 0) \cong H(S^1, 0)$ and $H_\Delta(S^1, 1) \cong H(S^1, 1)$ because $H_\Delta(S^1, 0) = q_* H \circ id(S^1, 0)$ and $H_\Delta(S^1, 1) = q_* H \circ id(S^1, 1)$. □

4.2. Homotopic Retraction Under Extended Dehn Twist

In this section, we consider that the three-space $A_{(F,a)} \subset F \times I$ can be topologically retracted and it is null-homotopic. If we first apply the extended Dehn twist to $A_{(F,a)}$ as $\Delta_{D(\pm m\varepsilon)}(A_{(F,a)})$, and next, we apply retraction under $r : A_{(F,a)} \to (B_{(F,a)} \subset A_{(F,a)})$, then we obtain the following equations:

$$\begin{aligned} &\Delta_{D(\pm m\varepsilon)}(p(\theta_{Dp}, a) \in \partial A_{(F,a)}) = p(\theta_{Dp} \pm 2\pi m\varepsilon a, a), \\ &(r \circ \Delta_{D(\pm m\varepsilon)})(p(\theta_{Dp}, a)) = p(\theta_{Dp} \pm 2\pi m\varepsilon a, a)_B \in \partial B_{(F,a)}. \end{aligned} \tag{6}$$

If we apply the extended Dehn twist and retraction in the reverse order, then it results in the following equations:

$$\begin{aligned} &p(\theta_{Dp}, a) \in \partial A_{(F,a)}, \\ &r(A_{(F,a)}) = B_{(F,a)}, \\ &p(\theta_{Dp}, a)_B \in \partial B_{(F,a)}, \\ &\Delta_{D(\pm m\varepsilon)}(p(\theta_{Dp}, a)_B) = p(\theta_{Dp} \pm 2\pi m\varepsilon a, a)_B. \end{aligned} \tag{7}$$

It leads to the following commutative diagram illustrated in Figure 2.

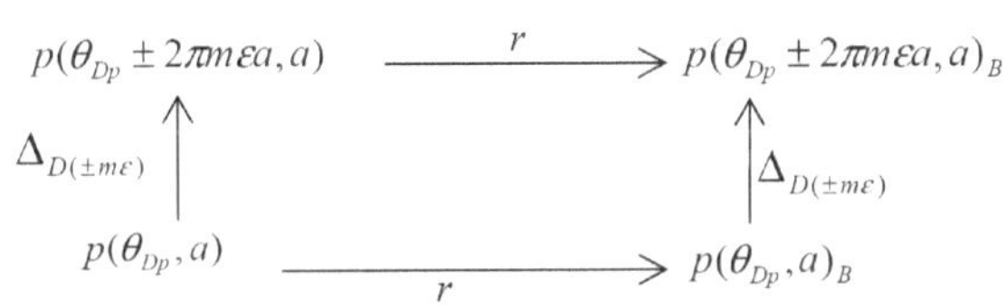

Figure 2. Commutative diagram for retraction and extended Dehn twist.

It is relatively easy to observe that the aforesaid commutative property is admitted for all points in the null-homotopic space. This results in the following theorem:

Theorem 6. *Let $H_{2*} : F \times I \to Y$ be a null-homotopic retraction up to $y_* \in Y$ in $(Y, y_*)_f$, where it preserves the $Hom(F, \overline{D_2})$ property. If $h : I \to \partial F \times I$ and $g : I \to \partial F \times I$ are two disjoint continuous functions, then it results in $H_{2*}(F \times \{g(1)\}) \cap H_{2*}(F \times \{h(1)\}) = \{y_*\}$ in $(Y, y_*)_f$.*

Proof. Let $F \subset X \subset R^2$ be a topological space such that the $Hom(F, \overline{D_2})$ property is maintained and $H_{2*} : F \times I \to Y$ is the corresponding homotopy. Let us consider that $H_{2*} : F \times I \to Y$ is a null-homotopy up to an $f - base$ point y_* in $(Y, y_*)_f$ such that $H_{2*}(A_{(F,1)}) = \{y_*\}$. This implies that there is a retraction with embedding $(i \circ r) : A_{(F,1)} \to (Y, y_*)_f$ such that $(i \circ r)(A_{(F,1)}) = H_{2*}(A_{(F,1)})$, where $r : A_{(F,1)} \to A_{(F,1)}$ is a retraction with $r(A_{(F,1)}) = \{x_{1b}\} \subset A_{(F,1)}$ and $i : A_{(F,1)} \to (Y, y_*)_f$ is the respective (injective) embedding with $i(x_{1b}) = y_*$. Thus, the homotopy $H_{2*} : F \times I \to Y$ is a null-homotopic retraction variety. Let us consider that $h : I \to \partial F \times I$ and $g : I \to \partial F \times I$ are two disjoint continuous functions such that $h(1) \in \partial A_{(F,1)}$ and $g(1) \in \partial A_{(F,1)}$. As $H_{2*} : F \times I \to Y$ is a null-homotopic retraction, we can infer that $H_{2*}(F \times \{g(1)\}) = H_{2*}(F \times \{h(1)\})$. Hence, we conclude that $H_{2*}(F \times \{g(1)\}) \cap H_{2*}(F \times \{h(1)\}) = (i \circ r)(A_{(F,1)})$ in $(Y, y_*)_f$. It results in the following commutative diagram as illustrated in Figure 3, where $u : I \to F \times \{1\}$ and $v : I \to F \times \{1\}$ are two constant (continuous) functions such that $u(I) = \{x_{1k}\}$ and $v(I) = \{x_{1c}\}$ within the topological space. □

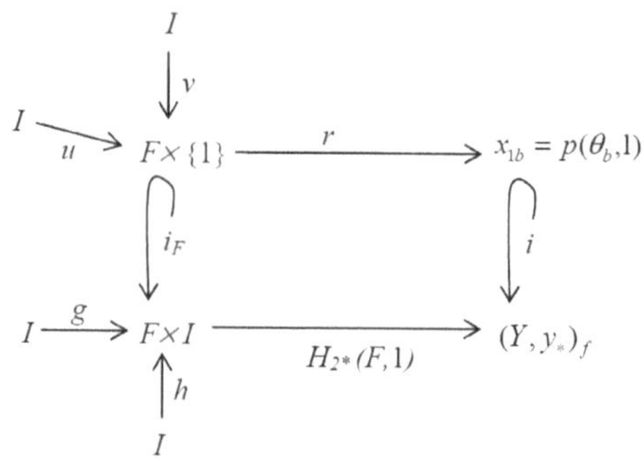

Figure 3. Commutative diagram representing Theorem 6.

This immediately leads to the following corollary:

Corollary 1. *There exist two injective embeddings under homotopy H_{2*} and the restrictions in $F \times I$, which are given as $i_{emH2*} : (F \times I)\big|_g \to (Y, y_*)_f$ and $i_{emH2*} : (F \times I)\big|_h \to (Y, y_*)_f$ such that $i_{emH2*}((F \times I)|_g) \cap i_{emH2*}((F \times I)|_h) = \{y_*\}$.*

We can view this as the admission of the base-point preservation principle within a based topological space.

Remark 6. *Finally, this is to note that the proposed concepts and formulations (excluding our proof of Theorem 1) in this paper are employing the elements of algebraic topology without resorting to the algebraic operator theory of twisted structures. Moreover, the proposed formulations generalize the Dehn twist under retraction in terms of algebraic topology. It would be interesting to investigate the relationships between the proposed concepts and the twisted (algebraic) K-theoretical structures in future.*

5. Conclusions

The general form of Dehn twists can be extended involving the pre-twisted topological based spaces and the orientations of twists, where the based space is formed through the continuous function retaining homeomorphism. Extended Dehn twists can be applied to homotopy under two conditions: (1) the non-retraction of a space and (2) under the retraction of the topological space. The resulting twisted homotopies behave differently. The Dehn twisted homotopy with non-retraction can admit a left lifting property (LLP) by following the modified form of Hurewicz fibration, avoiding pullback. However, the Dehn twisted homotopy under retraction up to the base point within a based space admits the point-wise continuity of two disjoint continuous functions at the base point. In a contractible space, the extended Dehn twists and retractions mutually commute.

Funding: This research (article processing charge) is partly funded by Gyeongsang National University, Jinju, Republic of Korea (ROK).

Data Availability Statement: The original contributions presented in the study are included in the article.

Acknowledgments: The author would like to thank the reviewers and editors for their valuable comments and suggestions during the peer-review process.

Conflicts of Interest: The author declares no conflicts of interest.

References

1. Chan, A.P.O.; Teo, J.C.Y.; Ryu, S. Topological phases on non-orientable surfaces: Twisting by parity Symmetry. *New J. Phys.* **2016**, *18*, 035005. [CrossRef]
2. Zhu, G.; Lavasani, A.; Barkeshli, M. Instantaneous braids and Dehn twists in topologically ordered states. *Phys. Rev. B.* **2020**, *102*, 075105. [CrossRef]
3. Heusler, S.; Schlummer, P.; Ubben, M.S. The topological origin of quantum randomness. *Symmetry* **2021**, *13*, 581. [CrossRef]
4. Ludkowski, S.V. Topologies on smashed twisted wreath products of metagroups. *Axioms* **2023**, *12*, 240. [CrossRef]
5. Donovan, P.; Karoubi, M. Graded Brauer groups and K-theory with local coefficients. *Inst. Hautes Études Sci. Publ. Math.* **1970**, *38*, 5–25. [CrossRef]
6. Hebestreit, F.; Sagave, S. Homotopical and operator algebraic twisted K-theory. *Math. Ann.* **2020**, *378*, 1021–1059. [CrossRef]
7. Farb, B.; Margalit, D. *A Primer on Mapping Class Groups (PMS-49)*; Princeton University Press: Princeton, NJ, USA, 2012; Chapter 3; pp. 64–88. [CrossRef]
8. Yusuke, K.; Massuyeau, G.; Tsuji, S. *Generalized Dehn Twists in Low-Dimensional Topology*; Topology & Geometry; EMS Press: Berlin, Germany, 2019; pp. 357–398. [CrossRef]
9. Słota, D.; Hetmaniok, E.; Wituła, R.; Gromysz, K.; Trawiński, T. Homotopy Approach for Integrodifferential Equations. *Mathematics* **2019**, *7*, 904. [CrossRef]
10. Hartmann, E. Coarse Sheaf Cohomology. *Mathematics* **2023**, *11*, 3121. [CrossRef]
11. Koropecki, A.; Tal, F.A. Area-preserving irrotational diffeomorphisms of the torus with sublinear diffusions. *Proc. Am. Math. Soc.* **2014**, *142*, 3483–3490. [CrossRef]
12. Addas-Zanata, S.; Tal, F.A.; Garcia, B.A. Dynamics of homeomorphisms of the torus homotopic to Dehn twists. *Ergod. Theory Dyn. Syst.* **2014**, *34*, 409–422. [CrossRef]
13. Doeff, H.E. Rotation measures for homeomorphisms of the torus homotopic to a Dehn twist. *Ergod. Theory Dyn. Syst.* **1997**, *17*, 575–591. [CrossRef]
14. Kuno, Y.; Massuyeau, G. Generalized Dehn twists on surfaces and homology cylinders. *Algebr. Geom. Topol.* **2021**, *21*, 697–754. [CrossRef]
15. Korkmaz, M. Stable commutator length of a Dehn twist. *Mich. Math. J.* **2004**, *52*, 23–31. [CrossRef]
16. Szepietowski, B. On the commutator length of a Dehn twist. *C. R. Math.* **2010**, *348*, 923–926. [CrossRef]
17. MCCullough, D. Homeomorphisms which are Dehn twists on the boundary. *Algebr. Geom. Topol.* **2006**, *6*, 1331–1340. [CrossRef]
18. Stukow, M. Dehn twists on nonorientable surfaces. *Fundam. Math.* **2006**, *189*, 117–147. [CrossRef]
19. Keating, A.M. Dehn twists and free subgroups of symplectic mapping class groups. *J. Topol.* **2014**, *7*, 436–474. [CrossRef]
20. Ishida, A. The structure of subgroup of mapping class groups generated by two Dehn twists. *Proc. Jpn. Acad. Ser. A Math. Sci.* **1996**, *72*, 240–241. [CrossRef]
21. Marden, A.; Masur, H. A foliation of Teichmüller space by twist invariant disks. *Math. Scand.* **1975**, *36*, 211–228. [CrossRef]
22. Hedden, M.; Mark, T.E. Floer homology and fractional Dehn twist. *Adv. Math.* **2018**, *324*, 1–39. [CrossRef]
23. Baykur, R.I.; Kamada, S. Classification of broken Lefschetz fibrations with small fiber genera. *Math. Soc. Jpn.* **2015**, *67*, 877–901. [CrossRef]
24. Lin, J. Isotopy of the Dehn twist on K3#K3 after a single stabilization. *Geom. Topol.* **2023**, *27*, 1987–2012.
25. Kronheimer, P.B.; Mrowka, T.S. The Dehn twist on a sum of two K3 surfaces. *Math. Res. Lett.* **2020**, *27*, 1767–1783. [CrossRef]

MDPI AG
Grosspeteranlage 5
4052 Basel
Switzerland
Tel.: +41 61 683 77 34

Mathematics Editorial Office
E-mail: mathematics@mdpi.com
www.mdpi.com/journal/mathematics

www.ingramcontent.com/pod-product-compliance
Lightning Source LLC
Chambersburg PA
CBHW041342210926
51850CB00013B/2958
9783725834150